ĀNANDABODHA YATI

(Life & Philosophy)

Dr. RABINDRA KUMAR PANDA

EASTERN BOOK LINKERS
DELHI : : (INDIA)

Publishers :
EASTERN BOOK LINKERS
5825, New Chandrawal, Jawahar Nagar,
Delhi-110007 Ph.: 2520287

First Edition : 1997

ISBN : 81-86339-38-8

Price EASTERN BOOK LINKERS EBL RS. 500-

Laser typesetting & Printing at :
UNIQUE PRINT MEDIA
Phone : 7252362

DEDICATED

TO

MY PARENTS:

SRI GADADHARA PANDA

AND

SMT. REVATI PANDA

विद्यया विन्दतेऽमृतम्

FOREWORD

Ānandabodha Yati is the only significant Advaita Vedāntist of eleventh century. Amidst the sway of such great Naiyāyikas like Jayantabhaṭṭa and Udayanācārya and of Mīmāṁsakas like Śālikanātha, it is Ānandabodha who keeps the flag of Advaita Vedānta flying and flying proudly. Out of necessity of his times, perhaps, he subjects Advaita tenets to regorous logic, and as a result, comes out with a classic import of Śaṅkara's own position. He accepts the views of post-Śaṅkara stalwarts also but not blindly. The logicality of his approach has also given him a freedom of views and an originality of thinking.

As the very titles of his seminal works, *Nyāyadīpikā*, (commentary on *Śābdanirṇaya* of Prakāśātman), *Nyāyadīpāvali*, *Pramāṇamālā* and *Nyāyamakaranda* suggest, he is almost a Naiyāyika turned Advaitist. A study of his works would have required a grounding both in Nyāya and in Vedānta. That is, perhaps, why a good study of this significant author was still lacking. The present work of Dr. Rabindra Kumar Panda fulfils this long-felt need in an able manner. He himself is a good Nyāya-student turning to Advaita Vedānta and as such he was eminently qualified to undertake such a comprehensive study of this uniquely significant Vedāntist. He has deservedly earned his doctorate on this study. Now, when his study is coming out in a book form, I am sure it will be received well by the scholars and be useful for further intensive research on these lines. I congratulate Dr. Panda and wish him well in his further scholarly pursuits.

May 1995 —**Prof. R.I. Nanavati**
Head, Deptt. of Sanskrit, Pali & Prakrit,
Faculty of Arts,
M.S. University of Baroda,
Baroda.

PREFACE

I have great pleasure in introducing to the world of scholars the present research-work- "Ānandabodha Yati: A Study" fully accomplished by Dr. Rabindra Kumar Panda, Lecturer, Department of Sanskrit, Pali & Prakrit, M.S. University, Baroda.

The whole study is divided into nine chapters in which the author has succinctly sketched biographical profile of Ānandabodha, his ontological, epistemological as well as soteriological theories with all their details. While doing so Dr. Panda has furnished with the complete account and philosophical tenets found in both heterodox as well as orthodox schools of Indian philosophy followed by their criticism and evaluation skilfully presented by Ānandabodha.

The present work which is both critical and comprehensive is based on Ānandabodha's four recondite texts viz. *Nyāyamakaranda*, *Pramāṇamālā*, *Nyāyadīpāvali* and *Nyāyadīpikā* studied meticulously by Dr. Panda who has illustrated the pertinent points by giving apt quotations from the several texts of celebrated authors belonging to ancient and medieval period.

Several thinkers and scholars like Citsukhācārya, Madhusūdana Sarasvati, Appayya Dīkṣita, Cāndu Paṇḍita, Vedānta Deśika have been immensely influenced by the versatile scholarship of Ānandabodha as cleverly pointed out by Dr. Panda. He has also critically evaluated the contribution of Ānandabodha profusely employing Nyāya-terms, syllosisms and dialectic methodology in order to refute the prima facie views and establish the main tenets of Advaita Vedānta.

The present work closes with bibliography and useful appendices comprising of a list of verses composed by Ānandabodha as well as syllogisms, maxims (Nyāyas) and epigrams contained in his works.

I know Dr. R.K. Panda for the last few years and am greatly impressed by his research acumen.

I hope that the present publication which significantly adds to the Indological literature in general and Advaita Vedānta in particular will be greatly appreciated by the scholars all over the world.

18.5.95 **—Uma Deshpande**

Baroda

Reader in Sanskrit, Faculty of Arts
M.S. University,
Baroda

AUTHOR'S PREFACE

The present work is a revised form of my doctoral thesis entitled as Ānandabodha Yati : A Study and approved by the M.S. University of Baroda for the degree of doctor of philosophy in 1993. It embodies the results of my long and meticulous study of Ānandabodha's philosophical works.

In the history of Indian philosophical literature in general and Advaita Vedānta in particular Ānandabodha Yati occupies a prominent place for his significant and substantial contribution to the prodigious growth of the post-Śaṅkara Advaita school.This eminent philosopher and profound thinker has distinguished himself from his celebrated predecessors like Prakāśātman and Sarvajñātman as the author of three outstanding independent works as well as a commentary. He has displayed unique genius and deep critical acumen in analysing, interpreting Sankaraite tenets and rebutting antagonistic views on logical grounds. Ānandabodha's role lies mainly in the enunciation and indoctrinisation of the Advaita standpoints on logical grounds employing syllogistic methods and technical terms against his opponents.It is because, at the time of Ānandabodha, rigorous logical methods of the Naiyāyikas like Jayanta Bhaṭṭa and Udayanācārya were prominently in vouge, particularly in the domain of philosophy. Ānandabodha, the only renowned Advaitin of the eleventh century, found that unless the basic concepts of Advaita were vindicated by strict and rigorous logic, they will become easy victims of attack from other systems, especially from the Nyāya and the Prābhākara school of Pūrva Mīmāṁsā. Hence he has dealt with the principal subject-matter in dialectic, syllogistic and analytic way. Coming quite distant in time from that of Śaṅkarācārya, the great architect of Advaitism, Ānandabodha had authentic intimations of what the great teacher meant of Advaita as implied in his celebrated commentaries on the *Brahmasūtra,* and Upaniṣads to us the classical import of Śaṅkarācārya's tenets. Thus, Ānandabodha is an interpreter and critic on his own and throws valuable light on various issues and aspects of Advaita Vedānta in a thought provoking manner, erudite style and dialectic method. Although Ānandabodha has borrowed some views from his prominent predecessors he does not blindly follow them in all respects. Sometimes he offers his unique opinions different from those of the earlier schools and also rejects their doctrines boldly and clearly. With this particular view an attempt has been made to present the distinct contribution of the prominent thinker Ānandabodha Yati to Indian philosophy in general and Absolute Monism (Advaita Vedānta) in particular in this present work. I have attempted to study his four polemic works entitled *Nyāyadīpikā* alias *Śābdanirṇayadīpikā,* a commentary on the *Śābdanirṇaya* of Prakāśātman, *Nyāyadīpāvali, Pramāṇamālā* and *Nyāyamakaranda.*

The present study attempts to examine and evaluate critically Ānandabodha's various principal tenets, views, and interpretations of several scriptural texts.

The study based on all four texts of Ānandabodha has been presented in the following chapters:-

CHAPTER I : A Brief Survey of Philosophical Doctrines of the Prominent Advaita Vedāntins upto Ānandabodha.

CHAPTER II : Ānandabodha : His Date and Works

CHAPTER III : Ontological Views

CHAPTER IV : Epistemological Views

CHAPTER V : Soteriological Views

CHAPTER VI : Predecessors and Successors

CHAPTER VII : Ānandabodha's Philosophy:A Critique

CHAPTER VIII : Ānandabodha's Distinctive Contribution

CHAPTER IX : General Estimate and Conclusion.

I take this opportunity to perform the most pleasant duty of expressing my deepest sense of gratitude to my most revered guide Dr. (Mrs.) Uma S. Deshpande, Reader, Department of Sanskrit, Pali and Prakrit for her excellent guidance and ever memorable help. Inspite of her heavy load of work and engagements, she had spent her most precious time in reading my work seriously, making necessary corrections repeatedly, in discussing some debatable points and enlightening me the right way by means of valuable suggestions and for writing an excellent, encouraging Preface to this book, I am highly grateful to her.

I am highly grateful to Prof. Dr. S.G. Kantawala, Ex-Head, Department of Sanskrit, Pali and Prakrit and Ex-Dean, Faculty of Arts, Ex-Director, Oriental Institute, M.S. University of Baroda for his valuable suggestions and constant inspirations to me for my study.

I express a deep and heart-felt sense of gratitude to Dr. R.T. Vyas, Director, Oriental Institute, M.S. University of Baroda, for allowing me to consult the manuscript of *Pramāṇamālā* preserved in the Oriental

Institute and collecting materials for my study from the Institute Library.

It is also a great pleasure to acknowledge my indebtedness to Prof. R.I. Nanavati, Head, Department of Sanskrit, Pali and Prakrit, Faculty of Arts, M.S. University, whose inspiration and encouragement in different ways for higher and deeper learning have given me a courage to walk ahead with conviction in my capabilities. I also express my thanks for writing a Foreword to this book.

I am greatly indebted to Dr. Jaydev A.Jani, Reader, Department of Sanskrit, Pali and Prakrit, Faculty of Arts, M.S. University who has helped me by supplying some valuable information and constant motivation. I am also thankful to my other collegues, Dr. L.M. Joshi and shri B.P. Pandya who had helped me with their inspirations.

I wish to place specially on record my gratitude to Professor Keshab Chandra Dash, Head, Department of Nyāya Philosophy, Shree Jagannatha Sanskrit University, Puri, Orissa for his affectionate encouragement and valuable advice. On the same line, I record my special thanks to Dr. M.L. Wadekar, Deputy Director, and S.Y. Wakankar, Research Officer, Oriental Institute for their encouragement and genuine interest in my scholastic and literary works.

My thanks are due to my friend Satyavalan, Teacher Fellow of CASE, Department of Education and Psychology, M.S. University who enormously helped me by collecting photo-stat copy of Ānandabodha's *Nyāyadīpikā* manuscript from the Govt. Madras Oriental Library, Madras.

I am grateful to U.G.C. for awarding me Junior Research Fellowship by which I was able to complete this study.

I also thank the authorities of the M.S. University of Baroda, Baroda for giving me permission to get the work published.

I also like to take this opportunity to note that I have been considerably helped by my wife Smt. Sweta R. Panda in bringing this work to the present shape. I enjoy my feelings of thankfulness to her.

I am very much thankful to my publisher Shri Shyam Lal Malhotra of Eastern Book Linkers, Delhi, without whose kind co-operation this book could not have seen the light of the day.

18th August,1995
Janmāṣṭamī

Rabindra Kumar Panda
Lecturer,
Department of Sanskrit,
Pali and Prakrit, Faculty of Arts
M.S. University of Broda
Broda

LIST OF ABBREVIATIONS

Aṣṭ	Aṣṭādhyāyī
BBV	Bṛhadāraṇyaka Upaniṣad-Bhāṣya-Vārttika
BG	Bhagavadgītā
BGŚB	Bhagavadgītā-Śāṅkarabhāṣya
Bhā	Bhāmatī
Bṛh. Up.	Bṛhadāraṇyaka Upaniṣad-Śāṅkarabhāṣya
BS	Brahmasiddhi
BSU	Brahmasūtra
BSŚB	Brahmasūtra Śāṅkarabhāṣya.
Chā.Up.	Chāndogya Upaniṣad
G.K.	Gauḍapādakārikā
HIP	A History of Indian Philosophy.
Iśa. Up.	Iśāvāsya Upaniṣad
IṢ.	Iṣṭasiddhi
JS	Jaiminisūtra
Kaṭh.Up.	Kaṭha Upaniṣad
Kp	Kāvyaprakāśa
MK	Mūlamādhyamika-kārikā
Muṇḍ.Up.	Muṇḍaka Upaniṣad
ND	Nyāyadīpāvali
NDI	Nyāyadīpikā

NM	Nyāyamakaranda
NMN	Nyāyamañjarī
NS	Nyāyasūtra
NṢK	Naiṣkarmyasiddhi
Nyā. bhā	Nyāyasūtrabhāṣya
Ny. Vā	Nyāyavārttika
PM	Pramāṇamālā
Pin. Up.	Pingala Upaniṣad
PP	Prakaraṇapañcikā
PPA	Pañcapādikā
PPV	Pañcapādikāvivaraṇa
PV	Pramāṇavarttika
RV	Ṛgveda
SD	Sāhityadarpaṇa
SI	Siddhāntakaumudī
SK	Sāṁkhyakārikā
SS	Samkṣepaśārīraka
Swet. Up.	Swetāśvetara Upaniṣad
SV	Ślokavārttika
Tait. Up.	Taittirīya Upaniṣad
VM	Vākyārthamātṛkā
VS	Vaiśeṣikasūtra
VIJ	Vishveshvarananda Indological Journal
YS	Yogasūtra

CONTENTS

CHAPTER I

A BRIEF SURVEY OF THE PHILOSOPHICAL DOCTRINES OF THE PROMINENT ADVAITA VEDĀNTINS UPTO ĀNANDABODHA

1.1 Significance of The Term Vedānta

The term *Vedānta* is generally explained to mean the *anta* or concluding portion of the *Veda*, taking *Veda*, with the commentators,to denote the *Saṁhitās* and *Brāhmaṇas*[1] (including the *Āraṇyakas* and *Upaniṣads*) of the different recensions of the *Vedas*. But all the *Vedānta* texts do not come at the end of the *Brāhmaṇas*. Some, like the *Īśa* or the *Bāṣkala*, form portions of the *Saṁhitās* themselves, while others, like the *Aitareya* and the *Taittirīya*, come in the middle of the *Āraṇyakas* and not at their very end, as it is the case with the *Chāndogya* or the *Bṛhadāraṇyaka*. As a consequence, another mode of interpreting the term *Vedānta* is at times resorted to wherby *anta* is taken to imply the final or ultimate teaching of the *Veda*. The major portion of the *Vedic* texts concern themselves with the details of the ritual,

1. *Mantrabrāhmaṇayorvedanāmadheyam;* Āpastamba, *Yajñaparibhāṣāsūtra,* I.34; *Mantrabrāhmaṇayorveda-śabdaḥ, Kauṣitaki-Gṛhyasūtra,* III.12.23

with the *Karmakāṇḍa* but the final teaching of the *Veda* i.e. *Vedānta* is salvation through knowledge.In this sense Vedānta is often styled the Uttara-Mīmāṁsā, or the science of exegesis as applied to the latter portion of the *Veda,* to distinguish it from the Pūrva-Mīmāṁsā which deals with the earlier or ritualistic part of the *Veda.*The name *Vedānta* does not signify one system only but it comprehends several systems differing from each other essentially in points of metaphysical doctrines, ranging from absolute idealism down to dualism, at the same time having some important features which are common and which may be the reason of their being designated by a common name, besides the fact of their professing to be based on the *Vedānta* or the *Upaniṣads.*

1.2 The Chief Periods of Advaita Vedānta

Advaita philosophy is *Philosophia Perennis* in its meaning and scope, in its theory and practice and in its ideology and methodology.Its tradition is oldest in the history of philosophy coming as it has been from the pre-historic days of the *Ṛgveda.* Radhakrishnan, the doyen of modern Indian philosophy divides[1] Indian philosophy in general and Advaita philosophy in particular into four periods, viz., the Vedic period, the Epic period, the Sūtra period and the Scholastic period. Sangamlal Pandey has classified[2]the same into five periods:-

I. The Vedic Period (2000 B.C. - 500 B.C.)[3]

II. The Upaniṣadic Period (700 B.C. - 600 B.C.)[4]

1. Radhakrishnan, S.*Indian Philosophy,* Vol.I, pp.56-59.
2. Pandey, Sangamlal. *Pre-Śaṅkara Advaita Philosophy,* p.l
3. Winternitz, M. *A History of Indian Literature,* p.310.
4. Dasgupta, S.N. *A History of Indian Philosophy,* Vol.I.p.28.

III. The Epic Period (600 B.C.[1] - 200 A.D.)

IV. The Aphoristic Period (200 A.D.[2] - 500 A.D.)

V. The Commentatorial Period (200 A.D.[3] -1400 A.D.)

The last period i.e. the Commentatorial period, has been classified into the following three periods :-

I. The Pre-Śaṅkara Period (500 A.D.[4] - 700 A.D.)

II. The Period of Śaṅkara (788 A.D.[5] - 820 A.D.)

III. The Post-Śaṅkara Period (800 A.D.[6] - 1400 A.D.)

1.3 The Vedic Period

The Vedānta philosophy begins with the *Ṛgveda* which includes about a dozen esoteric hymns like ṚV.X.129, X.90, 1. 164, 46, 1.115.1, X.81-82, X.172, X.171, X.121, X.12, and others. In these hymns, along with speculations on the universe and the creation, that great pantheistic idea of the universal soul which is one with the universe, appears for the first time-an idea, which since that time has dominated the whole Indian philosophy. Inspite of the reference to different deities like *Indra, Varuṇa, Yama, Agni, Mātariśvan,* the underlying monistic current is unmistakable. In these philosophical hymns the great idea of universal unity is foreshadowed, the idea that everything which we see in nature and which the popular belief designates as 'god', in reality is only the emanation of the one and

1. Radhakrishnan, S. op.cit. p.57.
2. Ibid. p.58.
3. Ibid. p.59.
4. Mahadevan, T.M.P. *Gauḍapāda; A Study in Early Advaita,* p.13.
5. Dasgupta, S.N. *A History of Indian Philosophy* Vol.I, p.418
6. Ibid. p.418.

only one; that all plurality is only imaginary - an idea which is clearly expressed in Ṛ.V.1.164.46, (*indram mitram varuṇamagnimahratho divyaḥ sa suparṇo gurutman ekam sadviprā bahudhā vadantyagnim yamam mātarisvānamāhu*). There are other *mantras* advocating oneness of the reality, like, That one (*tadekam*) is not personal; it is neither male nor female; it is neuter. It is an impersonal principle. There was nothing other than it (ṚV., 10.129.1,2). "Thus already in certain hymns of the *Ṛgveda*, there emerges a thought with which philosophy begins, - the conception of the unity of world, - which later rose upto Monism, perceiving through the veil of the manifold, the unity which underlies it."[1] In this connection may be particularly noticed the hymn X.121, where the *Hiraṇyagarbha* is described as existing in the beginning of the creation, the sole lord of being, supporting heaven and earth and X.90 where the whole world is conceived as one being, the *Virāṭapuruṣa* who having pervaded the earth from all sides, still remains over and above the mundane universe.

1.4 The Upaniṣadic Period

The monism adumbrated in the *Ṛgveda* is developed into idealistic monism in the Upaniṣads, which regard *Brahman*, the infinite, eternal, omnipresent, omniscient, and pure spirit as the Ultimate Reality. The temporal, spatial and causality bound world is the manifestation of this infinite and eternal spirit. *Brahman* is non-temporal, transcendental, indefinable, incomprehensible and unknowable. *Brahman* is without before and after, and inside and outside. It is *Ātman*. It is the one, undifferntiated, homogenious consciousness without inside and outside. The main idea of the oldest *Upaniṣads* i.e. the *Chāndogya*, vi.2.1, the *Bṛhadāraṇyaka*,

---

1. Ghate, V.S. *The Vedānta*, p.6.

II.4.14, IV.4.19, II.5.13, the *Muṇḍaka* and the *Kaṭha* can be summed up in the equation, *Brahman* = *Ātman* the world taken in the strictest and most literal sense from which it follows that the *Ātman* is the only Reality. (Bṛh.Up.I.4.10, II.5.1, II.5.14; Chā.Up.III.4.1). It is the metaphysical unity which is manifested in all the empirical plurality; all plurality thus by implication reducing itself to *Māyā*, that it is the knowing subject, is itself unknownable.Thus the doctrine of *Māyā* that the universe is illusory is found in some of the *Upaniṣads* like *Śvetāśvetara* 9-10.

1.5 The Epic Period

The *Mahābhārata* contains many and the varied developments of philosophy out of the *Upaniṣads*.It shows that the *Upaniṣads* gave rise, besides *Vedānta*, to several other schools of thought.*Brahmavidyā*, too, is not unknown to the Epic about which S.K.De has pertinently observes: "Indeed, the idealistic absolution of the Upaniṣads underlies most of the Epic teaching in its theoretic aspect".[1] But "the main contribution of the Epic to Advaita is the *Bhagavadgītā*".[2]

The *Bhagavadgītā* which forms part of the *Bhīṣmaparva* of the *Mahābhārata* (25-42) is the most popular religious poem of Sanskrit literature. It is a book conveying lessons of philosophy, religion and ethics.[3] The *Bhagavadgītā* transforms the metaphysical doctrine of the *Upaniṣads* into the philosophy of universal ethics and religion.It contributes, among others, the following main doctrines to Advaita.

---

1. *History of Philosophy, Eastern and Western*.Vol.I Ed. by Radhakrishnan and others, p.86.
2. Pandey, Sangamlal, *Pre-Śaṅkara Advaita Philosophy*, p.18.
3. Radhakrishnan, S. *Indian Philosophy*, Vol.I, p.519.

In the spirit of the *Upaniṣads*, the *Gītā* identifies the two principles i.e. the *Ātman* with the *Brahman*.Behind the fleeting senses and the physical body there is the *Ātman;* behind the fleeting objects of the world there is *Brahman*.The two are one, being of identical nature (XV.17, VIII.22, VIII.3).

The *Bhagavadgītā* removes the conflict of all pathways, i.e. *jñānamārga, yogamārga, karmamārga* and *bhaktimārga* and maintains that they are in reality one and the same. Dividing all these pathways into two classes, *Sāṁkhyamārga* and *Yogamārga,* it establishes the Advaita view that "he who sees *Sāṁkhya* and *Yoga* as one, really sees" (BG, IV.2, VII, 21-23, IX.3, 5, 23).This unity of all pathways is explicitly maintained in the *Bhagavadgītā*.

The *Gītā* develops the doctrine of *māyā* (IV.6, VII.14, VII.15, 25) when it solves the problem of the transformations of the impersonal Absolute into a personal God by the supposition that it is due to *māyā* or cosmic illusion that such a transformation takes place.In other words, the *Bhagavadgītā* states that this transformation is a mistery and explains in the same way the relation of the Absolute to the world as the *Upaniṣads* do. Although Śrīkṛṣṇa comes as a personalised God, the monistic principle is constantly kept in view in His utterences. The *Gītā* of Śrīkṛṣṇa lights the way of the *Bhāgavatadharma* which assures all, irrespective of caste, class or sex that they can achieve liberation by continuing their daily works and activities in a spirit of devotion and renunciation.

There is an allegorical interpretation of the *Gītā*. The blind Dhṛtarāṣṭra represents ignorance. Arjuna is the Individual soul. Śrīkṛṣṇa, the charioteer represents the universal soul, the indweller of the heart. Our body is the chariot, the sense motor organs being the horses.

Mind, egoism, senses, *samskāras*, desires, craving, anger, hatred, lust, jealous, greed, pride and hypocricy are our enimies. These battles within are being faught continously in life.

1.6 The Aphoristic Period

The *Brahmasūtra* written by Bādarāyaṇa is the main text in representing the aphoristic period in the Indian philosophy.The *Brahmasūtra,* also called the *Vedāntasūtra* is the exposition of the philosophy of the *Upaniṣads* which form the background of the orthodox systems of thought. All the commentators on the *Brahmasūtra* agree that the *Brahmasūtra* was intended to be a summary of the teaching of the *Upaniṣads.*

Bādarāyaṇa declares that *Brahman* is the cause of the origin, subsistence and dissolution of the world (1.1.2), cause both material and instrumental (I.IV.23), the *Brahman* having created the world even though it exhibits qualities divergent from those of the cause from out of itself, unaided by any extraneous means by the process of *Pariṇāma* (progressive modification). The world so created is not new object coming into existence out of an absolutely non-existent state. The *sūtrakāra* propounds that the Individual Soul is distinct from intellect, mind, sense-organs, and life- breaths (II.3.15, II.3.30, II.3.32, II.4.1, II.4.17, IV.2.10) as also from both the gross physical body and the subtle transmigrating body conceived as a totality. Individual Soul is minute in size (II.3.1). It has his abode in the heart (II.3.24, I.3.14) where he dwells along with the lord, the creator from whom he is distinct entity but is nevertheless related to Him like the drop to the ocean or the sparks to the fire. As the soul's essence is identical with that of *Brahman,* there is no creation of the soul as such.The soul is immortal and liable to transmigrations from life to life (II.3.19, III.1.1, III.1.13) until he is able to win his salvation through proper knowledge and discipline.

1.7 The Commentatorial Period

1..7.I(A) The Pre-Śaṅkara Period

Gauḍapāda (520-620 A.D.)[1] occupies an important place in the history of Advaita Vedānta as he is its first systematic exponent. In the traditional salutation formula repeated daily by the followers of Śaṅkarācārya, Gauḍapāda stands as the grand preceptor (*Paramaguru*) of Śaṅkara. Gauḍapāda's teaching provides the firm foundation on which Śaṅkarācārya and his successors in the Advaita field built their edifice of detailed, and analytical exposition of Advaita theory.[2] In the history of Advaita his name will ever remain as that of great pioneer who combined in himself a deep mysticism with a penetrating philosophy.

Gauḍapāda is known as the author of the following works[3].

1. *Gauḍapāda Kārikā* or *Māṇḍukyopaniṣad Kārikā*
2. *Bhāṣya on the Sāṁkhyakārikā of Īśvarakṛṣṇa*
3. *Uttaragītā*
4. *Subhagodayastuti*
5. *Śrīvidyāraṇyasūtra*

The Ultimate Reality, according to Gauḍapāda, is *Brahman*. Following the way of the *Upaniṣads*, he teaches the nature of *Brahman* both affirmatively and negatively. As related to and inclusive of the world, *Brahman* is *Īśvara* who is also called the lower (*apara*) *Brahman*. As

---

1. Sastri, Kuppuswamî. *Brahmasiddhi of Maṇḍana Miśra*, Intro. p.LVIII.
2. Karmarkar, R.D. *Gauḍapādakārikā*, Intro. p.XLVII.
3. *Ibid*. p.IX.

Īśvara, seated in the hearts of all, (G.K.I. 28) is the all-pervasive lord, impelling all being to activity. It remains the same in the three states of experience, viz. weaking, dream and sleep. The higher *Brahman (parambrahma)* i.e. *Brahman* per se, however, is not related to the world. It is devoid of sleep and dream; and transcends the three states of experience, and hence is called the fourth (*turīya*) (G.K.I.14). Gauḍapāda expounds the doctrine of non-duality (G.K.I.10, I.16, I.14) of the supreme spirit through citing important scriptural passages, and through reasoning. The creation-texts, he says, should not be interpreted literally; they are to be understood in a figurative sense, and should be regarded as providing an introduction to the texts which teach non-duality. Gauḍapāda gives an analysis of the three states of experience, and concludes as a result thereof that the real Self is not affected by the changing states, and it is the constant unvarying non-dual reality. Gauḍapāda sets forth the doctrine of *ajāti* (non-origination). The category of cause itself, which is the ground of the notion of origination, is unintelligible. Giving a critique of causality, "Gauḍapāda says that nothing could come out of nothing; nor could anything issue out of anything else. *Asatkāryavāda* and *Satkāryavāda* perish mutual conflict, and point to the truth of no-origination, the truth that nothing whatsoever is born".[1] *Brahman,* which is the eternal reality and is immutable, is neither an effect nor a cause. There is nothing other than it, either to produce it or to be produced by it. Gauḍapāda holds the view that the world of plurality is an appearance (*māyāmātra*). The one self seems to be many through its own *māyā* (G.K. 2.12.). The world with its things is an illusory projection of *Ātma-māyā* (G.K. III.10). Gauḍapāda teaches the

1. Mahadevan, T.M.P. op.cit, p.235

Vivartavāda or, to use his terminology, the *Vaitathya* of the world. *Māyā* which is the principle of illusion has not an independent ontological status. It is not an entity or reality having a substance of its own. As there are no real distinctions in ether and they are created by things like pot and pitches, similarly, according to Gauḍapāda, *Brahman* or the Self which is pure consciousness is undivided and indivisible. The truth is that no *jīva* is ever born. There is neither destruction nor origination, neither the bound souls nor those who seek the means to release, neither *mumukṣu* nor *mukta* (G.K. II.32). According to Gauḍapāda, *mokṣa* is not that what is attained *(sādhya)*. What is called *mokṣa* is really the attainment of what is really attained. The path thereto is *jñāna*. Gauḍapāda defines it as *ātmasatyānubodha* (realisation of truth of the self) (G.K.III.32). It is through the unborn knowledge that the unborn self is realised.

B) Maṇḍana Miśra - (750 A.D.)[1]

In ranking philosophical writers according to their contributions to the liberation of the human mind Maṇḍana Miśra, a great authority on Mīmāṁsā and Advaita Vedānta occupies a prominent place after Gauḍapāda in the history of pre-Śaṅkara Advaita Vedānta. He is the author of six works,[2] viz. 1. *Mīmāṁsānukramaṇikā*, 2. *Bhāvanāviveka*, 3. *Vidhiviveka*, 4. *Sphoṭasiddhi*, 5. *Vibhramaviveka* 6. *Brahmasiddhi*. Of these works, Maṇḍana's *Brahmasiddhi* occupies a unique place among the works on Advaita Vedānta not only because of its comparative antiquity but also because of the comprehensive and elaborate treatment of the various aspects of the Advaita doctrine.

---

1. Potter,K.H. op.cit. 19.
2. Sastri, S.K., *Brahmasiddhi*, Intro.

Maṇḍana maintains the *Sphoṭavāda* and *Śabdādvaita* of Bhartṛhari. He holds the view that the Upaniṣadic texts "*Aum iti Brahma, Aum iti idamsarvam:*" should be understood as establishing the identity of *praṇava* with *Brahman* and as supporting the *Śabdādvaita* doctrine.[1] Maṇḍana gives a prominent and honoured place to the *Bhāṭṭa* theory of *Viparitakhyāti* or *Anyathākhyāti* (BS. p.143, 150) with a slight variation.He maintains that the theory of *anyathākhyāti* is sound and when the nature of the object of erroneous cognition is examined, this theory reduces inevitably to a form in which it becomes hardly distinguishable from the *anirvacanīyakhyāti* (error of an indefinable object). Further, Maṇḍana recognises two kinds of *avidyā* (nescience), viz, non-apprehension (*agrahaṇa*). and misapprehension (*anyathāgrahaṇa*) (BS. p.149-50). Maṇḍana also utilises this distinction in explaining the purpose of meditation in his scheme of the attainment of the final liberating realisation of *Brahman* and considers meditation necessary for completely removing the second variety i.e. *anyathāgrahaṇa* of nescience and for converting the first indirect knowledge of *Brahman* (*parokṣajñāna*) into the direct *Brahman*-realisation (*aparokṣabrahma-sākṣātkāra*). Maṇḍana further avers that *Jīva* (the Individual soul) is the locus (*āśraya*)and *Brahman* is its object (*viṣaya*) (BS.p.50).According to Maṇḍana, the Upaniṣadic texts like '*Tattvamasi*' (Chā.Up.9.4, 10.2.3) reveal the identity of *Brahman* with *Ātman* and give rise to the true knowledge of the one Absolute Real.The knowledge which arises from such texts, however, is indirect (BS.p.99) and mediate (*parokṣa*) and necessarily involves relation in some manner (*samsṛṣṭaviṣaya*), like any other cognition arising from a valid verbal testimony (*śabdapramāṇa*). Maṇḍana advocates that the direct realisation which

1. Sastri, S.K., op.cit.p.XXVI.

springs from meditation based upon the indirect knowledge arising from the Upaniṣadic texts, is capable of bringing about the *mokṣa,* (final beatitude).

1.7.II The Period of Śaṅkara

Śaṅkarācārya (780 - 820 A.D.)[1] is one of the greatest systematic thinkers that India has ever produced.His Advaitism is a system of great speculative daring and logical sabtlety. From a purely philosophical point of view and apart from all theological considerations, Śaṅkara's doctrine is the most important and interesting one which has arisen on Indian soil.In him all lines of thought converge : Idealism and realism, pragmatism and rationalism, naturalism and mysticism, agnosticism and faith- philosophy.His system is one of the most valuable products of genius of mankind in its search for the eternal truth, and won him a place among the immortals. The works of Śaṅkara include eleven commentaries on the *Brahmasūtra,* the *Bhagavadgītā* and the prominent Upaniṣads etc., as well as five *Prakaraṇa granthas, Upadeśasāhasrī, Aparokṣānubhūti, Ātmabodha* etc., and eight *stotras* like *Ānandalaharī, Daśaślokī, Dakṣiṇāmūrti, Ṣaṭpadī* etc. making a net total of twenty four.[2]

Śaṅkara's doctrine is usually known by the name of *kevalādvaita* (absolute monism) according to which the Supreme Reality i.e. the *Brahman* is the only transcendental, absolute, emanent power and everything else including the individual soul being false gets merged with it after attaining the true knowledge. The *Brahman,* intelligence, without form, without qualities, without any limitations of time, space or causality and under-

1. Dasgupta, S.N. *A History of Indian Philosophy. Vol.II.p.100*
2. Belvalkar, S.K., *Shree Gopal Basu Mallik Lectures on Vedānta Philosophy,* p.230.

lying the unity is according to Śaṅkara, is the only absolute substratum of all aphemeral; and the empirical plurality is itself without the slightest touch of plurality. Śaṅkara's doctrine has two aspects, esoteric and exoteric, be it with reference to theology, cosmology or psychology.Esoterically the *Brahman* (the supreme spirit) is knowledge or realisation itself, without qualification and without possibility of change;exoterically it is qualified possessed of an infinite number of auspicious attributes, capable of producing this world from itself and reabsorbing in itself,- it is *īśvara*. The esoteric cosmology, however, says that all this is a mere appearance of truth. The manifold world is only an illusion, *māyā*, a dream; and the reality is to be attained not by reasoning (*tarka*), but by introspective realisation (*anubhava*). According to the esoteric psychology, the *Jīva* is *Brahman* itself in full and total possession of eternity, omnipresence, omniscience, etc., but these godly qualities lie concealed with it as the fire in the wood and appears only after the final deliverance of self-realisation.

The philosophical part of Śaṅkara's doctrine may therefore be summed up as follows:-

1) All plurality is false or unreal and superimposed upon one pure and eternal *Brahman* which is all-pervading; it is the *māyā* which makes us see plurality where there is unity and which itself has not independent existence.(BSŚB.I.3.5, II.2.2, IV.3.14, II.1.33, I.3.16. II.I.14.)

2) The Individual Soul is really nothing but *Brahman*.(BSŚB.I.3.46, I.1.1, I.2.20, Bṛh.Up.ŚB.II.1.20).

3) Knowledge in the form of self-realisation of the identity of these two i.e. the *Brahman* and *Jīvātman* is the only means to *mokṣa* (BSŚB I.1.4. III.2.5, III.4.1, Bṛh.Up.ŚB, IV.3.1, IV.4.7, BGŚB.XVIII.20).

4) The practical part of the doctrine amounts to this:- Actions must be performed only to purify the mind so as to make one fit to acquire the knowledge of this identity of *Brahman* and *Jīva*; but afterwards they must be all given up, since without complete abandonment (*sanyāsa*) of all actions, *mokṣa* is impossible; for, action (*karma*) and knowledge (*jñāna*) are opposed to each other like darkness and light.

1.7.III The Post-Śaṅkara Period

Sureśvara (800 A.D.)[1]

In the history of Advaita Vedānta Sureśvara occupies an important place in as much as he has presented the philosophy of Śaṅkara in clear and systematic way. This eminent Mīmāṁsaka is renowned as an immediate disciple of Śaṅkara after the latter defeated him in a debate and converted the former into an Advaitin.

The works[2] of Sureśvara :-

1. *Naiṣkarmyasiddhi*[3]
2. *Bṛhadāraṇyaka - Upaniṣadbhāṣya- vārttika*[4]
3. *Taittirīya-Upaniṣadbhāṣya-vārttika*
4. *Mānasollāsa*
5. *Pañcikaraṇavārttika*

Sureśvara propounds the theory of semblance (*ābhāsavāda*) according to which *Jīva* (Individual self) is

---

1. Dasgupta, *A History of Indian Philosophy*, Vol.II.p.98.
2. Raghavachar, S.S. *Naiṣkarmyasiddhi of Śrī Sureśvarācārya*, Introduction. p.IV.
3. Edited, p.19 with the Commentaries *Candrikā* and *Vidyāsurabhi*, Bombay Sanskrit and Prakrit Series, No.38/1925.
4. Ānandāśrama, pune.

the semblance (*abhāsa*) of the *Brahman* (NṢK II.51; BBV.I.II.157, I.IV.1328, II.IV.4.24, 25.III.IV.105). Sureśvara does not recognise any kind of differentiation between *āśraya* (locus) and *viṣaya* of *avidyā*. (NṢK.3). According to Sureśvara the immutable *Brahman* is the material cause of the world while the *māyā* is its secondary or mediate cause. Sureśvara maintains that the Vedic texts are capable of producing immediate cognition of the self as *Brahman* and repudiates the necessity of meditation (*dhyānābhāsa*) or repeatition (*prasaṅkhyāna*) as a means of producing immediacy (*aparokṣatva*) (NṢK III.89-93, III.123-126). This view of Sureśvara is called *Śabdāparokṣavāda*.

Sureśvara holds that *mokṣa* has nothing to do with the performance of action (*karma*). *Mokṣa* is not acquired by a combination of knowledge and performance of duties. (BBV.18, 28, 38, 39, 40, 73, NṢK.1.54-79) When self-knowledge dawns, the experience of ego (*ahaṁkāra*) vanishes. Duality is caused by the effects of *antaḥkaraṇa*. Knowledge breaks the bond of objectivity and illusory appearance. Hence *Jñāna* (pure knowledge) is the only means for the attainment of self-realisation (NṢK.1.99).

Padmapāda (820 A.D.)[1]

Amongst the immediate disciples of Śaṅkara, Padmapāda is universally reputed for his substantial contribution to the development of Śaṅkara's Advaita doctrine. The only work which Padmapāda is reputed to have composed is a commentary on the *bhāṣya* of Śaṅkara called *Pañcapādikā*[2] as it relates to the first five

---

1. Dasgupta, S.N. *A History of Indian Philosophy*, Vol.II.p.100.
2. *Pañcapādikā* of Padmapādācārya, Edited by Chandrasekhran, T., Madras Government Oriental Series, Madras, 1958.

pādas of the *Brahmasūtra* of Bādarāyaṇa and unfortunately that too is not available in a complete form but upto first four *Sūtras*. Padmapāda propounds that *māyā, avyākṛta, prakṛti, agrahaṇa, avyakta, tamaḥ, karaṇa, laya, śakti, mahāsupti, nidrā, kṣara,* and *ākāśa* are the terms synonymous with *avidyā* (P.P.p.98). It is this entity that obstructs the pure and independently self-revealing nature of *Brahman,* and thus, standing as the painted canvas (*citra-bhitti*) of ignorance (*avidyā*), deeds (*karma*) and past impressions of knowledge (*pūrvaprajñāsamskāra*) produce the individual selves (P.P. p.98-99). Undergoing its peculiar transformations with *Brahman* as its support, it manifests itself as the two powers of knowledge and activity (*vijñānakriyāśaktidvayāśraya*) and functions as doer of all actions and enjoyer of all experiences (P.P. p.98-99). In the association with the pure unchangeable light of *Brahman* it is the complex of these transformations which appears as the immediate ego (*ahaṁkāra*) (P.P.p.98-99). Through the association with this ego the pure self is falsely regarded as the enjoyer of experiences. This transformation is called *antaḥkaraṇa, manas, buddhi* and the ego or the ego- feeler (*ahaṁ-pratyayin*) on the vibratory side of its activity, it is called *Prāṇa* (biomotor functions). The association of the ego with the pure *Ātman,* like the association of the redness of a *japā* flower with a crystal, is a complex (*granthi*) which manifests the dual characteristics of activity of the *avidyā* stuff and the consciousness of the pure self (*saṁbhinnobhayarūpatvāt*) (P.P. p.100-102). Padmapāda avers that *avidyā* manifests itself in the individual person by obstructing the real nature of the *Brahman* as pure, self-luminosity and that the *Brahman* by its limitation (*avaccheda)* through beginningless *avidyā* which is the cause of the appearance of infinite individual selves.

Hastāmalaka[1]

Hastāmalaka is one of the immediate disciples[2] of Śaṅkarācārya. He is known as the author of *Dvādaśamañjarīvyākhyā* and *Hastāmalaka-śloka*. Hastāmalaka expounds that the self is eternally pure and it goes through transmigration *(samsṛṣti)* which is only temporary. The cause of this *samsṛṣti* is *Avidyā* (nescience) residing in *Ātman*, its object. *Īśvara* is the reflection of *cidābhāsa* in *māyā* consisting of three qualities, viz., *Sattva*, *Rajas* and *Tamas* while *Jīva* is a reflection of the *Cidābhāsa* of *Sattvaguṇa padhānamāyā*. *Īśvara*, the cause of this world is a reflection of the Highest *Brahman* called *Kūṭasthacidābhāsa* while the *Jīva* appears to be the further reflection of this *Īśvara* in *Jīvamāyā* (limited nescience) influenced by *Rajas* and *Tamas*.

Toṭaka (800 A.D.)[3]

Toṭaka alias Ānandagiri is not a major author still he is reckoned among the *Śiṣyacatuṣṭayī* (four pupils) of Śaṅkarācārya. He is credited with the authorship of two works[4], viz. *Toṭakaśloka* and *Kālanirṇaya*. Toṭaka propounds that the highest Reality is *dṛśirūpa* (comprising intelligence), *ananta* (infinite), *ṛta* (Highest Reality), *viguṇa* (void of qualities) and *hṛdayastha* (residing in heart). The plurality in the world is like the several appearances of the sun due to the distinction by water or like the ether-in-jar.[5]

1. Raval, C.V., *Śrīmad Śaṅkarācāryanu Tattvajñāna*, pp.21-25.
2. Potter, K.H.op.cit.p.19
3. Nachane, S.A., *A Survey of Post- Śaṅkara Advaita Vedānta*, p.237.
4. Raval, C.V., *Śrīmad Śaṅkarācāryanu Tattvajñāna*, p.21-25.
5. Nachane, S.A., *A Survey of Post-Śaṅkara Advaita Vedānta*, Unpublished Ph.D. Thesis, p.237.

Vācaspati Miśra (841-900 A.D.)[1]

After the four immediate disciples of Śaṅkarācārya, Vācaspati Miśra, a great Advaitin of versatile genius and encyclopaedic learning rose to fame. He is reputed as the propounder of a new sub-school of Advaita called "Bhāmatī school" by the name of his celebrated *Bhāmatī* on the *Brahmasūtra-Śāṅkarabhāṣya,* which is the first complete commentary in the entire history of post-Śaṅkara Advaita Vedānta.

The following are the works[2] of Vācaspati:

(1) *Nyāyakaṇikā,* a commentary on the *Vidhiviveka* of Maṇḍana;

(2) *Tattvasamīkṣā,* a commentary on Maṇḍana's *Brahmasiddhi*

(3) *Tattvabindu,* an independent treatise on *Vākyārtha;*

(4) *Nyāya-Vārttika-Tātparyaṭīkā* is a commentary on Uddyotakara's *Nyāyavārttika.* It is an epistemological work which discusses in detail the nature of the *Pramāṇas;* it reconstructs Nyāya-Vaiśeṣika philosophy on account of which Vācaspati became famous as *Tātparyācārya.* (5) *Nyāyasūcī,* the Nyāya work written as a supplement to *Tātparya;* (6) *Sāṁkhyatattvakaumudī,* a commentary on *Iśvarakṛṣṇa's Sāṁkhyakārikā;* (7) *Tattva-Vaiśāradī,* a commentary on Vyāsa's *Yogabhāṣya;* (8) *Bhāmatī,* a commentary on the *Brahmasūtra-Śāṅkarabhāṣya.* Besides these works Vācaspati is supposed to have written other works like (1) *Nyāyatattvāloka,* (2) *Nyāyaratnaṭīkā* (3) *Brahmatattvasaṁhitoddīpinī,* (4) *Yuktidīpikā,* a work on the

1. Rao, V.N.S. *Vācaspati's Contribution to Advaita.* p.7.
2. *Ibid* p.1-4.

Sāṁkhya, (5) *Vedānta-Tattva-Kaumudī*. The *Bhāmatī*[1] like the *Brahmasūtra-Śāṅkarabhāṣya* is known for its profoundity of spirit and subtlety of thought. It gives a clear and precise account of the central ideas of Advaita, and expounds uncompromising non-dualism setting forth its basic principles in cogent terms. In spirit, his view of Advaita is marked by depth of insight. Vācaspati's other Vedāntic work, viz., *Brahmatattva-samīkṣā*, a commentary on Maṇḍana's *Brahmasiddhi* has not found the light of the day. Vācaspati propounds that the locus (*āśraya*) of *avidyā* is the Individual Soul (*Jīva*) and *Brahman* is its object (*viṣaya*) (Bhā.I.4.3.) *Avidyā* differs from individual to individual. It is positive (*bhāvarūpa*) and specific to each *Jīva*. In fact there are as many *avidyās* as there are *Jīvas*. Vācaspati thus believes in plurality of even *mūlā-avidyās* and accepts *āvaraṇa-śakti* (veiling power) alone as dominant in the case of *avidyā*. Further, Vācaspati recognises two kinds of *avidyā* (1) *Mūlā-avidyā* or primal nescience (*kāraṇa-avidyā)* and (2) *Tulā-avidyā* or derivative nescience (*kārya-avidyā*).

Vācaspati propounds the theory of limitation (*avacchedavāda*) according to which the Individual self (*Jīva*) is the limitation (*avaccheda*) of the *Brahman*. (Bhā.II.3.17;II.3.28, II.3.30).

Vācaspati holds the view that *Śabda* (verbal testimony) causes only mediate knowledge which is to be made direct and immediate through constant practice of rational contemplation (*manana*) and meditation (*nididhyāsana*). This view is technically called '*Prasaṁkhyāna*'. For Vācaspati, constant meditation becomes the primary means to *mokṣa* (salvation).

---

1. With *Brahmasūtra-Śāṅkarabhāṣya, Kalpataru and Parimala* Ed. by Anantakrishna Sastri , Nirnaya Sagar Press, Bombay, 1917.

According to Vācaspati, what is veiled by nescience is the conditioned *Brahman* (*sopādhika Brahman*) in as much as the unconditioned *Brahman* is flawless; it cannot be veiled nor can it be revealed. What is revealed by final intuition must therefore, be conditioned *Brahman* (*sopādhika Brahman*).

Vācaspati advocates a distinct view as to the role of *Karma* in the scheme of Advaitic *sādhana*. *Karma*, says Vācaspati, only subserves the purpose of generating the desire to know *Brahman* (*vividiṣā sādhana*), not as a means to the knowledge of *Brahman* (Bhā.III.4.6, III.4.34).

Vimuktātman (850-1050)[1]

Another great writer who flourished after Vācaspati Miśra is Vimuktātman. He is earlier than Prakāśātman, the author of the *Pañcapādikāvivaraṇa* wherein his view is referred by the latter. His successors like Prakāśātman, Sarvajñātman, Ānandabodha and others profusely refer to his views in their distinguished works like *Pañcapādikāvivaraṇa*, *Saṁkṣepaśārīraka* and *Nyāyamakaranda* respectively. Vimuktātman is known as the author of the two works,[2] viz., *Iṣṭasiddhi*[3] and *Pramāṇavṛttinirṇaya*. The first work is published, while the second is still in the manuscript form.

Vimuktātman holds the view that the Ultimate Reality is pure intuitive consciousness (*anubhūti*). Nothing can be beginningless and external, except pure consciousness (IṢ.p.1). *Māyā* is indescribable (*anirvacanīya*) not from both i.e. being and non-being (*sat* and *asat*). but as involving the characters of being and non-being (*sat* and *asat*). It is thus regarded as a

1. Hiriyanna, M. *Iṣṭasiddhi*, Intro, p.XIII.
2. Dasgupta, S.N. HIP. Vol.II. p.198.
3. *Iṣṭasiddhi of Vimuktātman, with Vivaraṇa*, Cri. ed. by Hiriyanna, M. Oriental Institute, Baroda, *1933*.

power of ignorance (*avidyā-śakti*) which is the material cause of all objects of perception otherwise called matter (*sarvajaḍopādānabhūtā*). (IṢ p.69). But, just as fire springing from bamboos may burn up the same bamboos even upto their very roots, so *Brahman*-knowledge, which is itself a product of ignorance and its processes, destroys the self-same ignorance from which it is produced and at last itself subsides and leaves the *Brahman* to shine in its own radiance (IṢ.p.69).

The functions of the *pramāṇas*, which are all mere processes of ignorance (*ajñāna or avidyā*), consist only in the removal of obstructions veiling the illumination of the self-luminous consciousness, just as the digging of a well means the removal of all earth that is obstructing the omnipresent *ākāśa* or space; the *pramāṇas* have thus no function of manifesting the self-luminous consciousness and only remove the veiling *ajñāna*. So *Brahman*-knowledge also means the removal of the last remnants of *ajñāna*, after which *Brahman*-knowledge as conceptual knowledge, being the last vestige of *ajñāna*, also ceases. This cessation of *avidyā* is as inspeakable as *avidyā* itself (IṢ. pp.366-375). Vimuktātman does not consider *avidyā* to be merely subjective but regards it as being both subjective and objective, involving within it not only all phenomena, but all their mutual relations and also related to the pure consciousness, which is in reality beyond all relations.

Sarvajñātma Muni (900 A.D.)[1]

Sarvajñātma Muni alias Sarvajñātman, is the author of three works - *Saṁkṣepaśārīraka*[2] , *Pañcaprakriyā*,

1. Dasgupta, S.N. HIP. Vol.II P.III.
2. *The Saṁkṣepaśārīraka of Sarvajñātman*, Cri.ed. with Intro. and English Translation by N.Veezhinathan, Madras University Philosophical Series, No.18. University of Madras, 1972.

and *Pramāṇalakṣaṇa*. Of these three works his *Saṁkṣepaśarīraka* is very famous which contains the gist of the *Brahmasūtra-Śāṅkarabhāṣya*. In his text Sarvajñātman tries to describe the fundamental problems of the Vedānta philosophy as explained by Śaṅkara. He maintains that pure *Brahman* is the Ultimate cause of everything through the instrumantality of *ajñāna* (SŚ.I.2). The *ajñāna*, which rests on the pure self operates on it as its object (*viṣaya*), covers its real nature and creates delusory appearance (*vikṣipti*), thereby, producing the threefold appearance of God, Soul and the World. (SŚ.I.20.319). The *ajñāna* has no independent existence and its effects are seen only through the pure self (*cidātman*) as its locus and object, (SŚ.III.8) and its creations are all false. The pure self is directly perceived in the state of dreamless sleep as being of the nature of pure bliss and happiness without the slightest touch of sorrow. (SŚ.I.23). The *ajñāna* is defined as being positive in its nature (*bhāvarūpa*) and, though it rests on the pure *Brahman*, yet it melts away like butter in contact with fire (SŚ.I.317). The positive character of *ajñāna* is felt in the world in its materiality and in ourselves as our ignorance. The real ground cause, however, is the pure *Brahman*, and the *ajñāna* is only the instrument or the means by which it can become the cause of all appearances; but it is not the material cause of the world. (SŚ.I.322,323). When with the dawn of the right knowledge pure *Brahman* as one is realised, *ajñāna* disappears. It is only the light of *Brahman* as underlying the Individual souls that the *ajñāna* is perceived, as when one says, "I do not know what you say"; so it is neither the Individual soul nor the pure one which is *Brahman*, but the pure light as it reveals through each and every Individual soul.(SŚ.II.211).

Sarvajñātman maintains that the Supreme self itself undergoes transmigration and attains release. There is the transmigration of the self having the subtle body as the operating condition. The state of remaining in the pure consciousness constitutes its liberation. The transmigration is caused by its own *avidyā,* and liberation by the knowledge of its true nature (SŚ.III.7). The Individual soul is not accepted to be either a part of the Supreme self or its transformation or different from it, for there would arise conflict with the group of Upaniṣadic statements conveying the identity of the Supreme self and the Individual soul (SŚ.III.10). Sarvajñātman points out that *Śravaṇa, manana* and *nididhyāsana* along with *sama, dama,* etc., when pursued by ascetics remove the impediments present in their minds, and the direct experience of *Brahman- Ātman,* effective in dispelling *avidyā,* arises in this life itself, provided there is no obstruction to its rise by a variety of *prārabdhakarma.* If there is such obstruction, knowledge does arise to them in the next life irrespective of the stage of life which they lead then (SŚ,III,361). Sarvajñātman speaks of asceticism as the necessary condition for attaining direct experience of *Brahman.*

Prakāśātman (1000 A.D.)[1]

Another great Advaitin of the post-Śaṇkara Vedānta is Prakāśātman who had brought Padmapāda's *Pañcapādikā* to very great prominence. He is more famous as *Vivaraṇakāra* by his work named *Pañcapādikāvivaraṇa*[2]. Besides the *Vivaraṇa* Prakāśātman is the author of

---

1. Gode, P.K. *Studies in Indian Literary History,* Vol.p.228; Hiriyanna, M., *Outlines of Indian Philosophy,* p.340.
2. *Pañcapādika-Vivaraṇa* with Two Commentaries Ed. by S.Srirama Sastri and S.R.K. Sastri, M.G.O.S. Madras, 1958.

another work entitled *Nyāyanirṇaya*. But his *Pañcapādikāvivaraṇa* is the nucleus for the development of Advaitic thought known as "*Vivaraṇa- prasthāna*".

According to the Vivaraṇa school of Prakāśātman *Brahman* is both the locus (*āśraya*) and object (*viṣaya*) of *avidyā*. He maintains that the *Jīva* (Individual Soul) cannot be the locus of *avidyā* in as much as the former is the modification of *avidyā*. To say that *Jīva* is the locus of *avidyā* is to commit the falacy of mutual dependence (*anyonyāśrayadoṣa*), that is, without the *Jīva*, *avidyā* cannot be explained. (PPV pp.210-219). Thus, the *Vivaraṇa* school does not admit any distinction between the locus (*āśraya*) and the object (*viṣaya*) of *avidyā*[1].

The Vivaraṇa school postulates only one *avidyā*, that is common to all *Jīvas* but has different modes or potencies (*śakti*) to bind the *Jīvas. The* Vivaraṇa school holds that in the case of *avidyā*, both *āvaraṇa* (veiling)) and *vikṣepa* (projecting) powers (*śaktis)* are equally dominant. According to the Vivaraṇa school *avidyā* is one (*eka-avidyā-vāda)* (PPV.p.693).

The Vivaraṇa school advocates *Pratibiṁbavāda* (the theory of reflection) that is, *Jīva* (Individual self) is the reflection(*pratibiṁba*) of the *Brahman*. (PPV. p. 287. 288. 289. 294. 760).

The Vivaraṇa school moves to reconcile the plurality of *Jīva* with the singleness of *avidyā* by postulating many *śaktis* for the only one *avidyā*.

According to the Vivaraṇa school *śravaṇa* (hearing) is the principal cause of the realisation of the *Ātman* and *manana* (contemplation) and *nididhyāsana* (meditation) are subservient to it (*phalopakāryāṅge*). The *manana* and *nididhyāsana*, in other words, only effect the concentration of the mind (PPV.p.38).

---

1. Sengupta, B.K. *A Critique on the Vivaraṇa School*, p.249.

The mind is not an instrument for the realisation of the *Brahman,* and by mere instruction immediate knowledge is effected. The Vivaraṇa school holds that knowledge through verbal testimony (*śabdapramāṇa*) is only immediate (*sākṣāt*) (PPV. p.452). Prakāśātman in his *Vivaraṇa* asserts that though the Upaniṣadic texts impart immediate knowledge of *Brahman,* yet because of certain defects such as *Viṣayabhogavāsanā, Pramāṇa-sambhāvanā* and *Viparītabhāvanā,* it appears to be mediate. When these defects are overcome by the cultivation of virtues like the contṛol of the intellect (*buddhi*) etc., and by Vedāntic study, it ceases to be mediate and then gradually becomes immediate. For the Vivaraṇa school *śabda* (verbal testimony) alone is the means to *mokṣa* (PPV. pp.403-408).

The Vivaraṇa school maintains that pure *Brahman* unenveloped by any *upādhi* (adjunct) is an object (*viṣaya*) of *manovṛtti.* (PPV. p.211,213,224). The non-delimited *Brahman* is the object of *akhaṇḍārthavṛtti.* Self-realisation, according to the Vivaraṇa school, is possible only through the injuction (*vidhi*) '*Ātmā vāre draṣṭavyaḥ* (Bṛh. Up.II. 4.5). It is at the root of studying and understanding the Vedānta. Prakāśātman emphasises the realisation of the self only through this injuction (*vidhi*) (PPV. pp.36-38).

In the text of Vivaraṇa Prakāśātman advocates that "*ātmā vāre śrotavyaḥ*" is a distinct *vidhi.* And, on the *vidhi* (injuction), the Vivaraṇa school concludes that *Śravaṇa* is the principal one and *manana* and *nididhyāsana* are auxiliary to it. (PPV. p.32,33,352). Thus, the Vivaraṇa school is of the firm opinion that *vidhi* is plausible in the matter of self-realisation and only because it is an injuction, *vidhi* the aspirant of *mokṣa* determines to move on the path of self-perfection. Further, the Vivaraṇa school propounds a distinct view as to the place of *karma* (action) in the scheme of Advaitic *sādhana*. *Karma*, according to the Vivaraṇa school, useful in generating the knowledge of *Brahman* (*Vijñāna-sādhana*) and it is not conducive to desire to know *Brahman* (*vividiṣā*) (PPV. p.37, 546,554,546).

CHAPTER-II

ĀNANDABODHA: HIS DATE AND WORKS

2.1 Ānandabodha

Ānandabodha Yati, most popularly known as Ānandabodha, is a distinguished philosopher of post-Śaṅkara period. He introduces to himself by diverse ways of attributes like *Yati* (NM. p.360; PM. p.24), *Bhaṭṭāraka* (NM, p.360; ND, p.15), *Parivrājakācārya* (PM. p.24), *Sudhi* (ND, p.15), *Sukavi* (PM. p.360) and *Ācārya* (PM. p.24). Ānandabodha is a great philosophical writer who has contributed four celebrated works to Advaita philosophy, viz., *Nyāyadīpikā*, *Nyāyadīpāvali*, *Pramāṇamālā* and *Nyāyamakaranda*.

There are misconceptions regarding the name of Ānandabodha among the scholars since other eminent writers are also referred to by the same name Ānandabodha in several texts.

Aufrecht in *Catalogus Catalogorum* (part 1, p.48, 1962) refers to Ānandabodha by the name Ānandabodha Paramahamsa, who is the writer of *Nyāyadīpāvali* and its commentary *Pramāṇaratnamālā*, *Nyāyamakaranda* and *Nyāyāpadeśamakaranda*. This view of Aufrecht is not correct since Ānandabodha is known as the author of four works, viz., *Nyāyadīpikā*, *Nyāyadīpāvali*, *Pramāṇamālā* and *Nyāyamakaranda*. No such commentary named *Pramāṇaratnamālā* on the *Nyāyadīpāvali* is known to have been written by Ānandabodha and *Nyāyamakaranda* is not different from the *Nyāyāpadeśamakaranda* as stated by Aufrecht.

The New Catalogus Catalogorum edited by V.Raghavan and Kunjunni Raja Vol.II, p.108 refers to four Ānandabodhas who are:

1) Ānandabodha, pupil of Ātmāvāsa seems to quote Vimuktātman as *Guru*. Quotes, *Vivaraṇa* (Sarvajñātman). Circa. latter half of 11th and first half of 12th Century.

- *Nyāyadīpāvali*
- *Nyāyamakaranda*
- *Pramāṇamālā*
- *Śābdanirṇayavyākhyā or*

Nyāyadīpikā.

This chronological order of Ānandabodha's works as stated in the *New Catalogus Catalogorum* is found to be incorrect. It is as follows: (a) *The Nyāyadīpikā*, (b) *Nyāyadīpāvali*, (c) *Pramāṇamālā* and (d) *Nyāyamakaranda*.[1]

2) Ānandabodhācārya - quoted in Bhaṭṭaji's *Caturviṁśatimatavyākhyā* - a descriptive catalogue of *Samskṛta* and *Prākṛta* manuscripts in the Library of the Bombay Branch of the Royal Asiatic society by H.D. Velankar, 683.

3) Ānandabodhācārya quoted by Miśra Jagannātha, son of Rāma in his *Caṇḍīpīyuṣa*, New Indian Antiquary, Poona and Bombay Karnataka Publishing House, Chira Bazar, Bombay, p.683.

---

1. Vide, The Chronological Order of Ānandabodha's Works. p.59

4) Ānandabodhācārya - writer of *Bhaktibhūṣā* mentioned by Śivaśarmāsūri in his *Vāsudevarasānanda* p.193. l.27, Indian Press, Banaras, 1953 - 36.

Among these four scholars by the name of Ānandabodha, we are concerned with the first one who has written the Advaita texts and who amply quotes Prakāśātman's *Vivaraṇa* etc. Again, *The Bhāratīya Sanskṛti Koṣa*[1] speaks about another Ānandabodha who is the son of Jātaveda Bhaṭṭopādhyāya and has written a commentary entitled *Kaṇvavedamantrabhāṣya Saṁgraha* on *Kaṇvasaṁhitā*. The date of this Ānandabodha is not known.

R.M.Sarma introduces one Ānandabodha by saying "Advaitānandabodhendra (1149 A.D.) was the chief Ācarya of *Śaradāmaṭha* or *Kāmakoṭipīṭha* and he was the pupil of Bhumānanda Saraśvatī or Candraśekharendra Saraśvatī. He learnt the education of Vedānta from Rāmānanda Sarasvatī. Advaitānandabodhendra was also known by the name Cidvilāsa and Ānandabodha. He wrote *Brahmavidyābharaṇa*, *Śāntivivaraṇa* and *Gurupradīpa*."[2]

But Ānandabodha who has written the texts, viz., *Nyāyadīpikā*, *Nyāyadīpāvali*, *Pramāṇamālā* and *Nyāyamakaranda*, and belongs to 1150 A.D., is altogether different from these above mentioned Ānandabodhas who are quite different from the present Ānandabodha, as referred to by M.S. Joshi and R.M. Sarma.

2.2 Personal Life

It is the misfortune of almost all Sanskrit writers to remain as far as their personal history is concerned

1. 1st part, ed. by Mahadeva Sastri Joshi, Bharatiya Sanskrit Kosamandala, Pune, p.443.
2. *Some Aspects of Advaita philosophy*,p.102.

under a thick veil of obscurity or even darkness which under the present circumstances apppears a difficult task to remove. In this connection Whitney has rightly remarks "all dates given in Indian history are pins set up to be bowled down again".[1]

Ānandabodha, the author of the above said four works, like most of the Sanskrit writers is totally reticent about himself. In his works he tells nothing about himself. Perhaps, he was quite well-known in his days and did not feel the necessity of giving any details about himself. Moreover, tradition also does not supply any information about him.

Based on the four works, however, some general information regarding the personal life of the philosopher is gleaned as follows.

Ānandabodha calls himself in the colophon verses of all the four texts as a *Yati* (an ascetic, one who has renounced the world and controlled passions) (NM. p.360), as a *Bhaṭṭārakācārya* (a great learned man or venerable) (NM. p.1), as *Paramahaṁsa-parivrājakācārya* (an ascetic of the highest order, one who has controlled all his senses by abstract meditation and a wandering mendicant of the fourth religious order who has renounced the world), *Sudhi* (wise), and *Sukavi* (great thinker or poet). These epithets indicate that Ānandabodha was not only a wise and learned person gifted with poetic calibre but also an ascetic of a very high order. It seems that before renouncing this mortal world and adopting *Sanyāsāśrama* Ānandabodha was a house holder interested in different aspects of domestic, social and cultural life.This is evinced by some of the statements found in his works, viz. description of exuberant hair of the ladies, the happy conjugal married

1. Whitney, W.D., "*Sanskrit Grammar*", Introduction p.XVII.

life, the process of initial learning on the part of a small child, the belief of welcoming the birth of a male child with great joy, and social customs, such as the distribution of food to the poor people in the society.

These minute observations of Ānandabodha's works indicate that he was a householder who has experienced the happy family life and enjoyed good social status as an erudite scholar (*sudhi*) and learned preceptor (*Ācārya*) in initial stage of his life. Later on after the thorough studies of the Indian scripture probably the *Prasthānatraya* and the texts of Śaṅkara Ānandabodha might have inclined to become a sanyāsī and to live a life of recluse living in a solitary place.

2.3 Native Place

Nothing is known about the native place of Ānandabodha neither from the tradition nor from the historical sources nor from his works. Ānandabodha also does not speak at all about his ancestors. Under these circumstances the approximate place is being fixed on the basis of the internal clues found in the text in the following way.

In the *Nyāyamakaranda* Ānandabodha says:

Prasiddhayaiva bhāṣayā abhidhīyatām kim aprasiddhābhiḥ karṇāṭalāṭabhāṣābhirbhāṣate (NM.p.253). This statement of Ānandabodha indicates that he does not possibly belong to the place where *Karṇāṭa* and *Lāṭa* languages are spoken i.e. the western part of India. Another clue also arrests our attention, viz., Anubhūtisvarūpācārya (1300 A.D.) who has commented on all the three works of Ānandabodha[1]. "As at the end of his *Sāraśvataprakriyā* and *Candrikā* he invokes the

1. Dasgupta, S.N. HIP. Vol.II. p.116.

favour of God Hayagriva, a deity worshipped in the Southern India only it appears that Anubhūtisvarūpācārya was a native of the South."[1] Since this commentator of Ānandabodha belongs to the Southern part of India, it is inferred that Ānandabodha also belongs to the Southern part of India.

Secondly, Ānandabodha refers to Padmapāda in his *Nyāyamakaranda*. He "was a Keralite Brahmin who belonged to Vemannu Amsam in Alatur. His real name was Viṣṇu Śarmā and later named Sananda in his ascetic life. He came to be known later on by the title of Padmapāda".[2]

2) Ānandabodha tacitly criticises in his *Pramāṇamālā* Sarvajñātman's view regarding the nature of the *Ātman* or *Brahman* as pure bliss. Sarvajñātman lived in the 10th century A.D. when Munukuladitya ruled over Kerala. Sarvajñātman's connection with Kerala particularly Trivandrum is evident because of his reference to the temple of Padmanābha at Trivandrum in the colophon of the *Saṁkṣepaśārīraka*.[3]

3) Citsukha who has written commentaries on the works of Ānandabodha is known to belong to South India i.e. Andhrapradesh on the basis of the inscriptional evidence.[4] As we find that Sarvajñātman was ordained as *Sanyāsin* in the *Kāñicikāmakoṭipīṭh* by Sureśvara[5] and being very much influenced by his

1. *Tarkasaṅgraha of Ānandajñāna* edited by T.M. Tripathi, p.IX.
2. Nampoothiry, Ewsaran, *Contribution of Kerala to Advaita Vedānta Literature*, VIJ. edi. by Virendra Sharma, Vol.XXII, June - Dec. 1984, p.188.
3. *ibid.*
4. Sarma, V.A., *Citsukha's Contribution to Advaita*, p.1.
5. Veezhinathan, N.*Samkṣepaśārīraka of Sarvajñātman, p.61.*

philosophical thought wrote *Saṁkṣepaśārīraka* wherein the Sarvajñātman elucidates his Advaitic doctrines.

Similarly Citsukha, probably, being very influenced by Ānandabodha's philosophical views, method of dialectical argumentation and profound analytical ability, wrote commentaries on all the works of Ānandabodha and accepted most of his philosophical concepts in his prominent work *Tattvapradīpikā*. Dr. Sarma, on the basis of the inscriptional evidence proves that Citsukha belongs to Andhra region. We can, on the basis of Citsukha's place possibly presume the place of Ānandabodha as Andhrapradesh. In the works Ānandabodha repeatedly refers to the fruits like *Kadalī* (banana) and *tālaphala* (NM. p.60, 305) which grow on the sea coast, various types of lotuses such as *tāmarasa, indivara, nirājana* (NM.p.112), different types of rice such as *śāli-dhāna, yava, kalamavīja, dīrghaśuka* which are mainly grown and consumed in the South. Ānandabodha in his works prays to the Lord Viṣṇu by using different epithets like Mukunda (PM.p.1). We also see that the people of Andhradesa are attached to the worship of Mukunda or Viṣṇu (Shah Umakant Premanand, *Gīrvāṇapadamañjarī* and *Gīrvāṇavañmañjarī* of Dhuṇḍikavīśvara, p.25). These facts strengthen the conjecture that Ānandabodha might have been the resident of the Southern part of India, most probably of Andhrapradesh.

2.4 His Teacher

It is a critical problem to determine who was, in fact, the *Guru* (preceptor) of this celebrated philosopher Ānandabodha since no concrete information has been provided by Ānandabodha in his works. Notwithstanding this, two views with regard to the *Guru* of Ānandabodha have been found advocated by Prof. M. Hiriyanna, and by Prof. P.K.Gode in their works.

Prof.M.Hiriyanna, the learned editor of the *Iṣṭasiddhi* of Vimuktātman makes[1] a very cautious inference on the strength of a half stanza which is found both in the *Iṣṭasiddhi* of Vimuktātman and in the *Pramāṇamālā* of Ānandabodha.

Ānandabodha introduces this stanza with the words "*etadevoktam gurubhiḥ*". Hiriyanna also directs our attention to another stanza in the *Nyāyamakaranda* which contains the words analogous to the words "*etadevoktam gurubhiḥ*".

Prof. Hiriyanna observes (p.xiii): "there is a book with the title of *Pramāṇamālā* by Ānandabodha, a well-known exponent of the Advaita and in it he quotes the following half-stanza which is found in *Iṣṭasiddhi* (i.36) prefacing it with the words *etadevoktam gurubhīḥ* : *nānyatra kāraṇāt kāryam na cettatra kva tadbhavet* (NM. p.332).

We may deduce from this, though we cannot be at all sure about it, that, Ānandabodha was a disciple of Vimuktātman, There is nothing improbable in this, for, Ānandabodha was an early writer on the Advaita and, has shown by his reference to the *Iṣṭasiddhi* in another of his works, *Nyāyamakaranda*. He helds views in regard to many a detail of Advaitic doctrines which are identical with those maintained by Vimuktātman. But as Ānandabodha's date is not definitely known, this conclusion even if correct throws no light on the chronological position of the present work" (*Iṣṭasiddhi*).

Prof. Hiriyanna remarks further:

It is strange that the colophons in none of the three works of Ānandabodha included in the volume (Chowkhamba Series) mention his guru."

1. *Iṣṭasiddhi*, Gaekwad Ori. Series, Baroda, Introduction, pp.xiii-xiv.

P.K. Gode raises a question in his article - "Who was the Guru of Ānandabodha - Vimuktātman or Ātmāvāsa" (*Studies* in *Indian Literary History*, Vol. 1. pp.229-232). He considers Ātmāvāsa as the *Guru* of Ānandabodha on the strength of Ānandabodha's own testimony contained in the benedictory verse appearing at the end of a manuscript of a work called *Nyāyadīpikā*.

The verse is as follows:

Namaḥ nikhilasamsārasāgarottārasetave
samsritākhilasaṁkalpakalpavṛkṣāyasaṁbhave
namo nikhilavedāntakamalākarabhānave
ātmāvāsabhidhānāya gurave guṇavesmane.

P.K. Gode observes:

"This expression *ātmāvāsābhidhānāya gurave*" stating in unmistakable terms that Ātmāvāsa was the *Guru* of Ānandabodha directly contradicts Prof. Hiriyanna's cautious deduction that Ānandabodha was the disciple of Vimuktātman, the author of the *Iṣṭasiddhi*.

We must understand by the word *'Gurubhiḥ'* (Vimuktātman) only a respectful reference to a prominent Vedāntī instead of direct relation of the Guru with his disciple". Thus the expression *Ātmāvāsābhidhānāya* according to P.K. Gode, proves that Ātmāvāsa was the Guru of Ānandabodha (p.231).

This view of Prof. Gode is accepted by late Dr. S.A. Nachane.[1]

Ānandabodha does not furnish further information about Ātmāvāsa, his personality, date, life, place and works anywhere in his other three independent works. The colophons of all these also do not mention anything about Ātmāvāsa.

---

1. *A Survey of Post-Śaṅkara Advaita Vedānta,* Unpublished Ph.D. Thesis, p.217.

In the domain of Advaita literature, Ātmāvāsa, whom Ānandabodha refers as *Guru* is quite an unknown person about whom nothing is known. His works are not available. He also does not seem to be referred to by any Advaita writer besides Ānandabodha. *The New Catalogus Catalogorum* refers to Ātmāvāsa as an unknown *sanyāsin* (ascetic).

The opinion of P.K. Gode appears to me to be more plausible than that of Prof. Hiriyanna. As the text *Nyāyadīpikā* very clearly gives the name of Ātmāvāsa as his *Guru*, we can, on the strength of it say that Ātmāvāsa might be the *Guru* of Ānandabodha.

2.5 Family and Personality

Ānandabodha in his works does not directly speak anything about his genealogy, family, family-customs or traditions, norms or conditions of his society, and above all his own personal life. Because of his complete silence, the task of ascertaining the detailed account of his family and personality is a critical one. However, his works indirectly supply some clues which help in forming a brief account of his family and personal life. Ānandabodha says at the end of *Pramāṇamālā: Śrīmad paramahamsa parivrājakācārya śrīmadānandabodhācārya kṛtam*. And, at the end of the *Nyāyamakaranda, Śrīmadānandabodhabhaṭṭāraka viracita*. These epithets, viz. *Ācārya* (preceptor) and *Bhaṭṭāraka* (venerable or sage) indicate that Ānandabodha belongs to a brahmin-family since these epithets are found to be used for learned brahmins only. Further, Ānandabodha's family does not seem to be an ordinary but very learned and reputed one since Ānandabodha's encyclopedic scholarship and indepth study of the Vedic literature, the *Prasthānatraya* and diverse *śāstras* provide ample testimony to assume the orthodox and scholarly tradition of his family. It is almost impossible to imagine the family being devoid of the hidden treasure of śāstric knowledge could produce such an erudite scholar and philosopher like Ānandabodha. Ānandabodha's family most probably belonged to the *Yajurveda* school as he quotes profusely from the *Upaniṣads* like the *Bṛhadāraṇyaka, Taittirīya, Īśa, Śvetāśvetara* and *Kaṭha* belonging to the *Yajurveda saṁhitā.*

As his extraordinary works reveal Ānandabodha is a versatile scholar well-versed in several branches of knowledge. He is a recondite ācārya capable of setting aside various theories of heterodox as well as orthodox schools of philosophy ably asserting the tenets of absolute monism (Advaita Vedānta). At the end of the *Nyāyadīpāvali* he calls himself as '*Sudhi* (scholar)' :

Ānandabodhabhaṭṭārakasudhikṛta.......

Inspite of being a great scholar he appears to be a humble man as he says very frankly that his work i.e. *Nyāyamakaranda* is simply a *saṅgraha* (epitome, compotation) *nivandhapuṣpajālāni samālocya prayatnataḥ sannyāyamakarandānām saṅgraha kriyate mayā.*

The very purpose of his writing as Ānandabodha says, is not worldly gains, fame and riches or relief from evils but immediate bliss par excellence as pointed out by Mammaṭa in his *Kāvyaprakāśa* (1.3). As Ānandabodha says :

ānandaheturakalaṅkadhiyāvyadhāyī (NM p.360).

Ānandabodha being devoid of the desire of getting name, fame and social status has written his philosophical works with the only aim of experiencing highest transcedental bliss (*ānanda*). From this we can deduce that he was not only a lover of learning having genuine philosophical bent of mind but also a true *Yati* or *Parivrājaka* who was totally dedicated to the contemplation, meditation and devotion to the Supreme Reality, an abode of the highest bliss (*prajñānaghana* and *ānanda*)

2.6 As a Poet

Ānandabodha is also a poet as he introduces himself by the epithet *Sukavi* in the *Nyāyamakaranda*. He who has composed a number of verses in several metres like *anuṣṭubh*, (NM. p.43, 48), *Vasantatilakā* (NM. p.56, 360), *Mālini* (NM. p.179,p.24) *Upajāti* and others in order to support his own theories and views. His statements most of the time are ornamental and poetic. Ānandabodha has written the verses following the style of *Vaidarbhi* (a particular style of composition)[1] the main features of which are rhythmic words (*mādhurya*), and condescension (*prasāda*). The sentiment (*rasa*), he depicts, is *śānta*[2] (tranquility) and *bhakti* (devotion).

As for example :

ātmasvabhāvamadhikṛtya mukundameṣā
mānābhidhāna navaratnamanojñamālā/
Ānandabodha yatinā nidhinā guṇānām
ānandaheturakalaṅkadyiyāvyadhāī//

2.7 Ānandabodha's Scholarship

Ānandabodha occupies a significant place in the history of Advaita Vedānta for his multifaceted encyclopeadic scholarship. He is a meatphysician, a profound scholar, a poet, a honest critic, a distinguished prose writer and a recondite dialectician. The celebrated works of Ānandabodha make evidently clear all these above aspects of his scholarship.

Metaphysician

Ānandabodha is a distinguished Advaita philosopher and makes valuable contribution to Indian

1. *Kāvyādarśa*, 1. 41-53; *Sāhityadarpaṇa*, 9.3.
2. Jagannatha, *Rasagaṅgādhara*, p.35, 42. Mammaṭa, *Kāvyaprakāśa*, p.148.

philosophy in general and Advaita philosophy in particular. It is known from his works that he not only explains the subtle points of Advaita philosophy with sound logical reasoning , facile examples and epistemological arguments but some prominent doctrines of other schools of both orthodox and heterodox systems of Indian philosophy, viz., Jaina, Buddhist, Sāṁkhya, Nyāya-Vaiśeṣika and Pūrva-Mīmāṁsā are also set aside in scholarly manner. In his works Ānandabodha criticises and refutes the following systems and their doctrines.

1) Jaina Doctrines

Ānandabodha also criticises the Jaina theory of magnitude of *jīvātman* i.e. *madhyamaparimāṇavāda* (Individual soul has the size as that of the physical body) as set forth in the *Tattvārthasūtra* of Umāsvati. Ānandabodha also criticises and sets aside the Jaina theory of *mokṣa* found in the *Tattvārthasūtra* and its commentaries.

2) Buddhist Doctrines

Buddhist doctrines have been explained, criticised and refuted by Ānandabodha many times in his works. While he argues in favour of the Advaita theory of identity between *Brahman* and *jīvātman*, he explains and refutes the Buddhist theory of momentariness of consciousness (*kṣaṇikavijñānavāda* upheld by Yogācāra or Vijñānavādī Buddhist schools. Refuting the view i.e. *Vijñāna* (consciousness) is momentary, not eternal, Ānandabodha successfully proves the Advaita view that *Vijñāna* (consciousness) being identical with the transcendental Reality *Brahman* cannot be momentary (*kṣaṇika*) like any other inert wordly object.

Ānandabodha further criticises the theory of error, viz. *ātmakhyāti* advocated by the Buddhist Vijñānavādins in the *Laṅkāvatārasūtra* of Vasubandhu and Yogācāra school. Refuting these with sound logic Ānandabodha aptly establishes the Advaita theory of *anirvacanīyakhyāti* on the strength of the scriptural authority and logical reasoning.

Ānandabodha further refutes the theory of *nirvāṇa* or *mokṣa* propounded by the Yogācāra in the *Laṅkāvatārasūtra* of Vasubandhu and *Mādhyamikakārikā* of Nāgārjuna.

3) Sāṁkhya Doctrines

Ānandabodha criticises the Sāṁkhya system as the *Pradhāna Malla* for he devotes highest number of pages in his work like *Nyāyamakaranda*, and *Pramāṇamālā* to criticise and refute the Sāṁkhya view, profusely quoting from the Sāṁkhya texts, viz. the *Sāṁkhyakārikā* of Īśvarakṛṣṇa, its commentaries such as *Sāṁkhyatattvakaumudī* of Vācaspati Miśra, and the *Sāṁkhyasūtra*. The theory of the diversity of selves (*bahupuruṣavāda*) is criticised elaborately and refused aptly by Ānandabodha in his *Nyāyamakaranda*.

4) Nyāya-Vaiśeṣika Doctrines

Ānandabodha attempts in his works to set aside the prominent Nyāyā-Vaiśeṣika doctrines, viz. the diversity of individual selves, the theory of *anyathākhyāti* (misapprehension), the theory of *mokṣa* as expounded by the sūtrakāra Akṣapāda Gautama in the *Nyāyasūtra* and Jayanta Bhaṭṭa in his *Nyāyamañjarī*. Ānandabodha also criticises the Nyāya view i.e. dependence of *Ātman* for its luminosity on the mind (*mānasapratyakṣaviṣaya*).

It is remarkable to note that he adopts the method and technical words of the Nyāya system to refute the Nyāya view points like *anaikāntika, asidha, sādhyasama, dṛṣṭāntābhāsa, virodha, parasparāśraya* etc.

5) Mīmāṁsā Doctrines

Ānandabodha in his works also devotes a number of pages to criticise and refute the views of the Mīmāṁsā philosophers. In the *Nyāyadīpikā* Ānandabodha refutes the *Kāryānvayavāda* (action as the import) of the Mīmāṁsakas as expounded in the Mīmāṁsā texts, viz., *Mīmāṁsāsūtras* of Jaimini, and *Prakaraṇapañcikā* of Śālikanātha. He explains all subtle points of the Mīmāṁsā by quoting from authoritative Mīmāṁsā works like the *Prakaraṇapañcikā* of Śālikanātha (780 A.D.), and the *Nayaviveka* of Bhavanātha (800 A.D.). These passages on Mīmāṁsā are repeated in toto in the chapter of *Pravartakatva* in his *Nyāyamakaranda.*

In the *Pramāṇamālā* and the *Nyāyamakaranda,* Ānandabodha refutes Śālikanātha's views of diversity of individual souls, the *akhyātivāda, kāryānvayavāda,* theory of *mokṣa* and the doctrine of *karma* as a means to *mokṣa.*

Apart from being a metaphysician Ānandabodha is a profound scholar well-versed in numerous branches of Sanskrit Literature. His erudite scholarship in several systems are evidently clear from his examples which are as follows:

tatkim nanāmunijana sādhāraṇamapi kuṇḍamagasty kuṇḍamityā khyāyamānam indivarādisādhāraṇe ca nirabhijanane tāmarasameva nirajanham nābhijānāti.

(Linguistics) (NM p.112)

na khalvasya kriyāphalabhājopi karmabhāvaḥ, yataḥ svātmani vṛttir virudhyeta, parasamavetakriyāphalaśāli hi karmeti karmavidaḥ tathā sati nātmanaḥ karmabhāvo gantṛvad.

(Grammar) (NM. p.133)

tathāhi - varṇaharsvadīrghādayonyadharma api samāropitaḥ tattvapratipatti hetavo, na khalu laukika naga iti ca nāga iti vā padāt ku 1jaraṁ girim vā pratipadyamānā bhavanti bhrāntāḥ.

(Grammar) (NM. p.147)

Ānandabodha in his works quotes from the *Prasthānatraya*, *Gauḍapādakārikā* of Gauḍapāda, the *Bhāṣyas* of Śrī Śaṅkara, *Brahamasiddhi* of Maṇḍana, *Bṛhadāraṇyaka- bhāṣya-vārttika* of Sureśvara, *Bhāmatī* of Vācaspati, *Pañcapādikā* of Padmapāda, *Iṣṭasiddhi* of Vimuktātman, *Vivaraṇa* of Prakāśātman, *Saṁkṣepaśārīraka* of Sarvajñātma Muni.

He also refers to and quotes profusely from a number of texts belonging to the reputed philosophical schools and the prominent thinkers known to him, such as *Sāṁkhyakārikā*, *Yogasūtra*, *Nyāyamañjarī*, *Vaiśeṣikasūtra*, *Mīmāṁsāsūtra*, *Tantravārttika* and *Ślokavārttika* of Kumārila, *Prakaraṇapañcikā* of Śālikanātha and the *Nayaviveka* of Bhavanātha.

Ānandabodha makes use of his scholarship in his works in a very skillful and sucessful manner.Naturally therefore the learned people would appreciate his writing as he has expressed at the end of NM.

Ānandabodhasukaveḥ suktim ke nāvinandhanti/ no cedrucinidānam matsarasañja mahāpittam// (NM. *p.360).*

2.8 Critic and Dialectician

Ānandabodha as an honest critic also occupies a unique position among the Advaitins since his criticism of the opponents' views is not deliberate attempt aiming at refutation in a destructive motive. Like Śaṅkara he aims at removing the delusion that other systems are perfect and presenting the Absolute *Brahman* as Reality vouched by the highest authority i.e. the *Śruti* and then *Tarka*. As Nachane remarks, "his is a job of criticising others and thus strenghtening the Advaita with logic."[1] Ānandabodha's criticism is consistent, logically sound, without prejudice and to the point. Ānandabodha is one of the best dialecticians among the Advaita philosophers of the post-Śaṅkara period who has used the dialectic method in order to explain the Advaita principles. With the special purpose in mind, viz., to prove the logical validity of the Advaita doctrines and to point out the logical inconsistencies in the view points advocated by the opponents like the Jains, Buddists, Sāṁkhyas, Nyāya-Vaiśeṣikas and Pūrva-Mīmāṁsakas against Advaita, Ānandabodha, as it is seen from his exposition and refutation, employs the dialectic method.

The dialectical method used for the philosophical analysis, is not his invention. The Buddhists had made use of the dialectic method of logical discussions even from the time of Nāgārjuna. (300 A.D.).

Śaṅkara has also applied dialectic method for refutation of *Pūrvapakṣa* views in his *Bhāṣya* on *Brahmasūtra* and the *Upaniṣads.* His aim of employing dialectic method was, as Sarma remarks, "to establish the individuality of the system on the foundations of the Śruti freeing it from the shackles of the dualistic Sāṁkhya and Mīmāṁsā in which it had been caught up in its early phase."[2]

Dasgupta rightly observes: "Śaṅkara himself had started it in his refutation of the Nyāya and other systems in his commentary on the Vedānta-Sūtras II. II. Tarkapāda."[3]

---

1. Nachane, S.A. *A Survey of Post-Śaṅkara Advaita Vedānta,* Unpublished Ph.D. Thesis, p.339.
2. Sarma, V.A. *Citsukha's Contribution to Advaita,* p.17.
3. Dasgupta, S.N. HIP. Vol.II, p.118.

Hence K.Potter opines: "Śaṅkara is responsible for a group of dialecticians who conceive of the refutation of alternative views as the only function of philosophical analysis."[1] for "the post-Śaṅkara Advaita philosophy originates out of the different interpretations and commentaries of *Śārīrakabhāṣya*. The commentators of *Śārīrakabhāṣya* are fully manifest in their annotations. These annotations are mainly based on independent reasoning and sometimes insurmountable dialectic also is resorted to."[2]

Ānandabodha adopted the method of dialectics, the technical intricacies and the style of argumentation from the Navya Naiyāyikas since in those days i.e. ninth century onwards dialectic method was promiently used by Jayanta Bhaṭṭa (984 A.D.) and Udayanācārya (1000 A.D.)[3].Nachane aptly remarks,"This age was the age of big Naiyāyikas like Udayana, and Advaita was enhanced through the dialectical approach in order to defend Advaitic view points since they were seriously attacked by the Naiyāyikas".[4] The pioneering effort undertaken by Ānandabodha in this direction resulted in his four works.

Ānandabodha has maintained throughout his works the principles of dialectic such as applying the skills and techniques for the refutation (*khaṇḍana*) of the opponent's views. He employs the techinical terms most probably used by the Naiyāyikas called *doṣas* (faults) relating to argumentation which is the prominent feature of dialectical writing like *anavasthā* (inconstant gress),

---

1. Potter, K.H. *Presupposions of Indian Philosophers*, p.165.
2. Chakraborty, N.B. *The Advaita Concept of Falsity - A Critical Study*, p.41.
3. Dasgupta, S.N. HIP, Vol.II. p.116
4. Nachane, S.A. *op.cit.* p.100

ativyāpti (over-applicability), and *anaikāntika* (inconstant reason). Following are a few examples of the relevant and apt syllogisms furnished by Ānandabodha :

i) *Vivādapadam bhedasaṁvedanam na*
pramāṇanibandhanam
anirūpitapramāṇakatvād bhedasaṁvedanatvād vā
svapnabhedāvabhāsanavad (NM. p.55)

ii) *Samveditā na saṁvidadhīna prakāśaḥ*
saṁvitkarmaṇāmantareṇaparokṣatvāt
saṁvedanavat (NM p.135)

iii) *ānando daḥkhābhābo na bhavati*
tadanirūpyatvāt
Yadittham tat tathā
yathā ghaṭaḥ (PM. p.1)

iv) *Vivādpadam mithyā,*
dṛśyatvāt
yadittham tattathā
yathobhayavādyavivādpadam rajatam (ND. p.1)

2.9 Devotee of Viṣṇu

Though Ānandabodha was a staunch Advaita philosopher nevertheless he was a firm devotee of the God Viṣṇu. It is evident from his devout salutations offered to the God in the beginning and at the end of his works. (ND, p.1, ND p.1, PM. p.1, 20,NM.p.1). But his conception of God Viṣṇu is not the personal God as it is commonly understood but the transcedental Supreme Reality, *Brahman,* the supreme Bliss and self-luminous consciousness devoid of all differences and empirical defects. It can be deduced from this that though Ānandabodha had genuinly philosophical bent of mind still he had deep devotion to God Viṣṇu, whom he was totally dedicated even in his final stage of life as a great ascetic as evinced from the number of verses addressed to the God, e.g.

Yadbhasānikhilavibhāti viṣayo

yo na svayaṁ jyotiṣām/

yasyāhurbhūbanodbhavasthitilayān

lilāmayān sūrayaḥ//

yaṁ cāgocaramāmananti manasām

vācām ca viśvātmane./

tasmai śuddhasukhādvitīyavapuṣe

śsāsvannamo Viṣṇave//(NM p.2).

2.10 The Date of Ānandabodha

Though Ānandabodha is a person of wide repute still his date is enshrouded in mystery as there is total lack of exact chronology in the historical records of Advaitins. Since Ānandabodha does not furnish any information about his date in his works, the determination of his exact date becomes difficult. However, with the help of internal and external evidences available in his works Ānandabodha's probable date can be fixed. The authors and the texts which Ānandabodha refers to and comments on can be taken as the lower limit and the authors and the texts refering to him would be useful in deciding the upper limit of his time.

In this connection, some learned scholars have suggested certain dates of Ānandabodha, which are as follows :

T.M. Tripathi in the *Tarkasaṅgraha* (intro.p.xiv) of Ānandajñāna assigns Ānandabodha to 1200 A.D. However, he does not provide any ground on the basis of which Mr. Tripathi decides this date.

Prof. Dasgupta referring to T.M. Tripathi in his HIP. Vol.II, p.49 observes :- "Ānandabodha appears to have lived probably in the latter half of the eleventh century and the first half of the twelfth century".

Prof. M.R. Kavi mentions : "Ānandagiri (also called Ānandajñāna and Janārdana) was a contemporary of Citsukha and that he is generally assigned to A.D. 1200. Ānandabodha whose *Nyāyamakaranda* was commented by Citsukha, lived at least half a century prior to Ānandagiri (*Journal of Andhra Historical Society*, Vol.I, p.204).

Prof. P.K. Gode[1] observes :- "It is proposed now to fix the limits for the date of Ānandabodha and for this purpose the date A.D. 1200 assigned to Prakāśātman is useful as it gives us one terminus to the date of Ānandabodha who commented on the work of Prakāśātman in his *Nyāyadīpikā* as mentioned above by Mr. Kavi. The other terminus is furnished by the commentary of Cāṇḍupaṇḍita on the *Naiṣadhacarita* of Śrīharṣa. This commentary was composed in Samvat 1353 (A.D. 1297) and it quotes from *Nyāyamakaranda* of Ānandabodha in commenting on V.108 of canto XXI of the *Naiṣadhacarita*.

It will be seen from the foregoing data that Ānandabodha lived after Prakāśātman (A.D. 1200) and before Cāndupaṇḍita (A.D. 1297). We are, therefore, inclined to assign him to about A.D.1250 or the middle of the 13th century and not 11th century as Dr. Dasgupta has done in his *History of Indian Philosophy*."

---

1. Date of Ānandabodha Yati, the author of Nyāyamakaranda and other works on Vedānta - between A.D. 1200 and 1297 or the middle of 13th century, *Calcutta Oriental Journal*, Vol.II, pp.137-138; *Studies in Indian Literary History* Vol.I. p.224-225.

In another article Prof. Gode further observes :

"Mr. Hayavadana Rao rightly looks upon the date of Prakāśātman as other terminus to the date of Ānandabodha. If this date of Prakāśātman is finally fixed, we shall be in a position to clinch the issue with some certainty. At present, two dates for Prakāśātman are put forward. They are :

1) 1200 A.D. (Dasgupta)

2) 1000 A.D (Hiriyanna)

The date of Prakāśātman as 1200 A.D. is given several times by Prof. Dasgupta in the *History of Indian Philosophy* but in all these references the grounds for this date are not mentioned.

According to T.R. Cintamani the date of Prakāśātman given by Dasgupta is not correct, for it is widely known that Rāmānuja who lived between A.D.1015 and 1137 has criticised in his *Bhāṣya* the syllogism of Prakāśātman. In view of this fact, it is impossible to bring down Prakāśātman to any period later than A.D.1000. The date 1200 A.D. for Prakāśātman is definitely wrong. The Date of Citsukha is fairly correct (A.D.1200) and Ānandabodha who preceded Citsukha cannot be later than at least A.D.1150. He was probably slightly older."

The second view i.e. 1000 A.D. as the date of Prakāśātman is stated by M. Hiriyanna. This view appears to come nearer to Dr. Chintamani's view stated above that Prakāśātman is not later than A.D.1000.

The chronological order of the prominent Vedāntins, according to Prof. Gode, is as follows:

1. Prakāśātman : 1200 A.D. (Dasgupta).

1000 A.D. (Hiriyanna); not later than

1000 A.D. (Chintamani)

2. Rāmānuja : Between A.D. 1015 and 1137.

3. Ānandabodha : Before A.D. 1297 (Cāndupaṇḍita)

4. Citsukha : Between A.D. 1220 and 1289 (inscription)

Prof. P.K. Gode observes: "in the present state of the above date for Prakāśātman I am inclined to agree in general with Mr. Hayavadana Rao in his remarks about Ānandabodha's date, viz., Ānandabodha should be assigned to a date somewhat later than A.D.1000, say, cicra A.D.1050 but may go a step further and conclude that he may have flourished between 1050 and A.D.1100."[1]

Thus, Prof. P.K. Gode suggests two dates of Ānandabodha:

a) about A.D.1250 or the middle of the 13th century and b) between 1050 and A.D.1100.

The *New Catalogus Catalogorum* (Vol.2, p.108) speaks the date of Ānandabodha as "later half of 11th and first half of 12th century." Gopinath Kaviraja accepts the view of Prof. Gode about the date of Ānandabodha.[2]

Karl Potter[3] takes into account the first view of Prof. Gode i.e. 1200-1297 A.D.

Now, on the basis of the internal and external clues we can tentatively fix up the possible date of Ānandabodha.

---

1. Ānandabodha's Authorship of Nyāyadīpikā and limts for his date, *Journal of the Mythic Society*, Vol.XXVI, pp.153-156.
2. Quoted by H.Rao, Date of Iṣṭasiddhi, *Quarterly Journal of Mythic Society*, Bangalore, 1933-34, Vol.XXIV, pp.278-79.
3. *Bibliography of Indian Philosophies*, Vol.II, p.196.

Ānandabodha writes a commentary called *Nyāyadīpikā* on the *Śābdanirṇaya* of Prakāśātman. Hence undoubtedly it is known that Prakāśātman is his immediate predecessor. But the date of Prakāśātman according to Prof. Dasgupta[1] is 1200 A.D., which is not based on any ground.

This view is refuted by Chintamani. Acording to Dr. Chintamani the date of Prakāśātman is not later than 1000 A.D.[2] Prof. Hiriyanna assigns Prakāśātman to 1000 A.D.,[3] Since Prakāśātman has written a commentary i.e. *Nyāyadīpikā* on Prakāśātman's *Śābdanirṇaya,* Ānandabodha cannot be before 1050 A.D.

For the determination of the date of higher limit one reliable source is Citsukha who has written commentaries on all the independent works of Ānandabodha. The date of Citsukha is 1220-1284 A.D.[4] Since the commentator Citsukha's date is 1220 A.D., Ānandabodha cannot be later than 1150 A.D.

Secondly, Cāndupaṇḍita quotes a long passage from the *Nyāyamakaranda* in his commentary on the *Naiṣadhacarita (XXI.108)* of Śrīharṣa. The passage very clearly mentions Ānandabodha's name such as *Śrīmadānandabodhācāryairapinyāyamakarand bhedam nirākurvadbhiruktam*. This is related to the refutation of the notion of empirical difference (*bhedanirāsa*) and establishment of the Advaita doctrine of unity of Supreme Self with the Individual Self as discussed in (NM. p.54-56). The date of Cāndupaṇḍita is said to be the later half of the 14th century A.D.[5]

---

1. HIP. Vol.II, p.103
2. See Gode, P.K. Ānandabodha's Authorship of Nyāyadīpikā and Limits for his date, p.228
3. *Outlines of Indian Philosophy*, p.340.
4. Sarma, V.A. *Citsukha's Contribution to Advaita*, p.5.
5. Jani, A.N, *A Critical Study of Śrīharṣa's Naiṣadhīyacaritam*

This clue suggests that Ānandabodha cannot be later than 13th century A.D.

Thus it will be seen from the a foregoing data that Ānandabodha lived after Prakāśātman (1000 A.D.) and before Citsukha (1220 A.D.) and Cāndupaṇḍita (1250 A.D.). Hence on the basis of the a foregoing data we can say that Ānandabodha most probably flourished in the middle of the eleventh century A.D. i.e. 1050 A.D. to 1150 A.D.

2.11 Works of Ānandabodha

Ānandabodha like most of the Sanskrit writers does not say about the number of his works. However, some prominent scholars have focused their attention on this problem. Still it remains an open question as there are diverse opinions about the number of works written by Ānandabodha. The main reason for the uncertainty of works lies in the fact that none of his works bears any positive evidence which can help us arrive at a definite conclusion.

Aufrecht in *Catalogus Catalogorum* Part I, p.48 records the following works as the works of Ānandabodha Paramahamsa:

1. *Nyāyadīpāvali* and its commentary *Pramāṇaratnamālā*

2. *Nyāyamakaranda*

3. *Nyāyāpadeśamakaranda*

S.N. Dasgupta observes: "He wrote at least three works on Śaṅkara Vedānta, viz., *Nyāyamakaranda*, *Nyāyadīpāvali* and *Pramāṇamālā*"[1]:

---

p.41., See also Handiqui, *The Naiṣadhacarita* of Śriharṣa p.58.

1. HIP, Vol. 11, p.116.

R.M. Sharma says: "An Advaitin, Ānandabodhabhaṭṭārakācārya wrote three books namely, *Nyāyamakaranda, Pramāṇamālā* and *Nyāyadīpāvali*"[1]

Siddhesvara Sastri Chitrav also speaks[2] about these three works of Ānandabodha.

E.A.Solomon informs:[3] "He wrote *Nyāyamakaranda, Pramāṇamālā* and *Nyāyadīpāvali*". In the Chowkhamba Sanskrit Series (1907 A.D.). the following works of Ānandabodha have been published:

1. *Nyāyamakaranda,*
2. *Pramāṇamālā*
3. *Nyāyadīpāvali*

However, M.R. Kavi (*Journal of the Andhra Historical Research Society*, Vol. V, Part 3, p.188 (fn.) informs that Ānandabodha is the writer of another work called *Nyāyadīpikā*. He observes: "Ānandabodha, a pupil of Ātmāvāsa wrote a commentary on the *Śābdanirṇaya-dīpikā* of Prakāśātman. The commentary is known by the name of *Nyāyadīpikā*. Citsukha, a contemporary of Ānandagiri commented on the works of Ānandabodha." Dr. Kavi further informs that the above information about Ānandabodha's authorship of *Nyāyadīpikā* is based on the following verse occuring at the end of manuscript of the work described on p.4812 of Triennial catalogue of MSS, Vol. IV Part I (B) of the Govt. Ori. MSS Library, Madras.

"namo nikhilavedānta kamalākara bhānave
ātmāvāsabhidhānāya gurave guṇavesmane/
dustarkadhvāntapaṭalaprapāṭana paṭīyasī
iyamānandabodhena racitānyāyadīpikā//

1. *Some Aspects of Advaita Philosophy*, p.103.
2. *Bhāratavarṣīya Madhyayugina Charitrakoṣu*, p.105.
3. *Avidyā: A Problem of Truth and Reality*, p.57.

Supporting the above said view of Dr. Kavi, Prof. Gode observes: "In the beginning of the Ms the line *Śābdanirṇayasadarthabhāsikā dīpikeyamamalā vidhiyate"* clearly states that the work is a commentary on '*Śābdanirṇaya*' and not "on '*Śabdanirṇayadīpikā*' as stated by Mr. Kavi in the extract quoted above."

He further records the following reference to "*Nyāyadipikā* made by Ānandabodha himself in his *Nyāyamakaranda*. This reference appears as under in the Chowkhamba Edition of the *Nyāyamakaranda* referred to above:"

p.170 - "*diṅgmātramatra sūcitam vistarastu nyāyadīpikāyāmavagantavyaḥ*.

Evidently the "*Nyāyadīpikā*" in the above reference is identical with the *Nyāyadīpikā* referred to by Mr. Kavi as the commentary of that name on the *Śābdanirṇaya* of Prakāśātman (1000 A.D.). *Nyāyadīpikā* is thus the title of a commentary on the '*Śābdanirnaya* of Prakāśātman. It appears that Ānandabodha is referring in the above line to an earlier work written by him. However, C.Hayavadana Rao is not sure whether Ānandabodha, the author of *Pramāṇamālā* and *Nyāyamakaranda* is the same person who has written the *Nyāyadīpikā*.[1]

Prof. P.K. Gode observes : the author of the *Nyāyamakaranda* and *Nyāyadīpikā* appears to be identical for the following reasons:

1) Ānandabodha in his *Nyāyamakaranda* refers to the *Nyāyadīpikā*, which was presumably composed by him earlier as the following lines will show:

---

1. Date of Ānandabodha Yati, the Author of Nyāyamakaranda and Other Works on Vedānta - Between A.D.1220 and 1297 or The Middle of the 13th Century, *Calcutta Oriental Journal*, Vol.II, pp.137-138.

diṅgmātramatrasūcitam vistarastu nyāyadīpikāyāmavagantavyaḥ.

2) The manner in which the above reference is made by Ānandabodha shows that to save much in exposition he is pointing his finger to an exposition of the topic under discussion in the *Nyāyamakaranda*.

3) In the Madras Ms. of *Nyāyadīpikā* the following statement proves that the author of the treatise was Ānandabodha:

dustarkadhvāntapaṭalaprapāṭanapaṭiyasī

iyamāndabodhena racitā Nyāyadīpikā//

Prima facie, therefore, the above facts appear to clear up the doubt of Mr. Hayavadana Roa about Ānandabodha's authorship of both the works

1. *Nyāyamakaranda* and
2. *Nyāyadīpikā*[1].

Thus it is conformed that Ānandabodha is the author of the four works which have been arranged chronologically viz. *Nyāyadīpikā*, *Nyāyadīpāvali*, *Pramāṇamālā* and *Nyāyamakaranda*. These texts are philosophical treatises dealing with the principal tenets of Absolute Monism (*Advaita Vedānta*).

1. *Nyāyadīpikā*

This work being entitled as *Nyāyadīpikā* means *Nyāyasya dīpikā*, a light or illustrator of the Nyāya i.e. *Pramānaiḥ artha parīkṣaṇam nyāya* (*Nyāyakoṣa*, p.44) (an examination of the relevant content by valid means of knowledge).

---

1. Ānandabodha's Authorship of Nyāyadīpikā and Limits for His Date", *Journal of the Mythic Society*, Vol.XXVI, pp.153-156; *Studies in Indian Literary History*, Vol.1, p.226-229.

It is an unpublished commentary on the *Śābdanirṇaya*, an independent treatise of Prakāśātman alias Vivaraṇakāra. *Nyāyadīpikā* is preserved in Madras Government Oriental manuscript Library R.No.2986. Explaining the significance of this work Ānandabodha himself says:

dustarkadhvānta paṭala prapāṭanapaṭiyasī

iyamānandabodhena racitā Nyāyadīpikā//

Based on the original text *Śābdanirṇaya* of Prakāśātman Ānandabodha elaborately discusses mainly the nature of *śabda* (verbal cognition) arising from the *Śabdapramāṇa* (verbal testimony). He further explains the various theories of *Śābdabodha* or *Vākyārthabodha* (sentence-comprehension) and *anvitābhidhānavāda* (doctrine of the connected expression of words). The latter part of the work is devoted to the presentation and refutation of the *Kāryānvayavāda* of the Mīmāṁsakas. Ānandabodha discusses major subtle points of Mīmāṁsakas, by quoting from authoritative Mīṁāmsā works like the *Prakaraṇapañcikā* of Śālikanātha etc. No commentary has been written on Ānandabodha's *Nyāyadīpikā*.

II. Nyāyadīpāvali

The title is significant in the sense that it is a series of enlightening arguments to establish Advaitic doctrine (*Nyāyadīpānām āvaliḥ*), stated by Ānandabodha:

dustarkatimiraśreṇī vidāraṇaviśāradām

rūcirām nyāyadīpānāmāvaliṁ racayāmyaham//

i.e. Ānandabodha says that the purpose of writing this work is to dispel the wrong view points found to be spreading like dense darkness by the logical reasoning.

It is smaller than the *Pramāṇamālā*. Ānandabodha's dialectical method reaches its highest peak in this work.

Most of the *Navyanyāya* terms have been used in this work, such as *asiddha, sādhyasama dṛṣṭāntābhāsa, pakṣatvāsiddha, vādhita, avacchedaka, viruddha* etc., which envisages Ānandabodha's mastery over Nyāya category (*padārtha*) called *Vāda* (hypothetical argument). Dasgupta remarks about this work : "In his *Nyāyadīpāvali* he tries to prove the falsity of the world-appearance by inference on the anology of the falsity of the illusory silver."[1] Ānandabodha employs the following syllogism :

Vivādapadam mithyā dṛśyatvāt

Yaditham tattathā

Yathāubhayavādyavivādpadam rajatam

Tathaitat

Tasmāt tathā (ND p.16).

There are two commentaries written on the *Nyāyadīpāvali* viz. *Nyāyadīpāvali candrikā* of Anubhūtisvarūpācārya and *Nyāyadīpāvali Vyākhyā* of Sukhaprakāśa. These are published in the *Annals of Oriental Research*, Vol.XI, XII, 1953- 54, 1954-55.

III. Pramāṇamālā

The title of this work suggests that it is a garland of *Pramāṇas* (means of knowledge) *Pramāṇānām mālā*. Since Ānandabodha attempts in this work to prove some of the Advaitic tenets like nature of *Brahman* as Bliss, Bliss (*ānanda*) as positive *(bhāvarūpa)*, the self- luminosity of the *Ātman* etc., and to set aside the view points of the opponents by means of *Pramāṇa* i.e. scripture and valid reasoning, this work has been entitled as *Pramāṇamālā*. Ānandabodha finally calls it as a *Prakaraṇa grantha* i.e. a short manual of the *Pramāṇa* i.e. verbal authority.

1. HIP. Vol.II, p.118

The subject matter, which Ānandabodha discusses in this work does not much differ from his other text *Nyāyamakaranda.* The arguments which are briefly presented in the *Pramāṇamālā,* are elaborately discussed in the *Nyāyamakaranda*. Dasgupta rightly says : "There is practically nothing new in his *Pramāṇamālā*. It is a small work of about twenty five pages, and one can recognise here the arguments of the *Nyāyamakaranda* in a somewhat different form and with a different emphasis."[1]

The *Pramāṇamālā* deals with the essential nature of the transcendental Supreme Reality, *Brahman.* Ānandabodha explains that *Brahman* is *ānanda* (bliss) and bliss is positive (*bhāvarūpa*) and not negative (*abhāvarūpa*) as the absence of misery. The *Jīvātman* (individual self) being the creation of *anādi avidyā* (beginningless nescience) is non-different from the *Brahman* and hence in fact is of the nature of trans-empirical Bliss. Therefore Ānandabodha sets forth the Advaita theory of identity between *Brahman* and *Jīvātman* and proves the falsity of the difference (*bheda*) advocated by the opponents to be existing among the objects of knowledge (*jñeyapadārthas*). The locus of all the appearing differences (*bheda),* contends Ānandabodha, is a real entity which is *Brahman;* the empirical world is nothing but a superimposition of this Highest Reality. Finally Ānandabodha affirms the view that knowledge (*jñāna*) in the form of the realisation of *Brahman* or the cessation of *avidyā* is the only means to *moksa*.

Pramāṇamālā has got the following commentaries:

1) *Pramāṇamālā Nibandha* by Anubhūtisvarūpācārya

2) *Pramāṇamālā Vyākhyā* by Citsukha.

---

1. HIP. Vol.II, p.118

Both these manuscripts are unpublished.

The commentary by Citsukha i.e. *Pramāṇamālā Vyākhyā* has been wrongly attributed by Prof. P.P.S Sastri to Sukhaprakāśa, says E.P. Radhakrishnan (Sukhaprakāśa - His identity and works, *Annals of the Bhandarkar Oriental Research Institute*,Vol.XXIII, 1942, p.347).

IV. Nyāyamakaranda

The *Nyāyamakaranda* means *Nyāyasya makaranda* (essence of the Advaitic doctrines proved by examining different types of means of knowledge (*pramāṇa*). This work like his other works has been written in prose with the summary *kārikās* (*saṅgrahaślokas*) at the end of each theoretical discussion and final *siddhānta* precisely and clearly. Ānandabodha confesses in the colophon verses that this work is a collection of the doctrines in other celebrated Advaitic works:

nibandhapuṣpajālāni

samālocya prayatnataḥ/

sannyāyamakarandānām

saṅgraha kriyate mayā//

Ānandabodha also speaks about the purpose of the work, *Nyāyamakaranda* as the experience of the transcendental bliss (*ānanda*) other wise called *Brahman*.

nānānibandhakusuma

prabhavāvadāta

nyāyāpadeśamakaranda

kadamba eṣaḥ/

Ānandabodhayatinā nidhinā guṇānām

ānandaheturakalaṅkadhiyām

vyadhayi//(NM. p.360)

In this work Ānandabodha attempts to prove the logical validity of almost all the principal doctrines of Advaita philosophy in clear and comprehensive way, and refutes the views of the orthodox as well as heterodox opponent schools which are not on par with the Advaita view points. In this text Ānandabodha re-establishes firmly the views of Maṇḍana Miśra put forth in the *Brahmasiddhi* which were criticised by Śālikanātha in his *Prakaraṇapañcikā*. Ānandabodha refutes also the views of the Jains, Buddhists, Sāṁkhyas, Nyāya - Vaiśeṣikas and Pūrva-Mīmāṁsakas.

Although the contents, which Ānandabodha discusses in this work, are the same as those of the *Pramāṇamālā*, still in this work Ānandabodha attempts a more detailed discussion and adds new arguments.

There are three commentaries on *Nyāyamakaranda* by Citsukha and his pupil Sukhaprakāśa called *Nyāyamakaranda ṭīkā* and *Nyāyamakaranda Vivecanī* respectively. And Anubhūtisvarūpācārya (1300 A.D.) has also written a commentary on *Nyāyamakaranda* called *Saṅgraha*.[1] Citsukha's commentary *Nyāyamakaranda ṭīkā* or *Vyākhyā* is published with *Nyāyamakaranda* in the Chowkhamba Sanskrit Series at Benaras during the years 1901, 1903, 1905 and 1907.

2.12 Chronological Order of the Works :

Ānandabodha does not furnish any direct internal evidence in his works on the basis of which the chronological order of his works could be safely determined. Hence, by means of some indirect clues ascertained by the close study of the works the chronological order is stated below.

1. Dasgupta, HIP, Vol.II, p.116

It is found that Ānandabodha refers to his *Nyāyadīpikā*, the commentary on the *Śābdanirṇaya* in his *Nyāyamakaranda* by saying - *diṅgmātramatra sūcitam vistarastu nyāyadīpikāyāmavagantavyaḥ* (NM. p.170). This statement gives the clear indication that the subject matter, which Ānandabodha discusses in the *Nyāyamakaranda* i.e. import of Vedic statements is an established entity (*siddhe saṅgatigrahasattvastāpanam* had already been discussed comprehensively in his *Nyāyadīpikā*. This proves that the *Nyāyadīpikā* is Ānandabodha's first work and the *Nyāyamakaranda* is his later work.

Secondly, the *Nyāyadīpikā* is further determined as his first work for the reason that it is a commentary on *Śābdanirṇaya*. It appears that Ānandabodha possibly because of his lack of confidence has at first written a commentary before independent works which is little easier than the writing of any independent work. Further, in the beginning of the *Nyāyadīpikā* Ānandabodha pays salutation to many Gods and Goddesses like Gaṇapati, Sarasvati, Vedavyāsa, and his predecessor Prakāśātman along with his teacher Ātmāvāsa. But in his other independent works like *Nyāyadīpāvali*, *Pramāṇamālā*, and *Nyāyamakaranda* Ānandabodha does not do so.

2. Ānandabodha's second work seems to be the *Nyāyadīpāvali*. In this work Ānandabodha has used most of the technical terms found in the Nyāya system like *Upādhi*, *Viruddha*, *Vyāpti*, *Sāmānādhikaraṇya*, *Satpratipakṣa*, *Anadhyavasita*, *Kālātita*, etc. and syllogisms like:

I) *Vivādapadam mithyā dṛśyatvāt*

Yadittham tattathā

Yathobhayavādyavivādapadam rajatam (NDL, p.1)

II) *Vivādādhyāsitā pravṛttiḥ purovartigocararajatajñāna-*

pūrvikā

rajatechādhīna purovartipravṛttitvāt

yaduktasādhanam taduktasādhyam

yathā samyagrajatapravṛtti

sthatheyam tatasthathā (NDL. p.8)

III) *Vandhyāsuto vaktā na bhavati acetanatvāt*

pāṣāṇavat (NDL p.2)

The subject matter of this work covers only two prominent Advaitic tenets which are argued out by Ānandabodha in details in his *Nyāyamakaranda,* viz. falsity of the empirical world and establishment of *anirvacanīyakhyāti* (the object of error is indefinable). Ānandabodha discusses the nature of fallacies (*hetvābhāsas*) in this work in connection with the discussion of the falsity of the world.

3. *Pramāṇamālā* appears to be the third work of Ānandabodha. This work being very small seems to be a ground work made for the preparation of the *Nyāyamakaranda* wherein the same subject matter set forth in the *Pramāṇamālā* has been discussed comprehensively, clearly and systematically. On the *Pramāṇamālā* there is no systematic arrangement and logical order of the topics as it is found in the *Nyāyamakaranda.*

4. The *Nyāyamakaranda* occupies a prominent place among the four works of Ānandabodha. This work seems to be his last work on the basis of the following reasons:

The *Nyāyamakaranda* contains several Advaitic doctrines which are fully, precisely and critically discussed by Ānandabodha.

Secondly, in this work Ānandabodha develops novel theories like that of *mithyātva* (falsity) which is famous as fifth definition[1] of falsity differing from other three definitions propounded by Padmapāda and Prakāśātman, and of *avidyānivṛtti* (cessation of nescience) as of fifth kind (*pañcamaprakāra*).

Thirdly, the systematic order of the arrangement of the topics prove evidently that *Nyāyamakaranda* is the last work of Ānandabodha who has become quite mature and well-versed in the prominent scriptures by that time.

1. Gupta, Sanjukta, *Studies in the Philosophy of Madhusūdana Sarasvati*, pp.32-49;
Mishra Haramohan, *A Study in Advaita Epistemology;* pp.53-55; Madhusūdana, *Advaitasiddhi*, p.195.

CHAPTER III

ONTOLOGICAL VIEWS

This chapter embodies a comprehensive and critical analysis of the ontological views of Ānandabodha, viz., the transcendental Reality called *Brahman* or *Ātman* as non-dual (*advitīya*), self-illuminating consciousness (*vijñāna*) and supreme bliss (*paramānanda*).

3.1 Reality as Non-dual

In his three independent works, viz., *Nyāyadīpāvali*, *Pramāṇamālā* and *Nyāyamakaranda* Ānandabodha expounds the Advaita doctrine of identity of *Brahman* (Supreme Self) with the *Jīvātman* (Individual Self) as propounded in the *Prasthānatraya* and prominent Advaita Vedānta texts of his predecessors. His *Nyāyadīpikā* being a commentary on Prakāśātman's *Śābdanirṇaya* explaning the doctrine of *śābdapramā* (knowledge of verbal testimony) does not contain any significant discussion about the essential nature of the Supreme Reality.

In his *Nyāyamakaranda* and *Pramāṇamalā* these *pūrvapakṣas* are propounded by the orthodox schools, viz. Sāṁkhya, Nyāya-Vaiśeṣika and Prābhākara Mīmāṁsaka, which uphold the diversity of Individual selves. Ānandabodha explains all these above doctrines, examines logical validity of their arguments and finally sets aside them pointing out their flaws

(A) Sāṁkhya Doctrine

The Sāṁkhya school advocates the doctrine of diversity of *puruṣa* (self) as found in the *Sāṁkhyakārīkā* of Īśvarakṛṣṇa (400 A.D.) whom Ānandabodha quotes in his *Nyāyamakaranda* (p.18). It is stated there that plurality of *puruṣa* is established by three reasons - 1) definite adjustment of birth, death and the sense organs; 2) non-simultaneity of activity, 3) diversity due to three attributes (*guṇas) i.e. Sattva, Rajas* and *Tamas* (SK.18; NM. p.18). Kapila (900 A.D.) in his *Sāṁkhyasūtras* also advocates the diversity by saying that "Selves are many because of the wordly order" (*Vyavasthāto nānā)* (SS. 3.5). The main argument which the Sāṁkhya advocates that if there were one *puruṣa,* when one is born, all human beings would be born; when one dies, all would die; if there were any defect in the sense organs of one like deafness, then all would be deaf; but this is not perceptible in the worldly order and since there are several apportionments of death, birth and sense organs in the case of different human beings, the diversity of *Ātman* stands to reason. Moreover, there is no one kind of activity of all human beings in one particular time. While some are engaged in the activities full of virtues and non-attachment others are engaged in the actions prohibited by the scripture which lead to the bondage of the soul in this transmigratory world. Thirdly, by different modifications of the three attributes, the plurality of soul is proved, for instance, in ordinary life, one who is *sāttvika* is happy, another who is *tāmasika* is unhappy. Thus the *vyavasthā* (definite worldy order) is valid proof for the establishment of the diversity of *puruṣa,* according to the Sāṁkhya school.

Ānandabodha sets aside these arguments of the Sāṁkhya adduced in favour of the doctrine of diversity. He maintains that the phenomena of birth, death and activity (*janana, maraṇa* and *karaṇa*) cannot prove the diversity of *Ātman* since these are related to the physical body (*kṣetra*) and not to *Kṣetrajña* (knower of the field) i.e. the Supreme Self. These physical phenomena can only prove the plurality of physical bodies (*kṣetra*), not of the *Ātman* which is not different from the transcendental Reality. *Brahman* (NM. p.19).

(B) Nyāya - Vaiśeṣika Doctrine

Though the Nyāya and Vaiśeṣika originated as two different schools, yet because of the fact that the Nyāya accepts the Vaiśeṣika metaphysics and Vaiśeṣika accepts Nyāya epistemology and logic, both form jointly one system of philosophy which is known as Nyāya-Vaiśeṣika.

The Self (*Ātman*), according to this school, is a unique substance. It has been defined as "one who recognises (Ny.Vā. on N.S.1.1.10), *Ātman* as that which employs sense-organs to consciousness, which itself is a product and non-eternal. It is defined also as different from body, sense-organs, mind etc. (NS.III.1.1; III.1.2; III.1.3). Desire, aversion, effort, pleasure, pain and cognition are enumerated as special qualities of soul. (NS, 1.1.10). The souls are innumerable, because of the existing differences in the universe. (V.S. III.2.20). There are diverse souls in the diverse bodies. The Advaitin's view that the self is eternal consciousness is not acceptable to the Nyāya- Vaiśeṣika school.

In brief, according to this school, the diversity of souls is proved on the grounds of the impossiblity of explaining otherwise (*anyathā-anupapattiḥ*), the arrangement, order and distribution (*vyavasthā*) as perceived in the world, viz. when Chaitra is happy, Maitra is unhappy. If the soul were to be only one everywhere all should be happy or unhappy at one and the same time (NM. p.5). But this is not the case as seen in the world. Kaṇāda, therefore, declares *"nānātmāno vyavasthātaḥ* (the souls are many due to the order (V.S.III.2.20;NM.p.4).

Moreover, pain (*duḥkha*) and pleasure (*sukha*) are special attributes (*viśeṣaguṇa*) of the soul and not of the body, senses and the like. Therefore the difference cannot be explained with the help of *upādhis* like body and others. A soul in one body acts to remove the pain in different parts like head, or leg of that particular body only, and not in another. e.g. the soul in the body of Chaitra does not act to remove the pain in the body of Maitra. The syllogism to prove the diversity is given as follows :

Ātmādravyatvavyatriktāparajātyādhārabhedena nānā

aśrāvaṇa viśeṣaguṇādhikaraṇattvāt yaduktasādhanam taduktasādhyam yathā ghaṭādi(NM.p.5-6)

(The self differs with the subgenus other than the *dravyatva* being the locus of the special qualities which are different from those of ear.)

The *Ātman* is the locus of the special qualities (*viśeṣaguṇa*) like intelligence (*buddhi*), pleasure (*sukha*), pain (*duḥkha*) and others.

Another syllogism has been set forth to prove the diversity of *Ātman* as follows :

Ātmā nānā

Śarīrātmasambandhasambandhitvāt śarīravat

Śarīrāṇi svasaṁkhyāsaṁkheyā-

stmābhirātmavanti śarīratvāt

Sampratipanna śarīṛavad

(The souls are many because it is associated with the relation between soul and the body. The bodies bear the souls equal in number of bodies).

All these said arguments of the Nyāya-Vaiśeṣika school advanced to prove the diversity of the *Ātman* are rejected by Ānandabodha as follows :

The term in the *sūtra, vyavasthānupapatti,* employed in the *Nyāya-Vaiśeṣika* to prove the diversity of *Ātman* is confusing, says Ānandabodha. He questions the import of the very term *vyavasthā* (order). If the *vyavasthā* denotes the common experience as Chaitra is happy and Maitra is unhappy then *vyavasthā* cannot prove the diversity. For it depends on the difference between Chaitra and Maitra which cannot be established without assuming the *vyavâsthā*. Thus it leads to the fault of *parasparāśraya* (interdependent) as without *vyavasthā* difference cannot be proved, and without the difference (*bheda*) *vyavasthā* cannot be proved (NM. p. 9). If *vyavasthā* would mean, argues Ānandabodha, difference in pain and pleasure and not the difference in the locus (*ādhārā)* of pain and pleasure, then it cannot prove the diversity of the *Ātman* and their difference as the locus of pain and pleasure. The diverse attributes (*guṇas*) can reside in one locus (*ādhāra*) like the attributes such as cooking (*pacana*), burning (*dahana*) etc. as found in fire.

If the *vyavasthā* would mean the association of an object with different contradicting attributes (*virudhānekadharmatā vyavasthā*), it is not tenable, says Ānandabodha. It cannot be said that pain and pleasure being opposed to each other cannot co-exist or cannot have single locus since we find that a person whose upper part of the body is exposed to sun and the lower part immersed in cold water simultaneously experiences both the pleasure and pain. The contact of the mind with the *Ātman* produces heat and cold simultaneously. Likewise the contact of the mind with the *Ātman* produces both pleasure and pain at the same time. The process of the simultaneous experience of pleasure and pain takes place because single tactile sense-organ (*tvagindriya*) comes into contact simultaneously with cold and heat. Both these contacts are controlled by the mind through sense-organs just as contacts of eyes with jar and the like are controlled through eyes. These two contacts controlled by mind give rise to only one cognition which has both heat and cold for its content (*viṣaya*). Though the origination of the special qualities of the soul is accepted simultaneously (*aparyāyeṇa*) it is possible for pleasure and pain to be the object of one cognition due to the relation called *Samyukta-Samavāya* (connected inherence) with the internal sense-organs. Even though the origination of pleasure and pain is accepted in succession (*paryāyeṇa*) they can become the object of one single cognition, one vanishing and other arising immediately. Thus, so far as the factor of the time is concerned the co-existence of pleasure and pain is not impossible (NM. p.11).

The opposition (*virodha*) between pleasure and pain cannot be said to be the relation of destroyer and detroyed. for, one unborn cannot destroy other; or one object cannot destroy another existing in different place.

The opposition between pleasure and pain cannot be said as being of the nature of positive (*bhāvarūpa*) and negative (*abhāvarūpa*) which are not seen together, since pleasure and pain which are *pratidvandi* can be observed in one soul as a bird and its absence are found in ether (*ākāśa*). Thus, it is proved that pain and pleasure cannot prove any real difference with regard to their locus, the self (NM. p.18).

The two syllogisms in the *Nyāyamakaranda* put forth by the Nyāya school also cannot establish the diversity since the soul is not accepted by the Advaitins as the locus of special qualities. The special qualities, like pleasure and pain, being cognisable and perishable cannot be the attribute of the soul which is eternal, and knower. The ether which is given as the example for this phenomenon according to Advaita is non-sentient. Hence it is not a valid *dṛṣṭānta* (example). Ānandabodha finally employs the following syllogism:

Vivādapadam anityam jaḍatvāt

(Ether is non-eternal being non-sentient) (NM. p.21).

The *Śruti* (scripture) also supports this view, by declaring *Ātmanaḥ ākāśa sambhuta* (Ether is produced from the *Ātman* (NM. p.21). The syllogism - *Ātmanaḥ-* is not sound, says Ānandabodha, for the *hetu Śarīrātmasambandha-sambandhitvāt* is *anaikānta* with *sattājāti* and is also *sopādhika* since *kāryatva* is the *upādhi* (condition).

The other syllogism - *Ātmādravyatva* is involved with the fault of *siddhasādhana*. If diverse bodies are accepted as having souls, the diversity of souls need not be proved again (NM. pp.22-24).

(C) Pūrva-Mimāṁsā Doctrine

Ānandabodha in continuation of the refutation of the doctrine of diversity puts forth the view of Śālikanātha Miśra (700 A.D), a distinguished advocate of the Prābhākara school of Pūrva-Mīṁāṁsā. In his famous work, *Prakaraṇapañcikā,* Śālikanātha advocates that the selves are many because of the following reasons :

The diversity of souls in diverse bodies can be inferred from their activities (*prayatna*). When one perceives the activities of other people he infers the diversity of the souls since all these souls are not the same that the perceiver has, but different from it, as the object of its knowledge. The diversity or difference among the souls is proved by inference (*anumāna*) since the perceiver never infers that the activities of his body are due to the effort of his soul residing in his body, because of the efforts of his own soul. The different bodies of others are infered. Thus, diversity of souls is proved.

Secondly, Śālikanātha argues that there is no valid means of knowledge (*pramāṇa*) to prove the identity or unity of the *Brahman* with *Jīvātman* (Individual Self). Direct perception (*pratyakṣa*) cannot prove it since it reveals form (*rūpa*), taste (*rasa*) and other objects differently and does not reveal all of them as one series of form (*rūpa*) or taste (*rasa*) or other objects and therefore direct perception does not prove the existence of the one and non-dual Reality. If there would have been the cognition of series of forms (*rūpadhārā*) in the series of tastes (*rasadhārā*) the direct perception (*pratyakṣa*) might have established the Advaita. But there is no such experience of such cognition *homosapiens*. Hence Advaita or the unity of all selves cannot be established by the testimony of the direct perception (*pratyakṣa*). Since *pratyakṣa* fails in proving Advaita all other means of knowledge (*pramāṇa*) cannot prove Advaita since they all depend on perception (*pratyakṣa*) (NM. p.292, PP.336).

Thirdly, Śālikanātha argues that the *Veda* (*Śruti* or Scripture) cannot prove Advaita, for the object of the Vedas is action (*kriyā*). Hence the *Veda* is not *pramāṇa* to know *Brahman*. Even if it be argued that the Vedic statements reveal the existence of objects, then how can the Vedic statements generate the idea of the existence of *Brahman*, for Vedic statements generate the ideas of many objects other than the *Brahman* (NM. 290-1, PP.337). Ānandabodha rejects the arguments of Śālikanātha by saying that just as the *vyavasthā* (order) of the *grāhyagrāhaka* relationship can be explained as imaginary different conditioning parts for the soul, so there is possibility of havirg an additional ground of the existence of efforts and their absences on the part of the soul. For instance, even though there is cognition of sound existent in the space of ether by one's own ear, there is non-cognition of that sound by other person, similarly the experience of efforts (*prayatna*) and its absence can be explained by presuming special parts of the (*parikalpitapuruṣapradesaviśeṣāt*, NM. p.29). Ānandabodha further argues that by perceiving different types of physical body doing the works and others being inactive the diversity of souls cannot be proved.

The difference between the two things viz. one perceptible and other non-perceptible is not directly seen like the wind shaking the trees. Thus Ānandabodha avers that the scripture is the only means of knowledge to prove the supreme Reality, *Brahman*. Ānandabodha quotes two verses from Maṇḍana's *Brahmasiddhi* to substantiate his view which are as follows :

Sarvapratyavedye vā brahmarūpe vyavasthite,
prapañcasyapravilayaḥ śabdena pratipadyate/
pravilīna prapañcena tadrūpeṇa na gocaraḥ,
mānāntarasyeti matamanāyaikanivandhanam,//
(B.S. IV.3.4; NM. p.298)

(*Brahman* in the form *Sat* appears as the locus of all cognitions and the Vedic word declares it as devoid of everything. It cannot be the object of any other valid means, ultimately scriptures are the only authority for this Highest *Brahman*).

Ānandabodha further contends that although the scriptures are the sentences, made of many words, yet they convey one homogeneous meaning. The word '*eṣa*' in the sentence *sa eṣa neti neti* can be construed with the absolute absence of dualism. Thus Ānandabodha repudiates the doctrine of diversity and establishes the Advaita doctrine of unity of the Supreme Self, *Brahman* with the Individual Self. *Jīvātman,* according to Ānandabodha, being a false creation of the beginningless nescience (*anādi avidyā*), has no separate existence from *Brahman,* since *Brahman* is the true essence of the Individual Self. The false notion of *Jīvabhāva* continues as long as *avidyā* persists. Ānandabodha also quotes numerous *Śruti* statements in support of his view which negate the diversity of Individual Selves :(Bṛh.Up. 4.4.19; Pin.Up. 1.1; Śve.Up 6.11).

If it be argued that the *Śrutipramāṇa* only proves the oneness of the *paramātman* (supreme self) and does not prove the unity of the Individual Selves since the purpose of the Upaniṣadic statements is only to prove the oneness of the *Paramātman,* it is not correct, as the analogy of moon given in the Upaniṣadic statement i.e. *eka eva hi bhūtātmā bhūte bhūte vyavasthitaḥ/ ekadhābahudhā caiva dṛśyate jalacandravat//* (Bṛh. Up.11; NM.p.24) denotes the refutation of the difference *(bheda)* among the *Jīvātman* and does not refer only to the unitive nature of the *Paramātman.* The word *eva* of the above Upaniṣadic sentence clearly indicates the refutation of the difference between the *jīvātman* and *Brahman.* Hence the purport of the *Śrutivākyas* is not the repudiation of the difference supposed to be existing in the *Paramātman* since no difference (*bheda*) is possible in *Brahman.*

Again, it cannot be argued that as in the state of worldly life it is seen that when any object, for instance, a jar (*ghaṭa)* is negated in one part of the ground it is presumed that *ghaṭa* exists somewhere else. Similarly the difference (*bheda*) though negated in the *Paramātman,* it still can be found somewhere else. Because the

Brahman is accepted as the cause of the whole universe, and so when anything negated in the cause (*kāraṇa*) gets absolutely nullified in its effect (*kārya*) also. To substantiate his view Ānandabodha quotes from the *Iṣṭasiddhi* of Vimuktātman - the effect does not exist elsewhere than the cause. If a particular quality is absent in the cause where else can it be ? (IṢ. 1.3; PM.p.4). Ānandabodha proves that since the difference is negated in the *Paramātman,* any other object cannot be the substratum of the difference. Ānandabodha employs a syllogism:

Vivādapadam bhedasamvedanam na pramāṇa-

nivandhanam

anirūpitapramāṇakatvād

bhedasaṁvedanatvād

svapnabhedāvabhāsanavad

(NM. p.55).

Ānandabodha further holds the view that the difference which are cognised in the phenomenal world are caused by the *upādhis* (adjuncts) like physical body, and sense organs (*dehendriya*). The *Ātman* which is in reality, *Brahman* is attributeless. It is not the enjoyer (*bhoktā*) of pleasure (*sukha*) and pain (*duḥkha*) etc., which are not qualities of the *Ātman* or *Brahman*. The diverse feelings of pleasure and pain etc. can be explained with the help of the different *upādhis*. Just as one *mahākāśa* (ether) appears to be many in the form of *ghaṭākāśa* or *gṛhākāśa* etc. because of the diverse *upādhis* like a jar, a house etc., likewise the embodied self (*Jīvātman*) in one body feels pain or pleasure in different parts of the body like head or feet etc., which are the adjuncts of the self.

3.2 The Self-luminosity of the Ātman

Ānandabodha expounds the Advaita doctrine of the self-luminosity (*svayaṁprakāśatā*) of the *Ātman* or *Brahman* as propagated in the *Upaniṣads* and earlier Vedānta texts (Bṛh. Up. IV. 3.9; Kaṭh up. 11.2.15, BG.xiii.17; 34). The Self-luminosity of the *Ātman* follows from the fact that unlike any other empirical inert object, for instance, a jar (*ghaṭa),* the *Ātman* does not require any other light or object for its manifestation but it manifests everything else existing in the emperical world. Apart from the *Ātman,* no object of the world is self-illuminating, but all objects depend entirely on the *Ātman* for their manifestation.

The self-illuminating nature of the *Ātman* is proved by the fact that men after knowing the real nature of the object whether favourable or unfavourable, endeavour to achieve only favourable ones and withdraw themselves from unfavourable objects (NM p.130; PM. pp.17-18). The real nature of the objects whether good or bad is not known by the objects themselves as they are insentient but known by the sentient *Ātman.* This wordly capability of determining the nature of the objects as good or bad undoubtedly proves that the *Ātman* is self-luminous.

Ānandabodha employs the following syllogism to prove the self-luminosity of the *Ātman* in his *Nyāyamakaranda* (p.131).

Vijñānam avacchedakātmaprakāśādhīnam

avacchinnaprakāśatvāt

Ya uktasādhana

Sa uktasādhya

Yathā daṇḍaprakāśādhīnodaṇḍaprakāśaḥ.

In his *Pramāṇamālā* Ānandabodha also discusses this point *mutatis mutandis* but in this text the above syllogism has been modified as follows :

Idam avacchedakaprakāśādhīnam

avacchinnaprakāśatvād

daṇḍiprakāśavat (PM. p.4).

In this connection Ānandabodha refutes the *pūrvapakṣa* view which upholds that the *Ātman* can become the object of mental perception (*mānasapratyakṣaviṣaya*). The *Ātman* cannot be self-luminous since it depends on mind for its menifestation (PP. p.333).

Ānandabodha refutes this view by saying that the *Ātman* cannot be manifested by the mental perception since the *Ātman* cannot be the object of its own cognitive operation or psychosis (*vṛtti*) as one object cannot be both *kartā* (subject) and *karma* (object). For example, a sword which cannot cut as well as touch itself or a finger-tip which cannot touch itself at one and the same time. (NM. p.131, pp.335). Since the *Ātman* is the subject of all cognitions it cannot be an object of cognitions. Hence the *pūrvapakṣa* view is not valid, says Ānandabodha. He further refutes the view of Śālikanātha who in his *Prakaraṇapañcikā* advocates *Ātman* as the subject of the cognition (*vijñāna*). Śālīkanātha argues that the *Ātman* not perceived through the direct mental perception (*mānasapratyakṣa*) cannot be said to be self-luminous . For the *Ātman* is manifested in all the object-cognitions (*sarvam-artha-samvitsu*) which depend on the sense organs (*indriyādhīna*) (NM.p.132). It cannot be said that the *Ātman* is the receipient of the ultimate result of the action (*kriyā*). It (*Ātman*) is the object of the action since that would go against the functioning capability of the *Ātman*. (*na khalu asya kriyāphalabhājaḥ api karmabhāvaḥ yataḥ anātmani vṛttiḥ virudhyate.* (NM. p.132).

For those who know the concept of *karma* (object) well, they advocate the object (*karma)* to be one connected with the fruit of the action inherent in something else, i.e. in the *kartā* (*parasamaveta kriyāphalaśāli karma iti karmavidaḥ*) (NM. p.132). This being the case, the *Ātman* is not the object like the person who strives to reach the town. (*tathā sati na ātmanaḥ karmabhāvaḥ gantṛvat*) (NM, p.133), e.g. when Chaitra, goes to a town through the action of going inherent in him i.e. Chaitra, he becomes the enjoyer of the ultimate result i.e. reaching the town, yet Chaitra is not the object nor is the *Ātman's* functioning is contradictory in any manner. It is only the town that is the object being connected with the fruit, produced by the action of going inherent in Chaitra. Śālikanātha further argues that the *Ātman* cannot be perceived mentally since perception or cognition implies some object for it and as the *Ātman* cannot be the object (*karma*), it follows that the *Ātman* cannot be perceived. The cognition of a blue object manifests the *Ātman* which is its locus as 'not this ' (*nedam*) and the blue object as 'this' (*idam*).

Ānandabodha briefly refutes the above mentioned view of Śālikanātha. He opines that if the *Ātman* would have been different from its cognition and at the same time would not have been the object (*karma*) thereof, it would not depend on cognition (*vijñāna or samvid*) for its manifestation. That which is manifested by cognition is necessarily its object. As the *Ātman* cannot be the object of its cognition (*vijñāna)* it logically follows that it cannot be manifested by cognition (*vijnāna*) because being manifested by cognition (*vijñāna*) is being pervaded (*vyāpya)* by "being an object of cognition just as 'simsapāness' *(simsapātva)* is perveded (*vyāpya*) by treeness (*vṛkṣatva*). When 'treeness' is denied *(vyāvartamāna)* as a particular object, it is obvious that 'simsapāness' is also per se absent there. Similarly, if the *Ātman* is not the object of cognition (*vijñāna*) it cannot be manifested by cognition (NM. p.135). Ānandabodha finally employs the syllogism:

Samveditā na saṁvidadhīnaprakāśaḥ

Samvitkarmaṇāmantareṇāparokṣatvāt

Samvedanavaditi (NM p.135).

(The cogniser does not depend on cognition for his manifestation because he is not the object of cognition but is self-luminous like cognition itself).

Thus, Ānandabodha refutes Sālikanātha's views and proves the Vedāntic doctrine of self-luminosity of the *Ātman*, as propounded in the earlier texts of the Advaita Vedānta.

Ānandabodha in his *Pramāṇamālā* and *Nyāyamakaranda* expouses the Advaita doctrine of Reality as consciousness (*vijñāna*) as expounded in the fundamental texts[1] of *Prasthānatraya* and those of his celebrated predecessors. With the help of a number of scriptural statements *(śrutivākya)* and valid reasonings he establishes the Advaita doctrine that *Brahman* is of the nature of pure consciousness (*viśuddhavijñāna*) which constitutes the essential nature of *Brahman*. As *Brahman* is devoid of attributes consciousness cannot be its attribute. Consciousness, according to Advaita Vedānta, being itself Brahman is not identical with the empirical knowledge expressed by the terms like *jñāna, buddhi* etc., and consciousness (*vijñāna* or *samvid*) is trans-empirical and transcendental.

1. Bṛh. Up. III.3.28; Tait. Up.II.1; BG.XIII.17.

According to Ānandabodha pure consciousness (*viśuddha vijñāna*) is self-luminous (*svayamprakāśa*) (PM. p.13; NM. p.137) which does not require any other object for its luminosity. Since all the empirical objects are manifested by this supreme light no object can illumine supreme consciousness, *Brahman* which is therefore self-luminous and self-proved.

Ānandabodha differs from the view put forth by the Nyāya school which does not aprove the theory of self-luminosity of the consciousness (*vijñāna*), as expounded by the preceptors of the Advaita philosophy. According to the Nyāya school the Self (*Ātman*) is essentially a pure substance (*dravya*). The knowledge (*jñāna or buddhi*) being one of the adventitious qualities of the *Ātman* (NS.3.2.8), resides in the *Ātman*. Hence *samvid* or *Vijñāna* is not self-luminous (*svayam prakāśa*).

Ānandabodha asks the question whether *vijñāna* (consciousness) cognises objects when in itself it is luminous or otherwise (NM. p.137). If consciousness manifests objects being itself unmanifest then there would arise doubt whether a pot is cognised or not, i.e. when a person cognises a pot after that pot-cognition, he does not doubt whether he has seen the pot or not as he is sure of the pot-cognition. Hence it is proved that consciousness at the time of manifesting an object manifests itself since there does not arise any doubt concerning the cognition. Without admitting the self-luminosity of the cognition (*vijñāna*) the determination of the cognition of an object would not be possible (NM. p.137). Ānandabodha therefore employs the following syllogism:

Vijñānamarthaprakāśanasamaye prakāśate

tadupādhāvanantaram sandehāyogyatvāt arthavat

(NM. p.138).

(Consciousness manifests itself at the time of manifestation of object because after the cognition of an object doubt does not arise about that cognition like the object)

If it is said that consciousness (*vijñāna*) manifests an object being itself manifest by another consciousness then it does not stand to reason. For it will lead to infinite regress (*anavasthā*), because, for the manifestation of the first cognition second will be necessary, and for the second, a third (NM. p.138-139). Thus, the process would not come to a logical end. Moreover, numerous cognitions of the worldly objects cannot occur at one and the same time. The worldly objects like the jar (*ghaṭa)* and others are insentient by nature and consequently they are not self-luminous. Nor they manifest by one another. If it be argued that consciousness though insentient, manifests an object, like the eyes, which though insentient manifest a visible object, Ānandabodha rejects this view saying that the alternatives involved in it are not admissible. Manifesting is producing manifestation. The manifestation produced by consciousness should be either non different from the object of the cognition or different from the object of cognition. The manifestation (*prakāśa*) is not the nature of the object since an insentient object and manifestation (*prakāśa*) cannot be identical with each other like a liquid and a solid, and the momentary manifestation cannot be identical with an object which is subtle in nature (NM. p.141-2).

Nor can it be said that *prakāśa* (manifestation) is something other than the object, and is an attribute of the object *(arthadharma)* generated by the cognition (*vijñāna*); for, if it would have been the case, there would not have been manifestation of the past and future objects, though actually such a manifestation is always seen (*asti ca tayorapi avabhāsaḥ*).

Again, if manifestation were to be internal (*antaram*) it is nothing but the cognition (*vijñāna*); if it were to be non-sentient, (*jaḍa*), it would manifest neither the object nor its nature. Then the entire world would be blind (*jagadāndhyam prasajyeta*). Therefore it must be admitted that cognition (*vijñāna*) is self-luminous and also manifests the object. (NM. p.142). Just as light dispelling darkness helps the eye sight in its operation and illumines itself and the object without requiring any other light, in the same way the *Ātman* manifests itself and the object without the need of any intervening object (NM. p.143).

The Yogācāra, one of the four schools of the Buddhist philosophy otherwise known as Vijñānavādins for advocating *vijñāna* (consciousness) as the Supreme Reality, argues that the *vijñāna* is not eternal (*nitya*) but momentary (*kṣaṇika*). To prove the validity of the momentariness (*kṣaṇikatva*) of the *vijñāna* this school points out that cognition of blue (*nīla*) is different from the cognition of yellow (*pita*). The individual cognitions like the cognition of blue etc., arise and perish and so no cognition can be said to be eternal, maintains the Yogācāra school.

Ānandabodha refutes this view by saying that the momentariness (*kṣaṇikatva*) of cognition cannot be proved by any means of knowledge. The argument, viz. "when 'blue' is cognised 'yellow' is not cognised" is not capable of proving the momentariness of the cognition. In all individual cognitions (*samvedanavyakti*) like the cognition of blue (*nīla*) etc. there underlies one basic cognition (*vijñāna*) which is identical with all these subsequent cognitions. Hence the eternality of the cognition or consciousness is absolutely valid and logical.

Secondly, the contention of the Yogācāra school, viz. the individual cognitions like the cognition of blue are momentary, is not tenable according to Ānandabodha because there would not be the cognition of difference (*bheda*) among the cognitions without a conscious self or *vijñāna*, the perceiver of their differences. The cognition of different cognitions presupposes the *Ātman* which is of the nature of *vijñāna*. Since no other object or entity except *Ātman* or *vijñāna* can determine the difference, the consciousness is proved to be eternal (*nitya*) (NM. p.134-44).

3.3 Bliss (Ānanda)

Following the *Prasthānatraya* and the texts of his predecessors Ānandabodha in his *Pramāṇamālā* contends that as the Individual Soul (*jīvātman*) is identical with the Supreme Self both are of the nature of absolute bliss[1] *'tathācāyamānandasvabhāvaḥ syāt ātmatvāt paramātmavat* (p.3). This blissful nature (*ānandasvabhāva)* of the Self is experienced in everyday life as the object of supreme love. To substantiate his view Ānandabodha quotes the statement of Yājñavalkya from the *Bṛhadāraṇyaka Upaniṣad, Ātmanastu kāmāya sarvam priyam bhavati* (2-4-5) i.e. the *Ātman* is dearer than any other object in the transmigratory world. It is seen in this empirical world that there is hiararchy among the objects loved by a person e.g. a son is dearer than a friend, and a wife is dearer than a friend. Following the hiararchy the Self is the dearest of all. (PM. p.2).

Ānandabodha asserts that the blissful nature of the *Ātman* is further proved by *Ātman's* non-relation with any kind of evil which is non-self (*anātman*). If the nature of the *Ātman* were not *ānanda* it would have not

---

1. Bṛh.Up.III.9 p.28; IV.2.19,20,21, 32,; I.4.8; II.4.5; III.4.2; III.5.1; Chā.Up.VII.23.1; VII.24; Tai.Up.II.4, 7,9; III.5.1.

been loved by all the beings and would have been devoid of *paramapremāspadabhāva* (being the receptacle of the supreme love), for without the nature of supreme bliss (*paramānandasvabhāva*), the nature of the supreme love of the *Ātman* (*paramapremāspadabhāva)* is impossible since the nature of supreme bliss *(paramānandasvabhāva)* is co-related with the supreme love of the Self. (NM. p.175).

Ānandabodha further says that the expression of a living being such as "I should not be born again (*mā na bhūyām bhūyāsam*) indicates the blissful nature of the *Ātman,* because all human beings experience suffering in this transmigratory world caused by nescience (*avidyā)* and they endeavour to attain the supreme bliss, which is the essential nature of the *Ātman*. They also desire not to come back again to this mundane world. Since all the human beings love their own selves they therefore endeavour to achieve only those mundane objects which are favourable to the *Ātman,* rather than to our physical body.

The opponent argues that the expression of human beings like "I should not be born again in this mundane world." (*mā na bhūyām bhūyāsam)* does not denote blissful nature of the *Ātman,* but fear of suffering (*duḥkhabhaya*) which a man tries to avoid along with the birth in the *saṁsāra* in best possible way. This is because of the fear of pain, caused by the destruction of the physical body etc. (NM. p.175) as pointed out in the *Bhagavadgītā* (XIII.8).

Then Ānandabodha sets aside this *pūrvapakṣa* argument by saying that though there is fear of suffering arising out of pain caused by the destruction of the physical body etc., still pain belongs to the *upādhis* (adjuncts) like the body (*śarīra*) etc. Hence pain cannot be the cause of fear of suffering but the enjoyment of the mundane objects (*bhoga*) is the cause of suffering. A person becomes miserable because of his enjoyment of undesirable objects. Hence the enjoyment of objects resulting in misery and painful experience creates an urge in the person to attain the supreme bliss which is nothing but the Self dearly loved by a person.

In the *Pramāṇamālā* Ānandabodha argues that unlike the worldly objects the *Ātman* endowed with the supreme bliss is only whole heartedly loved by every person. Hence every person hates the worldly objects and finally attempts to attain the supreme bliss after experiencing the miserable condition of the mundane world and realising the blissful nature of the self which is both all-pervasive and transcendental.

To prove this Ānandabodha employs the following syllogism:

Jivaśca paramānandasvabhāvaḥ

parapremāspadatvāt

ya uktasādhyo na bhavati

nāsābuktasādhanaḥ

yathā ghaṭaḥ

na cāyamuktasādhano na bhavati

tasmānna noktasādhyaḥ (PM. p.2).

(Individual Soul has the nature of highest bliss since it is the subject of the supreme love as the object which is not of the highest nature of bliss, cannot be the subject of supreme love as a jar which has not the nature of supreme bliss. Hence it is not the subject of supreme love).

Ānandabodha explains the nature of bliss (*ānanda*). He firstly differentiates *brahmānanda* (*Brahman*-Bliss) from the mundane pleasure and then explains the positive nature of bliss (*ānanda*).

Brahmānanda, according to Ānandabodha, is eternal (*nitya*), obiquitous (*vyāpaka*) and not limited by any *upādhi* (adjunct). It is transcendental and all together different from the mundane pleasure expressed by the terms like *sukha* or *duḥkhābhāva* etc. *Brahmānanda* is not an object of love as a source of enjoyment (*upabhogasādhana*) like a piece of sandal (*candana*) or a woman (*vanitā*) (NM. p.174). These are perishable and always prone to painful experiences.

Ānandabodha argues that there is difference between *Brahmānanda* and *Sāṁsārika-ānanda* (worldly happiness), otherwise no difference in one's delight and the delight of another in the empirical world would be found. The empirical pleasure experienced in the achievement of the dearest objects is non-sentient (*jaḍa*), finite, limited and mere semblance (*ābhāsa*) of the Supreme bliss, for all the creatures are originated from the bliss. Ānandabodha quotes from the Bṛh. Up. in his *Pramāṇamālā* to substantiate his position (PM. p.1; Bṛh. Up. 4-3-32).

According to Ānandabodha, *Brahmānanda* is positive (*bhāvarūpa)* and not negative by nature (*abhāvarūpa*) such as absence of misery (*duḥkhābhāva*). Ānandabodha in his *Pramāṇamālā* employs the following syllogisms to prove it.

Ānando duḥkhābhāva na bhavati

tadanirūpyatvāt

Yadittham tattathā

Yathā ghaṭaḥ (PM. p.1).

(Bliss is not absence of misery since it cannot be proved like a jar).

Ānando bhāvarupaḥ

Pratiyogyanirūpyatvāt

Ghaṭavat (PM. p.1).

(Bliss is positive because it does not depend on its counter-entity like a jar.)

Ānandabodha explains in his *Pramāṇamālā* that the knowledge of the absence of the jar (*ghaṭābhāva*) depends on the knowledge of *ghaṭa* since *ghaṭa* is the counter-entity (*pratiyogī*) of *ghaṭābhāva* (absence of jar) (PM. p.4). But the knowledge of a jar does not depend on the knowledge of its absence (*abhāva).* So *ghaṭa* is a positive entity (*bhāvapadārtha*). Similarly *ānanda* (bliss) is experienced without the knowledge of its absence. Therefore *ānanda* is a positive entity (*bhāvapadārtha*) like a *ghaṭa.*

Ānandabodha further maintains that *ānanda* (bliss) and *duḥkhābhāva* (absence of misery) are two different entities. Hence the relation of entity and counter-entity cannot exist between them. (PM. p.1). As *ānanda* and *duḥkhābhāva* are experienced separately by a person since without the latter the former i.e. *ānanda* is experienced in this world. For exmple, says Ānandabodha, when a person hears all of a sudden a sound of a lyre (*vipañcī*), he experiences *ānanda* which is positive by nature and not merely the absence of misery. Thus, Ānandabodha establishes the Advaita view that *ānanda* is of positive nature (*bhāvarūpa*). According to Ānandabodha, the nature of the Supreme Reality is bliss, pure and simple without any tinge of *duḥkha* or *duḥkhābhāva* (absence of misery).

3.4 Individual Self (Jīvātman)

Following Śaṅkara Ānandabodha states that Individual Soul (*Jīvātman)* is not different in reality from the *Brahman,* the transcendental Reality (*na ca paramātmā jivātmānostatvato vyatiricyata ityapāditamadhastāt* (NM. p.25-26). Ānandabodha employs the following syllogisms in his *Pramāṇamālā* to prove the non-difference as follows:

a) *Jīvāḥ paramātmanastatvato na bhidyante*
ātmatvāt
paramātmavat (PM. p.3).

b) *VivÂdÂdhyÂsitÂ jÏvÂÌ prativÂdinastatvato na vyatiricyante*
jīvatvādātmatvādvā
prativādivat (PM. p.3).

According to Ānandabodha, the Individual soul (*jīvātman*) is a false projection of *avidyā* (nescience) which has in reality no existence. It is *Brahman* which because of the beginningless nescience does not realise its essential nature i.e. existence, consciousness and bliss (*sat-cit-ānanda*) and considers himself as *jīvātman*. Ānandabodha like his predecessors uses example of the eather (*ākāśa*) to explain the jīvahood of the *Ātman*, the Supreme Self. He says that as the ether though one and all-pervasive, appears to be numerous because of limitations of ear-hole (*karṇaśaṣkuli*), similarly the *Brahman* being limited by the physical body appears to be diverse which is a false notion (*tattatkarṇaśaṣkulīmaṇḍalāvacchinnasya nabhasa statratatra-śrotrabhāvavat tattadbhogāyatanādyavacchedalabdhajīva-bhāva bhedasyatatratatrabhogopapattau kimanekātmakalpanā-durvyasanena*) (NM p.26-27). Ānandabodha also uses the example of reflection or type (*pratibiṁba*) and proto-type (*biṁba*) to elucidate the same. As the one *biṁba* appears to be diverse in the form of *pratibiṁbas* (reflections) similarly one *Brahman* appears to be numerous Individual selves. (*biṁbapratibiṁbayoḥ pratibiṁbānāmiva ca parasparamalikanirbhāsa eva*, PM. p.3).

Ānandabodha further asserts that the difference (*bheda*) which is found in this transmigratory world among the Individual Selves as one is a scholar and other is a fool, is unreal (*asatya*) and illusory based on *avidyā* (PM. p.8).

As *Jīvātman* is identical with *Brahman,* the Supreme Reality, it is also of the nature of supreme bliss (*paramānanda*). Ānandabodha employs the following sylloism:

Jīvaśca paramānandasvabhāvaḥ

paramapremāspadatvāt

ya uktasādhyo na bhabati

nāsābuktasādhanaḥ

yathā ghataḥ (PM. p.2).

Thus, Ānandabodha proves that *jīvātam* (Individual soul) is not a real entity but *Brahman* itself. The difference (*bheda*) is unreal and *aupādhika* (conditional).

3.5 The Problem of the World

Ānandabodha following the *Prasthānatraya* and the texts of his predecessors explains the nature of the world (*jagat*) in his three works, viz., *Pramāṇamālā, Nyāyamakaranda* and *Nyāyadīpāvali.* He puts forth the view that the world (*jagat*) is false (*mithyā*) designed by *anādi avidyā* (beginningless nescience). However, the phenomenal world is not absolutely unreal (*tuccha*) like sky- flower (*ākāśakusuma*) and also real like *Brahman.* Although the world thus has phenomenal reality, compared to the Ultimate Transcendental Reality i.e. *Brahman,* the world is false (*mithyā*).

To prove the falsity (*mithyātva)* of the world Ānandabodha in his *Nyāyamakaranda* and *Pramāṇamālā* employs the following syllogism :-

Prapañcaḥ avidyāvijṛmbhitaḥ

jāḍyadṛśyatvahetubhyām

rajatasvapnadṛśyavat (NM. p.128; PM, p.11).

(The world is a product of *avidyā*, because it is non-sentient and perceptible like the perception of silver and dream).

Explaining the nature of two *hetus* (reasons) i.e. *jaḍatva* (non-sentient) and *dṛśyatva* (perceptible) in the *Pramāṇamālā* Ānandabodha says that the non-sentient (*jaḍatva*) nature means the absence of self-luminosity (*anātmaprakāśatva*) or being the nature of *asamvidrūpatvam* and therefore is of the nature of the negation or exclusion with regards to the Supreme Reality. While perceptibility (*dṛśyatva*) as a rule means being seen by something other than itself (*sva-atirekidarśana dṛśyatvam*). These two *hetus i.e. jaḍatva* and *dṛśyatva,* according to Ānandabodha, are not possible in case of the *Ātman* or *Brahman* since it is pure consciousness (*viśuddhavijñāna*) and self-luminous (*svayaṁprakāśa)* as proclaimed by the *Upaniṣads* (Bṛh 3-9-28; Kaṭh.15, Śweta. Up.6.14; Muṇḍ Up.2.2.10).

In the *Nyāyadīpāvali* (P.1) Ānandabodha employs one more syllogism as follows :-

Vivādapadam (jagat) mithyā

dṛśyatvāt

yathā rajatam ubhayavādyavivādāspadam (ND. p.1).

(The object of dispute i.e. the world is false because it is an object of perception like the silver in the shell).

Ānandabodha proclaims that the said syllogism is devoid of fallacies (*hetvābhāsa* or *hetudoṣas*).

The opponent argues that if the phenomenal world is unreal (*vivādapadam mithyā*), then the world cannot be a substratum of the *hetu* i.e. *dṛśyatva* (perceptible) since the substratum should be always existent or real object, otherwise the *hetu* cannot be in *pakṣa* (locus).

Ānandabodha refutes by saying that though the world is accepted as unreal, it is not absolutely unreal (*tuccha*) like the sky-flower (*ākāśakusuma*) as its phenomenal reality has been accepted. The world being false also can be a substratum (*pakṣa*) as implied in the above syllogism. Thus the *pūrvapakṣa* argument does not stand to reason.

Ānandabodha further contends that an absolutely non-existent object can be a substratum in a negative inference (*vyatireka anumāna*) e.g.

Vandhyāsutaḥ vaktā na bhavati

acedtanatvāt

pāṣāṇavat.

Ānandabodha says that though a positive or an affirmative term (*astivācaka*) is impossible with reference to an absolutely non-existent object, the negative term (*nāstivācaka*) can be used for a non-existent object. Otherwise there would not be a single term to express the non-existent entities. When one expresses a statement that a negative term is not possible in case of absolutely non-existent entities, he admits a negative term, since negation (*abhāva*) means absence of something. To substantiate this view, Ānandabodha quotes a verse from the *Pramāṇavārttika* of Dharmakīrti (600 A.D) the great Buddhist philosopher.

Vidhānaṁ pratiṣedham ca muktvā śābdosti nāparaḥ/

Vyavahāraḥ sa cāsatasu neti prāptātra mūkatatā//

(ND, p.2; PV.4.225)

Ānandabodha further maintains that the *hetu*, (*dṛśyatva*) is not involved with any of the following defects.

1) *Svarūpāsiddha hetvābhāsa* (unproved)

For, *Svarūpāsiddha* occurs if the *hetu* remains absent in the *pakṣa*. In the given syllogism - *Vivādapadam mithyā dṛśyatvāt,* the *hetu* i.e. *dṛśyatva* remains present in the *pakṣa* i.e. the world. Hence it is bereft of *Svarupāsiddha* fallacy.

2) *Vyāpyatvāsidha* (unproved)

It is not involved with *vyāpyatvāsiddha,* since the condition (*upādhi*) required for this fallacy is not present in the given syllogism.

3) *Viruddha* (Contrary reason)

The *hetu* i.e. *dṛśyatva* is not involved with *viruddha* (contrary reason). For *viruddha-hetvābhāsa* occurs if the *hetu* proves the absence of *sādhya*. But here *dṛśyatva* does not prove the absence of *sādhya* i.e. *mithyātvābhāva* because the *Ātman,* the transcendental reality is not accepted as the object of perception like a jar (NDI p.5).

4) *Savyabhicāra* (discrepant reason)

Ānandabodha further maintains that the *hetu* i.e. *dṛśyatva* is free from the fallacy called *savyabhicāra* (discrepant reason) since *savyabhicāra* co-exists with the *sādhya* partially. But it is not possible because unlike *jagat* the *Ātman* cannot became the object of perception as it is self-luminous. The other thing that could be urged as real as well as perceptible is the cessation of *avidyā* which would be perishable if it is different from the *Ātman.* If *jagat* is identical with the *Ātman,* the former would be self-illuminating and not an object of perception. Thus, there is no scope for the fallacy called *savyabhicāra.*

5) *Bādhita* (annulled)

According to Ānandabodha, the *hetu, dṛśyatva* is not involved with the *bādhita* (annulled) fallacy for it occurs only when the absence of *sādhya* becomes established by another *pramāṇa* (means of knowledge). But in case of the said syllogism, - *Vivādapadam mithyā dṛśyatvāt* there is no other means of knowledge to prove the reality of the world which is *sādhyābhāva.* Direct perception (*pratyakṣa*) cannot prove the reality of the world for it only illuminates the object, not its reality. Inference (*anumāna*) also cannot prove the reality of the world since it depends on perception. Comparision (*upamāna*) shows only similarity between two objects and does not prove reality or unreality of any object. Presumption (*arthāpatti*) also proves a thing which is seen or heard but which is impossible to be explained by other means of knowledge. But presumption cannot prove the reality of the world since the worldly objects cannot be explained as those seen in a dream. Finally non- perception (*abhāva*) also cannot establish the reality of the world which is a positive entity (*bhāvapadārtha*). Hence as there is no means of knowledge to prove the absolute reality of the world, the *hetu* i.e. *dṛśyatva* is not *bādhita* (annulled).

6) *Satpratipakṣa* (inconclusive reason)

The *hetu* becomes involved with the fallacy called *satpratipakṣa* (inconclusive reason) if there is another *hetu* to prove the absence of *sādhya,* but in case of the said syllogism i.e. *Vivādapadam mithyā jaḍatvāt* two *hetus* can be accepted, viz. *abādhyatva* (not being nullified) and *arthakriyākāritva* (serving an useful purpose). Both of these *hetus* cannot prove the reality of the world since *abādhyatva* is contradictory to *sādhya* i.e. *mithyātva* itself and *arthakriyākāritva* (serving an useful purpose) can be applicable even to the objects in dreams, which are not real. Thus, the *hetu* i.e. *dṛśyatva* is devoid of all fallacies and it is a valid reason (*sadhetu)* to prove the falsity of the world, contends Ānandabodha.

Moreover, Ānandabodha rejects the difference (*bheda*) supposed to be existing among the objects of knowledge (*jñeya- padārthas*). Since it is unreal caused by *Avidyā* and perishable, no means of knowledge (*pramāṇa*) can prove the validity of difference (*bheda*). Direct perception cannot cognise *bheda* (difference) for the following reasons :-

Firstly, direct perception (*pratyakṣa*) cannot manifest the difference alone, for without the knowledge of an object and its counter-entity (*pratiyogī*), the difference alone cannot be perceived.

Secondly, direct perception cannot manifest the difference (*bheda*) first and then the objects, or the objects first, then the difference, since the cognition being momentary cannot have more than one function (*vyāpāra*) at one and the same time, though cognition (*vṛtti* or *jñāna*) dces not disappear immediately in the next moment and continues for two or three moments. There cannot be any other function (*vyāpāra*) of cognition other than its own origination (*utpatti*) (NM. p.33).

If it be argued that origination (*utpatti*) of cognition is not a function (*vyāpāra*) of cognition since it cannot be related to that which is originated (*jāta*) as origination (*utpatti*) of *jāta* (who is born) is virtually impossible. Nor the origination of cognition can be realised to *ajāta* (which is not originated), since function (*vyāpāra*) can be of an existent object (*bhāvapadārtha*) (NM. p.34).

Ānandabodha refutes this saying that cognition (*vṛtti* or *jñana*) is not *kāraka* (agent) since *kāraka* produces an effect (*kārya*) but cognition does not create any addition to the worldly object as it is impossible with past and future objects. It is never seen that a locus (*ālambana*) has vanished or has come into existence and its attributes have an existence in the present (NM. p.34). Hence the manifestation of the object (*arthāvagraha*) is the nature (*rūpa*) of cognition. The notion of difference is understood in the secondary sense (*lakṣaṇā*) as in the statement there is a head of Rāhū (*rahoḥ śiraḥ*). As Rāhū, (one of the nine planets) has, *ipso facto,* no head and the head (*śira*) is itself Rāhū, similarly difference (*bheda*) is not a real entity but an illusion as that of the head of Rāhū. Ānandabodha further says that cognition depends on its origination and therefore this very origination is accepted as its function (*vyāpāra*) (NM. p.35). To substantiate Ānandabodha quotes from the *Brahmasiddhi* of Maṇḍana Miśra, *api ca janma eva buddheḥ vyāpāraḥ arthāvagraha rūpāyāḥ*. (BS. p.45; NM. p.35). The very origination of cognition which has nature of the manifestation of object is its function.

Thirdly, perception (*pratyakṣa*) cannot manifest both objects and difference since the cognition of difference depends on the objects and its counter-entity (*pratiyogī*) e.g. to know the difference seperately from the object from a distant place which is beyond perception, the remembrance (*smṛti)* of that object has to be admitted along with the perception of the object in front. Similarly, to know the difference seperately from the object at hand the two different cognitions of objects and counter-entity (*pratiyogī*) have to be admitted. These three cognitions, i.e. the object, the counter-entity and the difference cannot be cognised simultaneously. Thus perception cannot manifest the difference as well as the objects. Ānandabodha maintains that since direct perception (*pratyakṣa*) cannot cognise the difference (*bheda*) no other means of knowledge (*pramāṇa*) can cognise it since all of them depend on the direct perception. Inference (*anumāna*) depends on the perception (*pratyakṣa*) for the knowledge of relation of *vyāpya* and *vyāpaka*. Hence inference fails in proving the reality of the difference. (NM. p.38). Verbal testimony (*śabda*) also depends on the knowledge of difference between word and its meaning. Presumption (*arthāpatti*) is of the nature of a necessary assumption as oil can be had only from the sesamum. It also depends on the perception. Hence for the presumption (*arthāpatti*) also the knowledge of difference is necessary and for the knowledge of difference the knowledge of presumption is necessary. This leads to the fault of interdependence (*parasparāśraya*). Thus, presumption cannot prove difference (*bheda*). Similarly *upamāna* also cannot be the means for cognising difference, since it has for its objects the similarity in two things that are proved by other means. Non-cognition (*abhāva*) also does not cognise difference since its existence depends upon difference between the things excluded. Non-cognition (*abhāva*) is dependent on the knowledge of difference and hence cannot be a valid means for establishing difference (NM. p.38).

In the *Nyāyamakaranda* (pp. 44-51) Ānandabodha refutes two characteristics of difference (*bheda*); a) it is of the nature of the thing (*vastusvarūpa*) and b) it is the attribute of a thing (*dharmasvarūpa*). It is argued that difference (*bheda*) is the very nature of positive entities (*bhedasvabhāvāḥ sarve bhāvāḥ* NM. p.44). Perception (*pratyakṣa*) which cognises the things as such, has for its objects also the mutual exclusion (*pratyakṣa parasparavyāvṛttiviṣayam* NM.44). In direct perception (*pratyakṣa*) the objects appear as having an exclusive nature. The experience establishes the existence of blue and establishes also its difference from yellow and the like. Indeed, difference (*bheda*) as distinct from the things cannot be explained. If it is accepted as distinct from the object, it should be experienced differently. Difference between the two, i.e. the object and its difference (*bheda*), must be known by another difference. Thus it would lead to the fault of *anavasthā* (infinite regress). If *vidāraṇa* (dichotomy) is accepted as the very nature of difference, it is easier to accept the same as the object (*atha na bhedo bhedāntarabhedyaḥ tasya svabhāvato bhedāt hante astu vastu eva tathā lāghavāt.*) (NM. p.44).

Ānandabodha refutes this prima facie view by saying that if that whose nature is *vidāraṇa* (*bheda*) would be identified with object, then there would not be unitive feature of the objects since oneness or unity of co-existence with non-difference conflicts with difference. (*bhedasya vidāraṇātmano vasturūpatve na kiñcana ekam vastu syāt*) (NM. p.46). The knowledge of difference consists of two parts i.e. the locus (*ādhāra*) and counter-entity (*pratiyogī*) of difference, as in the form this is different from that where this is the locus of difference and 'that' is the counter-entity. If difference is identical with the locus, then one and the same object would be cognised in two forms, viz., the object, and the counter-entity. Then there would not be the knowledge of the one object. Like the oneness of the objects the plurality which is the collection (*samāhāra*) of many individual things, would become impossible. Again, the difference cannot be the third entity apart from oneness and plurality, as flavour (*gandha*) is from form (*rūpa*) and taste (*rasa*) because oneness and plurality are opposed to each other. The denial of one leads to the existence of others like perishability and non-perishability where if perishability denied, non-perishability becomes affirmed.

Difference is of the form of blue only in relation to yellow and the like and not in relation to the blue itself. The object is only one in the form of blue and different in relation to other entities. But Ānandabodha explains that the difference (*bheda*) being of the nature of a positive entity, is originated from the cause of that entity and hence should not require the counter-entity (*pratiyogī*). If it requires, then that would be contradictory, for the object by itself does not require any such thing. Thus difference (*bheda*) does not require any other thing for its origination, or existence. If establishment of one's individual nature is mutually dependent, not even one will be established.

3. If the existence of blue is dependent on the existence of yellow and vice versa, the existence of any one of the two will not be proved for the obvious flaw of interdependence (*parasparāśraya*).

4. For blue and the like, there is no requirement of mutual dependence in case of dealing with empirical objects (*arthakriyā*) for the person desirous of blue never takes up yellow and like. Hence positive entities do not require another positive entity. From this, it is clear that if difference is a positive entity (*bhāvapadārtha*) it cannot require any other positive entity, for as difference (*bheda*) requires the counter- entity (*pratiyogī*) it could not be of the nature of a positive entity. Thus difference (*bheda*) cannot be said to be positive in nature according to Ānandabodha.

5. It is argued that difference is the attribute (*dharma*) of the object, and it can be perceived. Though another difference between difference and the object is admitted still there cannot be the fault of infinite regress (*anavasthā*). Because when the very basic idea is not in danger and nullified, the *anavasthā* (infinite-regress) is not a fault in the argument. The root (*mūla*) here means the original reason, i.e. the primary knowledge of the difference (*bhedajñāna*). This can be had in the indeterminate knowledge (*nirvikalpakajñāna*). In the indeterminate knowledge (*savikalpakajñāna*) the difference and the object appear simultaneously; then in the deter-

minate knowledge one appears as the difference and the other as the counter-entity (*pratiyogī*, p.49).

Ānandabodha refutes this view by saying that the knowledge of locus-attribute relation (*āśrayāśrayibhāva*) between the difference and the object is impossible without the knowledge of difference. e.g. for the knowledge of a man possessing stick (*daṇḍī*) one must know both the stick and the man differently. Similarly the knowledge of difference, whether it appears as a locus as in 'the difference of jar' or as an attribute as in 'jar is different from the pillar' should necessarily be preceded by the knowledge of difference. In the *Pramāṇamālā* (p.5). Ānandabodha remarks that one cannot know the locus-attribute relationship (*āśrayāśrayibhāva*) or (*dharma-dharmibhāva*) between the two objects from distance. Thus the knowledge of difference does require the knowledge of another difference which is of the nature of difference. Thus the succeeding differences cannot be proved without the establishment of the preceding differences. The preceding ones cannot be proved without proving the original difference. Thus it leads to infinite regress (*anavasthā*).

6. Ānandabodha points out further that as difference (*bheda*) cannot be proved either as the *svabhāva* (nature of the object) *or a-svabhāva* (different from the object) it also cannot be proved as *svabhāvāsvabhāvasammuccaya* or *svabhāvāsvabhāvavilakṣaṇa*. The combination (*samuccaya*) of *svabhāva* and *a-svabhāva* would be contradictory like the combination of a positive and negative characteristics. The third alternative (*vilakṣaṇa*) from *svabhāva* and *a-svabhāva* is also impossible. Thus, the nature of difference is inexplicable.

Thus *Brahman* or *Paramātman* is the one, non-dual, transcendental Reality. The plurality of the *Ātman* as propounded by the orthodox schools like the Sāṁkhya, the Nyāya-Vaiśeṣika and the Prābhākara schools of Pūrva-Mīmāṁsā is untenable, according to Ānandabodha , as it is not based on valid reasoning and scriptural authority. Secondly, *Brahman* is of the nature of pure consciousness (*viśuddhavijñāna*) and self-luminous (*svayaṁ prakāśa*). Further this consciousness is eternal and not momentary as advocated by the Yogācāra school of Buddhist philosophy. Thirdly, *Brahman* or the *Ātman* is of the nature of pure bliss (*paramānanda*). The nature of bliss is positive (*bhāvarūpa*) not as the cessation of misery (*duḥkhābhāva*). This supreme bliss is experienced in the state of *mukti* (emancipation) when the individual soul (*Jīvātman*) is completely devoid of beginningless nescience (*Avidyā or Māyā*).

Fourthly, the Individual Self (*Jīvātman*), according to Ānandabodha, is not a real entity; it is not different from *Brahman*. The difference (*bheda*) which appears between the *Brahman* and the *Jīvātman* is illusion created by the binding and blinding *Avidyā*.

Fifthly, the world (*jagat*) is not real like the *Brahman*. Though it has empirical reality nevertheless it is false (*mithyā)* in comparision with the transcendental reality, *Brahman*.

Sixthly, the difference (*bheda*) supposed to be existing among the objects of knowledge in this empirical world is in reality false (*mithyā*), an illusion designed by the *avidyā*. Hence there is no means of knowledge (*pramāṇa*) to prove the reality of the differences (*bheda*) as it is not a real entity.

CHAPTER IV

EPISTEMOLOGICAL VIEWS

This chapter embodies Ānandabodha's epistemological views in two sections. In the first section, the following topics, viz., empirical validity of means of knowledge (*pramāṇas*), validity of the vedic scripture in obtaining the knowledge of the *Brahman*, an established entity (*siddhavastu*), import of the Upaniṣadic statements and *pravartaka* (inducer or the motivator) and in the second, the problem of *avidyā*, nature of *avidyā*, and the theories of error have been discussed.

SECTION I

4.1 Empirical Validity of Pramāṇas

In the *Nyāyamakaranda* and *Pramāṇamālā* Ānandabodha like his predecessors expounds Advaitic view that the *pramāṇas* (means of knowledge) viz., *pratyakṣa* (perception), *anumāna* (inference), *upamāna* (analogy), *arthāpatti* (presumption) and *anupalabdhi* or *abhāva* (negation) except the *śruti* or *śabda* (scripture or valid verbal testimony) are false because they form a part of this illusory empirical world. These above said *pramāṇas* including the perception (*pratyakṣa*) which is considered to be the supreme means of knowledge on which other *pramāṇas* depend for their validity, according to Ānandabodha, are products of indefinable and beginningless *avidyā* and eventually valid only in the limited spheres of phenomenal world in a restricted sense. These *pramāṇas* based on *avidyā* possessing the limited empirical validity cannot generate the highest knowledge of the trans-empirical reality called *Brahman* or *Ātman*. Hence the scripture (*Śruti* or *Veda*) is the only means of knowledge of the Supreme Reality called *Brahman* not being originated from the *avidyā* and so not limited to the false phenomenal world. (NM. p.145; PM. p.16).

In the *Pramāṇamālā* Ānandabodha at some length explains the reason why the vedic scripture (*śrutipramāṇa*) is the only valid means in comparision with the direct perception (*pratyakṣa*) etc., about the knowledge of the *Brahman,* the Supreme Reality. He points out that the validity (*prāmāṇya*) of any means of knowledge (*pramāṇa*) is determined by its cognition of an object which is absolutely unsublated (*abādhita*) by any other later cognition belonging to the present, past and future times. But the *pramāṇas* like perception etc. apart from the scripture, are not capable of generating the cognition of an absolutely unsublated object (*atyantābādhitaviṣaya*) either by themselves (*svataḥ*) or *parataḥ* (depending on other objects). Though perception and other *pramāṇas* are self-valid in connection with their origination (*utpatti*) and cognition (*jñapti*) nevertheless these are not valid means for the knowledge of the Absolute Reality, *Brahman*. It is because without proving the *Brahman* which is totally beyond sublation (*atyantābādha*) a *pramāṇa* cannot prove its validity. (*sva samvedana pakṣe'pi svārthasyātyantikamabādhamanavagamya tatham tadupahitamaryādātmanaḥ prāmāṇyamadhyavasyet* (PM. p.12). Moreover, absolute non-sublation of an worldly object cannot be grasped by the limited direct perception (*pratyakṣa*) because the sublation (*bādha*) which might occur in the future cannot be the object of the present perception (*kālāntarabhāvino bādhasyedānimayogyatvenānupalambhasambhavāt*, NM. p.12). In case of a series of direct perceptions succeeding ones cannot prove the validity of the preceding ones as the latter contain the same potency as the former and ultimately fail in generating the cognition of the Supreme Reality, *Brahman*. As the direct perception (*pratyakṣa*) is not capable of giving the knowledge of the Reality, other *pramāṇas* such as *anumāna* (inference) etc. cannot also be authoritative means of knowing the Supreme Reality because all of them depend on the perception and without perception they cannot function independently (*yadā tu pratyakṣasya eva etādṛśigatistadā kaivakathā tadgocaravyāptyupajīvino varakasyānumānādeḥ* (PM. p.12). Ānandabodha further points out that the validity of perception and other *pramāṇas* cannot be ascertained by *parataḥ* (depending on other object) also as it will lead to the obvious fault of *anavasthā* (infinite regress) because the validity of the first perception will depend on the second, and the second on the third and so on and thus the cycle would not come to an end. Ānandabodha proves that the validity of perception and other *pramāṇas* neither by *svataḥ* (independently) nor by *parataḥ* (depending on other objects) cannot generate the supreme intuition of the Transcendental Reality called *Brahman* or *Ātman*.

To prove the validity of the scripture (*śrutipramāṇa*) regarding the *brahmajñāna* Ānandabodha maintains that the objects (*viṣaya*) of the Vedic scripture are beyond the limits of time, i.e. past, present and future and therefore the scripture can generate the cognition of the objects which are unlike that of the perception etc., unsublated (*abādhita*) by any succeeding sublating knowledge (PM. p.4). The validity of the scriptural means as the only means of the *brahmajñāna* can be verified from the positive and negative concomittance (*anvayavyatireka*) as the *Brahman* is known from the Vedic scripture only and not by any other means as specified by the Upaniṣadic statement like *satyam jñānamanantam brahma* (Tait. Up. 2.1.1).

In the *Pramāṇamālā* Ānandabodha refutes the prima facie view which holds that the scripture (*śrutipramāṇa*) belonging to the phenomenal world cannot generate the knowledge of the Transcendental Reality. Ānandabodha maintains that as the unreal reflection (*pratibiṁba*) is considered as the means for the proof of real original object (*biṁba*) similarly the Vedic scripture belonging to the empirical world is capable of illuminating the supreme reality i.e. *Brahman*. To substantiate his view Ānandabodha quotes the authority of Bādarāyaṇa's *Brahmasūtra, sūcakaśca hi śruterācaskṣate ca tadvidaḥ* (3.2.4) (a dream is indicative of future events according to the *śruti*, those well-versed in the science of dreams declare so). Śaṅkara comments this text that notwithstanding the illusory nature of dreams, they are indicative of future events. The sight of a woman in a dream is considered as a sign of success in the work undertaken. (Chā. Up. V.2.8; PM. p.16):

Yadā karmasu kāmyeṣu striyam svapneṣu paśyati/
samṛdhim tatra jānīyāt tasmin svapnanidarśane //

Just as a dream is suggestive of the good or bad events in the future similarly the *Śruti* leads to the realisation of the *Brahman*. It cannot be argued that the knowledge of the reflection (*pratibiṁba*) is real and that real knowledge serves as a source of knowledge of the real proto-type and not the unreal reflection itself. Ānandabodha asks whether the knowledge in general becomes a source, or the knowledge that is limited by its object becomes the source? Both the alternatives, according to Ānandabodha, are not tenable, for in the first alternative any knowledge, even of the jar, would be the cause of the knowledge of the proto-type (*pratibiṁba*) which really is not the case. In the second option, knowledge limited by object is accepted to be the source of knowledge of the proto-type (*pratibiṁba*), the unreal reflection which is also the part of the original *biṁba*. Thus, according to Ānandabodha false means like Vedic scripture can become the source of knowledge of the real entity called *Brahman*. Ānandabodha explains this point following another instance in his *Nyāyamakaranda* in a clear manner. He maintains that the non-sentient vowels also denote the same real worldly objects. The momentary longness (*dīrgha*) or shortness (*harsva*) of vowels which are superimposed on them become the cause of the knowledge of the real objects as the word *nāga* clearly conveys the meaning of a serpent and the word *naga* of a mountain. In the same way the unreal reflection or the *pramāṇas* which are the products of *avidyā* can produce the real cognitions and those cognitions which have conformity with the objects are valid and those which have not, are invalid. To substantiate Ānandabodha quotes from *Pramāṇavārttika* of Dharamkīrti as follows:-

> *maṇipradīpaprabhayoḥ maṇibudhyābhidhāvataḥ /*
> *mithyājñānaviśeṣepi viśeṣortha kriyām prati //*
>
> (NM. p.148; PV. II.58)

In the *Nyāyamakaranda* Ānandabodha sets aside the prima facie view which holds that the scripture is weaker than perception when there arises any conflict between the scripture and the perception (NM. p.149) and that is why perception is the first and the strongest of all *pramāṇas*. Ānandabodha maintains that there is no conflict between the scripture (*śrutipramāṇa*) and perception. The scripture is not weaker than the perception since the validity of the perception is only confined to the realm of the phenomenal world. On the contrary, the scripture, being able to give the knowledge of the transempirical objects is different from the perception and the other means of knowledge. The scripture is authoritative and strongest of all *pramāṇas* since it deals with the highest and faultless Reality. The indicatory marks[1] i.e. (*upakrama*) (beginning), *upasaṁhāra* conclusion, *abhyāsa* (repetition) *apūrvatā* (newness), *phala* (result) and *arthāvāda* (praise or censure) and *upapatti* (logic) indicate the import of the Vedānta texts as non-dual *Brahman* which is real (*sat*) as it is not sublated (*abādhita*). In the *Chāndogya Up.* we see the *upakrama* when Uddālaka teaches his son - *sadeva saumyedamagraṃ āsit* (6.2.9). Starting the teaching of *Brahman* the father concludes (*upasaṁharati*) - *etadātmymidam sarvam* (Chā. Up. 6- 8-7-16). *Tattvamasi* is repeated nine times there which is *abhyāsa*. The *apūrvatā* lies in this that *Brahman* who is devoid of form etc., is to be known only by means of the Vedānta and not by any well-established means of knowledge like *pratyakṣa* etc. The *phala* of *Brahmajñāna* is laid down in *tasya tāvadeva ciram yāvanna vimokṣe atha sampatsye*. The only delay in his becoming *Brahman* is due to his body. As soon as the body is destroyed he becomes *Brahman*. The *arthavāda* is illustrated in *yenaśrutam śrutam bhavati* etc. - that by means of which even-unheard-of thing is heard, is *Brahman*. *Upapatti* is illustrated in *yathaikena mṛtpiṇḍena sarvam mṛṇmayam vijñātam bhavati*, etc. This *upapatti* proves that *Brahman* is changeless and it is only the *Prakṛti* which is changing (*satvikārā*). On the contrary, the objects of

---

1. *Upakramopasaṁhārābhyāso'pūrvatā phalam/ arthāvādopapattiśca liṅgam tātparya nirṇaye//*
Sharma, Haradutta, *Brahmasūtra Catuḥsūtri*, p.98; Radhakrishnan, S.*Brahmasūtra*, Introduction.

direct perception and other *pramāṇas* are sublated, by the posterior real cognition, i.e. "this is not a serpent" uttered by a trustworthy person (*āpta*). Thus, the latter, i.e. "this is not a snake, is stronger than the former i.e. "this is a snake". To substantiate Ānandabodha quotes the *Jaimini-sūtra* i.e. *Paurvāparye pūrvadaurvalyam prakṛtivat* (JS.6.5.59; NM.p.150). (Among the preceding and succeeding causes, the preceding is the weaker. Ānandabodha also quotes Kumārila Bhaṭṭa's *Tantravārttika* (2.18; NM. p.151):

Pūrvātparavalīyatvam tatranāma pratīyatām,/
anyonyanirapekṣāṇām yatra janma dhiyām bhavet //

(Among the cognitions which are independent in respect of their knowledge, the latter one is stronger than the former one.)

According to Ānandabodha, the *Śruti* or *Āgama* is self-valid (*svayam siddha*) and divine. Hence it does not depend on other means of knowledge like direct perception etc., for the origination (*utapatti*) and cognition (*jñapti*) of the objects and therefore it is stronger than the perception. Moreover, according to Ānandabodha *vaidika āgamas* are different from the *Bauddha-āgamas* as these latter are the human creations and so are defective and prone to deception and invalidity. But unlike these *Bauddha-āgamas* the scripture i.e. *Veda* being divine in nature is completely devoid of defects. But all the statements of the scripture are not relevant because those statements which deal with action (*kriyā*) and recommend same (*karmakāṇḍa*) are meant for the ignorant ones who are eligible to perform these rituals[1]. But the injunctive sentences are of no use to the persons who have realised the Supreme Reality as enunciated in *jñānakāṇḍa* following the direct method of

1. BSŚB 1.1.4.5

the *śravaṇa* (hearing), *manana* (meditation) and *nididhyāsana* (contemplation) and winning over the evils like anger, (*krodha*) desire (*kāma*) and so on. Thus there is no opposition between these two sentences as they are meant for two different types of persons, i.e. *ātmavid* and *anātmavid*.

According to Ānandabodha, the activity based on *mithyājñāna* (false knowledge) continues upto the realisation of the Supreme Reality called *Brahman* as a person being affected by the disease called bile (*pitta*) though very well knows the sweetness of sugar but experiences it as bitter and therefore throws it away. In the same way, the persons knowing very well the false nature of the *pramāṇas* carry on their worldly activities and realising the essential nature of the Reality by means of the Vedic scripture only set them aside after realising the supreme nature of the Reality.

4.2 Import of the Upaniṣadic Statements

Like his predecessors Śaṅkara, Sureśvara and others Ānandabodha in his works, mainly in the *Nyāyamakaranda* (p.178-179) and *Pramāṇamālā* (p.17-19) makes an attempt in expousing the Advaitic view i.e. the import of the Upaniṣadic statements (*Vedāntavākya* or *Āgamavākyas*) as an established entity (*siddha or parinispanna vastu*), which is the supreme Reality. In this connection Ānandabodha puts forth the prima facie view of Śālikanātha (700-750 A.D) as expounded in his *Prakaraṇapañcikā* (p. 239-241). He argues that the import of the Upaniṣadic statements can only be action (*kārya* or *niyoga*); but not any *siddhavastu* like *Brahman* as the Upaniṣadic statements cannot have any *saṅgati* (connection or relation) with the *siddhavastu* like *Brahman*. This view of Śālikanātha has been completely refuted by Ānandabodha. He has established succintly the Advaita view with sound logical reasoning.

Śālikanātha in his *Prakaraṇapañcikā* adduces the following arguments:-

The Upaniṣadic statements cannot denote a *siddhavastu* (an established entity) like the *Brahman* since the *saṅgati* (connection or relation) of the Upaniṣadic statements with reference to an established entity (*siddhavastu*) is not possible. People learn the meaning of words only by watching the usage and activity of older people. When a set of words is addressed by one person to another - whereupon the latter person acts in a certain manner, it is clear to the observer that the meaning of the words pronounced must have been in the form of an injuction (*vidhi*) to do what the other person has done in the case of words where such an interpretation related to an activity is not possible, (*sarvapuruṣāṇām tāvadvṛdhavyavahāre eva prathamaśabdānām vyutpattirangikaraṇiyā, na khalu vyavahāramantareṇa siddhārthanvākhyāne vyutpatti ravakalpyate* (PP. p.240). Comprehension of the meaning must depend upon something indirectly connected with the terminations like imperative[1] *(liṅ)* express the injuction directly[2] while other words denote things related to that injunction *(vidhi)* as the name of the act enjoined, the person enjoined and so on. Thus, the direct denotation of the *Veda* must lie in the enjoining of something to be done (*kārya*). As laid down by Jaimini, viz. *amnāyasya kriyārthatvādānarthakyamatadarthānām* (I.2.1), the purpose of the *Veda* lying in the enjoining of actions, those parts of the *Veda* which do not serve that purpose are useless.

---

1. *Vidhinimantraṇāmaṇtraṇādhiṣṭasampraśnapārthaneṣu liṅ*. Aṣṭ, 3.3.161.

2. *Śabdāntarāṇi svārtheṣu vyutpadyante yathevati/ āvāpodvāpabhedena tathā kārye liṅgādayaḥ//* VM. II.10;12

The *saṅgati* of the sentences is understood only through actions of elders[1] e.g. a teacher addresses his student - "*māṇavaka samidhamānaya*" (Māṇavaka! bring fuel sticks) and Māṇavaka immediately attempts to fetch the *samidhas* (fuelsticks). A child who stands nearby and hears the sentence of the preceptor and observes the action (*kārya*) of Māṇavaka, also acts similarly following the action of Māṇavaka. Thus, the injunctive power in the verbal form *ānaya* motivates a person for doing any kind of action (*kārya*). This *kārya* is expressed by the injunctive affix *liṅ* in the verb *ānayana* (bring) and other words in the sentence like Māṇavaka, *samidha* and others which express their own meanings being related to *kārya* i.e. Māṇavaka as the agent of the *āharaṇakārya* and *samidha* as the object (*karma*) of it.

It cannot be said that when a person hears a sentence, *putraste jāta,* he becomes happy and his happiness can be inferred from the beaming expression of his face etc. As the cause of his happiness is the knowledge about the attainment of a desired object i.e. a son which is expressed by a sentence, *putraste jāta*. Thus the sentence itself that has been heard is the cause of this knowledge. As the listner is having a keen desire for the birth of a son, the happiness of the listner, therefore, is the result of the knowledge or understanding of the sentence, *putraste jāta* which simply states the fact and does not denote any *kārya*. Each and every word in a sentence would express its own individual meaning and nothing else (NM.p.147-148).

Though the cause of the happiness of the person who hears the sentence *putraste jāta* is the sentence itself, nevertheless the very sentence i.e. *putraste jāta*

---

1. *Vyavahāreṣubṛddhānām vākyaśravaṇdibhiṣuāvāpodvarā/ bhedena padānām śaktiniścayaḥ //* VM, I.6...

does not express the particular cause of the happiness, viz. the birth of a son.[1] As there are numerous causes of happiness belonging to the past, present and future, at hand and at distance *pariśeṣa-anumāna* (remnant inference) cannot prove a particular cause in this case. Śālikanātha quotes the definition of the *pariśesa-anumāna* from the *Nyāyabhāṣya* : *Prasaktapratiṣedhe sati anyatra aprasaṅgāt śiṣyamāṇe saṁpratyayaḥ pariśeṣaḥ*. (Nyā.bhā on NS 11.5; NM. p.230). (Other possible things being denied and other different thing being impossible, the definite understanding about the remaining one is called *Pariśeṣa*). Since a number of causes of happiness of listener are possible, the *pariśeṣa anumāna* cannot determine the particular cause i.e. birth of a son.

Verbal communication (*vyavahāra*) can also denote particular connotation of the particular words. Since the verbal communication (*vyavahāra*) could be understood only after the knowledge of *kārya*, all words in a sentence should express the *kārya* only. When common usage of words is found referring to the established entities (*siddhavastu*) it should be understood in the secondary sense (*lākṣaṇikārtha*), as the principal meaning is incompatible with the rest of the sentence[2] and should express *kārya*. (PP. 241). And the *kārya* indicated by the sentence '*putraste jātaḥ*' is that of seeing the child born and would be equivalent to 'beholding it'. When a person uses any word for the established entity he uses it in the secondary sense (*lākṣaṇikārtha*) understanding the relation of words to actions (*kārya*). Thus, in the verbal communications also the *saṅgati* (connection) of the sentences is found with reference to *kārya* only.

---

1. *Yadyapi mukhaprasādi ..... atyantaduṣkaratvāt*, PP. p.240.
2. *Mukhyārthavādhe tadyukto yayānyorthaḥ pratīyate/ ruḍheḥ prayojanādvāsau lakṣaṇāśaktirarpitā//* Viśvanātha, SD, II.9.

The Upaniṣadic statements like *satyam jñānamanantam Brahma* (Tait. Up.2.1.1) should either denote the *kārya* or should be related to the *kārya* (action) of knowing the *Brahman*. In the injunctive sentence (*vidhivākya*) i.e. *ātmāvāre draṣṭavyaḥ śrotavyo mantavyo nididhyāsitavyo maitreyātmano vā are darśanena matya vijñānenedam sarva viditam* (Bṛh. Up. 2.4.5; 4.5.6) the reward (*phala*) of the *kārya* is knowledge of the *Ātman* which is expressed by the sentence *etāvadare khalu amṛtatvam* (Bṛh. Up. 4.5.15). Applying the maxim of *rātrisastra* Śālikanātha maintains that as the *phala* (reward) of the *rātrisastra* is not mentioned in the injunctive sentence viz. *aharmāsena rātrim pivasamspe yusena ghṛtam rasena* (Rai. S.5.7.20) and is taken from the nearby subordinate sentence i.e. *pratitiṣṭhanati ha va ya eta upayanti; brahmavarchasvinonnadi bhavati ya eta upayanti*[1] (those who have recourse to these sacrifices become famous; those who have recourse to these become endowed with Brahmic glory and also partake rich food) where *'pratiṣṭhā* is pointed out as the *phala*. In the above case also no *phala* (reward) is expressed in the sense i.e. *ātma vāre śrotavyaḥ* (Bṛh. Up. 4.5.6); it should be taken from the nearby subordinate sentence i.e. *etāvadare khalu amṛtatvam* where *amṛtatva* (immortality) as the *phala* is expressed, which one obtains after realisation of the *Brahman*.

The Upaniṣadic statements cannot prove the reality of the non-dual *Brahman* with its nature of supreme bliss as they are in conflict with other means of knowledge such as perception (*pratyakṣa*). The *Brahman* or *Ātman* shines in all perceptual cognitions and memory as the subject of the notion of I-consciousness (*ahaṁpratyaya*). The *Brahman* being self- luminous cannot

1. *Śābarabhāṣya* on *Jaiminisūtra* IV-III.17, 18.

be veiled by any other object by which it would not shine in its essential nature. Thus, the *Brahmavādins* are creating a grand confusion regarding the Upaniṣadic texts as the means of the knowledge of *Brahman* (NM. p.161-162). Ānandabodha rejects all these arguments of Śālikanātha as follows:-

It is incorrect to say that the *pariśeṣa anumāna* cannot prove the particular cause of the happiness of the person who hears the sentence *putraste jāta* since the *pariśeṣa anumāna* can very well prove the particular cause i.e. the birth of a son. Gautama in his *Nyāyasūtras* speaks of three types of *anumāna*[1] (inference): viz., *pūrvavat, śeṣavat* and *sāmānyato dṛṣṭa*. Explaining it Vātsyāyana says that posterior (*śeṣavat*) is *pariśeṣa*[2] when cause is inferred looking at its effects as inference of rain from the swelling of a river.[3] In case of the person who becomes happy hearing the statement putraste jāta the effects like *vadanavikāsanādi* indicate very well the *putrajanma* which is the cause of happiness by *pariśeṣa anumāna* (posterior effects).

It is not correct to imagine in this context the objects belonging to the past, present and future which are not seen as the cause of the happiness of the listener especially when the particular cause of happiness i.e. the birth of a son is very clearly known. A person after hearing the statement *putraste jāta* feels very happy on account of the birth of a son. Hence only *putrajanma* is the cause of his happiness and nothing else. Quating from Vācaspati's *Brahmatattvasamīkṣā*, a commentary on the *Brahmasiddhi* of Maṇḍana, Ānandabodha severely

---

1. *atha tatpūrvkam trividhamanumānam pūrvavat śeṣasvat sāmānyatodṛṣṭaśca*, Nyā. Sū.1.1.5; see SK.4.
2. *Śeṣavannāma pariśeṣaḥ; sa ca pasakta-pratiṣedhe anyatrā prasaṅgāt śiṣyamāṇe sampratyayaḥ, Nyā. bhā,* on 1.1.5.
3. *Yatra kāryeṇa kāraṇānumīyate. Ibid.*

criticises this attitude of the Mīmāṁsakas like Śālikanātha who does not accept the visible cause directly perceived. Vācaspati maintains that those who entertain doubts about the meaning of scriptural statements may also entertain doubts about the chastity of their mothers and therefore about their parentage and family lineage. They thus doubting their own priestly class would not be eligible for the duties prescribed by them and so they would better leave the study of Mīmāṁsā (NM. p.163). Though there is possibility of other causes as a person never loves only one thing like birth of a son, but he may love and desire many other things like safe delivery of his beloved wife and others, as argued by Bhavanātha (780 A.D.) in his *Nayaviveka* (p.44 ; NM. p.164), still these other causes of the happiness i.e. safe delivery etc., negated by *anvayavyatireka* and by *āvāpodvāpābhyām* the meaning of the word *putra as tanaya* becomes clear. Thus, the *pariśeṣa anumāna* explicitly suggests the particular cause of the happiness of the listener which is birth of a son expressed by the sentence *putraste jāta*.

In sentences (*vākyas)* which are a collection of words possesing compatiblity, expectancy and proximity mutual relation[1] exists between *padas* (words) and *padārthas* (meaning), but *padas* do not have relation with *kārya* (action). There are so many sentences like *putraste sukhi* where the word *putra* not being related to any action serves as the cause of happiness since the father becomes happy when he knows the son to be happy. Hence it is reasonable to hold relation between *pada* and *padārtha* (meaning) and not necessarily between *pada* (word) and *kārya* (action). The denotative power of words is related to an appropriate word but not

1. *Vākyam sāt yogyatākāṅkṣāsattiyuktaḥ padoccayaḥ*. SD.2.2.

necessarily to the *kārya*. Ānandabodha employs the following syllogism :

Vivādapadāni na kāryānvita svārtha niyata

sāmārthyāni padavat

Kāryapadatvāt (NM. p.168; PM.p.17).

As the very word *kārya* (action) conveys the sense of action and expresses its own meaning only without a relation with any other particular action, similarly the power of all words should be related to objects in a general manner, not being related with any particular *kārya* (NM. p.170).

It is not proper to say that all the Vedānta texts are injunctive (*vidhivākyas*) and therefore lay down the action of knowing *Brahman,* since the laying down of the knowledge of the *Brahman* is of three types, viz. *śābdi* (verbal), *bhāvanātmikā* (contemplative) and *sākṣātkārarūpā* (direct realisation), and injunction is not necessary for these three kinds of the knowledge of the *Brahman*. Firstly, there is no need of any injunction (*vidhi*) for the verbal understanding of the *Brahman* (*śābdipratipatti*), for a person who knows the meaning of the words properly and the power of the words in denoting particular meanings, could understand the import of sentences from the words themselves without any injunction (*vidhi*). Secondly, there is no need of any injunction for the *bhāvanātmikā pratipatti* (contemplative knowledge) as repeated meditation and thinking of the subject of the study is the cause of excellent knowledge (*jñānaprakāśa*) of the soul since no such excellent knowledge takes place in its absence. Thirdly, injunction (*vidhi*) is not necessary for *sākṣātkārarūpā pratipatti* (direct realisation) since the *sākṣātkāra* means either becoming the nature of *Brahman* (*Brahmasvabhāva*) or attainment of a complete state of supreme bliss and infinite peace by transformation of heart (*antaḥkaraṇa*). The first i.e. *brahmasvabhāva* (the nature of *Brahman*), being eternal naturally cannot be a *kārya*. The second i.e. *antaḥkaraṇapariṇati* is a reward (*phala*), which attracts a person by its natural excellence i.e. purification of mind, without any injunction (NM. p.170).

There would not be any kind of difficulty in knowing the essential nature of the *Brahman* as Supreme bliss and consciousness since the Upaniṣadic statements directly denote the established entity (*siddhavastu*) i.e. *Brahman*.

The Upaniṣadic statements cannot command something other than *siddhavastu* or direct any action (*kārya*), as their relation or connection (*saṅgati*) is with reference to the established entity like *Brahman*, but not with the *kārya* as wrongly pointed out by Śālikanātha (NM. p.171).

Following Śaṅkara, Sureśvara and Sarvajñātman, Ānandabodha in his *Pramāṇamālā* (p.19) and *Nyāyamakaranda* (pp.257-269) points out that the Upaniṣadic statements like *Vijñānamānandam brahma* (Bṛh. Up.3.9.34) and *tattvamasi* (Chā. Up.6.8.7) denote the impartite or unitary sense (*akhaṇḍārtha*). He maintains that the import derived from the Upaniṣadic statements - *vijñānamānandam brahma* and the like is *akaṇḍārtha* (homogeneous), that is, free from all differences and relations and above all distinctions of subject and predicates or generic and particular etc. Ānandabodha sets forth the *pūrvapakśa* view as follows:-

The words *vijñāna* and *ānanda* in the Upaniṣadic statement *vijñānamānandam brahma* (Bṛh. Up. 3.9.34) cannot denote homogeneous meaning (*akhaṇḍārtha*) since *vijñāna* and *ānanda* cannot have the same primary meaning. If both the words would denote the same meaning they would be synonyms and being so they could not be used simultaneously in the same sentence. As the synonyms only express the individual meanings one after the other in a sentence and do not give collective sense, they are called synonyms and hence the simultaneous use of the synonyms is not logical (NM.p.258; PM.p.19).

The faculty of implication (*lakṣaṇā)*[1] cannot also give the secondary meaning of the words *vijñāna* (consciousness) and *ānanda* (bliss) since in the case of implication (*lakṣaṇā*) one word either *vijñāna* or *ānanda* would suffice to denote the desired object i.e. *Brahman* following the literary rule i.e. if a thing is produced by one cause, then the other cause, not contributing and acting in a distinct manner from the first cause, becomes unnecessary. (*nispāditakriye karmaṇyaviśeṣabhidhāyinaḥ sādhanasya sādhananyāyātipāta*, NM. 259*)*. Thus the words *vijñāna* and *ānanda* would denote the attributes of the *Brahman* instead of the homogeneous meaning (*akhaṇḍārtha*), i.e. partless, non-dual *Brahman*.

The locus-attribute relationship (*guṇaguṇibhāva*) is neither possible between two mutually altogether different objects, for instance, cow and horse, nor two identical objects, like the relation of a locus and its nature. Therefore, to prove the logical tenability of the relation i.e. *guṇaguṇibhāva* (locus-attribute relationship) existing between the *Brahman* i.e. *guṇi* (locus) and *vijñāna* or *ānanda* as *guṇa* (attribute), some sort of difference (*bheda*) is to be admitted. Thus, the appropriation of difference will lead to the sublation of the doctrine of absolute identity promulgated by the Upaniṣadic statements like *ekamevādvitīyam* (Chā. Up.6.2.1).

---

1. *Mukyārthabādhe tadyoge ruḍhitotha prayojanāt/ anyortho lakṣyate yatsa lakṣaṇāropitā kriyā //* KP, II, 9.

Ānandabodha sets aside this prima facie as follows:—

The words *vijñāna* and *ānanda* in the statement *vijñānamānandam brahma* denote the *akhaṇḍārtha* (homogeneous meaning). Though there is no difference (*bheda*) between the indicated meaning (*lakṣārthas*) of the words, *ānanda* and *vijñāna* nevertheless there is difference (*bheda*) as to what they intend to exclude (*lakṣārthabhedabhāvepi vyavacchedya vibhedataḥ/ vijñānānandapadayoḥ paryāyavyarthātā kutaḥ//* (NM. p.260).

Although in the said statement *vijñāna* and *ānanda* have only one indicated sense (*lakṣārtha*) i.e. *Brahman,* nevertheless they are useful as they differ in their 'exclusive capacity (*vyavachedya*) and required for negating different objects.

The word *vijñāna* (consciousness) excludes the objects which are different from itself (*vijñānetara*) and similarly the word *ānanda* from that which are *ānandetara* (different from *ānanda*). Ānandabodha explains this fact by an *prakṛṣṭaprākaśaḥ candraḥ* (that is which is resplendent with light is moon).

When a person is asked which is the moon among the luminaries in the sky he answers, the one which is having protracted resplendent light is moon. In this sentence there is neither reference to any quality of the moon nor the relation of the moon to that quality except an identity of the moon with the profuse light. It is known from this identification that though shinning is common to all other lights still the moon is different from them since it is having superior brightness. And protractive (*prakṛṣṭa*) alone cannot be proper answer to above question for the identification of the moon since the protractive (*prakṛṣṭa*) is possible in a place with dense darkness. Similarly, brightness (*prakāśa*) alone cannot be an appropriate answer, for it is in the sun which has not the same nature or characteristic as that of the moon. The answer i.e. *prakṛṣṭaprakāśaḥ candraḥ* aims at showing particularity and thus, there is the difference between implied sense of the words '*prakṛṣṭa* and *prakāśa*' as well as the identity between them and moon's own definition. Hence the word *prakṛṣṭa* (resplendent) is not irrelevant in so far as it dispels the doubt that it is the glowworm which is not full of bright light; the 'word' light (*prakāśa*) is not irrelevant as it also dispels the doubt that it is pitched darkness. (NM. p.261). Thus, although the implied meaning (*lakṣārtha*) is one still the different words have each a distinct purpose in excluding this or that thing. In view of this fact it cannot be argued that the words become mere synonyms and therefore redundant in a sentence.

Ānandabodha employs the following syllogism :

Vijñānādivākyamakhaṇḍārthaparam

lakṣaṇavākyatvād

yadittham tattathā

yathā prakṛṣṭaprakāśaḥ candraḥ

yathā vā pṛthubughnodarākāra kumbhaḥ.

(NM. p.263; PM.p.19)

Ānandabodha here also quotes from the *Pañcapādikāvivaraṇa* of Prakāśātman who asserts that each of the words in the statement *vijñānamānandam brahma* though has a distinct meaning of its own, still they, on account of their one content, denote a homogeneous meaning (*akhaṇḍārtha*). The words *vijñāna, ānanda* and *sat* denote the *para* (higher), *apara* (lower) and highest *sāmānya* (generality) respectively. The word *sat* (existence) conveys the highest generality since it is omnipresent pertaining to all objects but the meaning of the word *vijñāna* comparatively limited as it is seen in the lesser number of objects and the same of the word *ānanda* is still further restricted because it is almost non-existent apart from the *Brahman*. But all these three words are used in the same *sāmānādhikaraṇa* (same case relation or same location or predicament or apposition) and therefore they express their own *sāmānya* or *jāti* (generality) in a general sense and the *Brahman*, which is bliss in a particular sense (NM. p.249; PV.415).

Ānandabodha further maintains that in the statements of definitions or definitives (*lakṣaṇavākyas*) like *gandhavatī pṛthivī* words never occur for exclusion directly, but denote particular qualities of an object and by themselves exclude the opposite entities. Thus, the exclusion is not the meaning of any word in a *lakṣaṇavākya* but a secondary function. The *lakṣaṇavākyas* only describe the nature of the objects and therefore they impart *akhaṇḍārtha*. Quoting from Vācaspati's *Brahmatattvasamīkṣā*[1] Ānandabodha points out that in case of the *bahubrīhi samāsa*[2] (the attributive compounds) two or more words ending in the first case affix form a compound, denote another new thing not connected by those words individually, for example, *daṇḍī kamaṇḍalu* and *vaiśvadevī āmikṣā*. In the *bahubrīhi samāsa* the word *daṇḍī* denotes the person who carries the stick and not the stick itself; similarly, in the other case *vaiśvadevī* denotes *āmikṣā* (curd of milk and a mixture of boiled and coagulated milk) that is offered to *Vaiśvadevas*. Thus, though there are two words having distinct meanings still in *bahubrīhi* both of them impart an unitary meaning (*akhaṇḍārtha*).

---

1. NM. p.264.
2. *anekamanyapadārthe*, Aṣṭ. 2.2.24; *anekam prathamāntamanyapadārthe vartamānam vā samasyate sa bahubrīhi*.

Ānandabodha maintains that the theory of *akhaṇḍārtha* has been accepted not only by the Advaitins but by another systems of philosophy also. The *Vaiyākaraṇas* (Grammarians) accept the *akhaṇḍārtha* (one single meaning) of the *Prātipadika*[1] (the crude form of a substantive; a noun in its uninflected state before receiving the case-terminations) and *Prathamāvibhakti*[2] (first class affix). For example, the word, pot in the statement "pot is black" (*kṛṣṇaḥ ghaṭaḥ*) and nominative case signifies the same pot also.

The Buddhists admit *akhaṇḍārtha* with regard to the words *vjñāna* and *bhinna* (different) when they say *vijñāna* is different. Everything being a form of cognition (*vijñana*) for the Buddhist *vijñānavādins* there is no difference anywhere[3] apart from the *vijñāna* by which one could determine the meaning of the word difference. The Prābhākara Mīmāṁsakas also admit *akhaṇḍārtha* as they admit difference (*bheda*) as the very nature of objects and hence the word denoting the object and the word *bhinna* (different) have the same meaning. The Naiyāyikas and Bhāṭṭa Mīmāṁsakas also admit *akhaṇḍārtha*. Thus the statement- *vijñānamānandam brahma* denotes the unitive *Brahman* and not *ānanda* (bliss) and *vijñāna* (consciousness) as the attributes of the *Brahman* as wrongly pointed out by the *pūrvapakṣa*.

---

1. *arthavaddhāturapratyaḥ prātipadikam,* Aṣṭ. 1.2.45.
2. *Prātpadikārthaliṅgaparimāṇavacanamātre prathamā.* Aṣṭ. 2.3.46.
3. *Dṛśyam na vidyate vāhyam cittam citram hi dṛśyate/ Deha-bhoga-pratiṣṭhānam cittamātram badāmyaham.// Laṅkāvatārasūtra, cittamātra, verse* 23.
   b) *Vijñāna-pariṇāmoyam vikalpo yad viklpyate/ Tenattannāsti tenedam sarvam vijñāptimātrakam// Triṁśikā-vijñapti verse* 17.

Ānandabodha further points out that all sorts of difference i.e. *sajātīya* (homogeneous), *vijātīya* (dissimilar) and *svagata* (belonging to one's self) are negated by the Upaniṣadic statements like *ekamevādvitīyam* (Chā. Up. 6.2.1) and *neha nānāsti kiṅcana* (Bṛh. Up.4.4.19) etc. Therefore the locus-attribute relation (*guṇaguṇibhāva*) based on difference is not possible for the *Brahman.* The identity that implies an absence of difference (*bheda*) and the locus-attribute relation (*guṇa-guṇi sambandha*) which implies a difference cannot go together because of the obvious flaw of the contradiction as found in case of a jar (*ghaṭa*) and the absence of it which is not possible in one and the same substratum. Since the *guṇaguṇibhāva* is impossible in the case of the *Brahman* it is established that *vijñāna* and *ānanda* denote homogeneous meaning (NM. p.267).

Ānandabodha maintains that the statement *Tattvamasi* (That thou art) (Chā. Up. VI.8.7) indicates the identity of *jīva* (the individual self) and the *Brahman* (supreme self). The above *mahāvākya* signifies the partless ultimate reality when viewed under three relations as has been postulated by Sureśvarācārya in his famous work *Naiṣkarmyasiddhi.* The three relations are that of apposition (*sāmānādhikaraṇa*) between the terms, that of substance and attribute (*viśeṣaṇa-viśeṣya*) and that of the implied and the implying between the deeper self and what is denoted by the two terms (*lakṣalakṣaṇasaṁbandha*). Of these the appositional relation (*sāmānādhikaraṇya*) is in the proposition 'That is this Devadatta' (*so'yam Devadattaḥ*) where that (*saḥ*) signifying Devadatta as related to past time, and 'this' (*ayam*) signifying Devadatta as related to present time are both intended to refer to one and the same individual. So also in the case of the present *mahāvākya 'Tattavamasi.* It is the intended reference to one and the same spirit in 'that' (*tat*) signifying spirit characterised by mediacy (*parokṣatvaviśiṣṭa*), etc. and in 'thou' (*tvam*) signifying spirit characterised by immediacy (*aparokṣatvādiviśiṣṭa*), etc. The relation of substance and attribute (*viśeṣaṇa-viśeṣya*) is as in the statement 'This is that Devadatta' the relation of substance and attribute is between Devadatta as related to past time which is the primary meaning (*vācyārtha*) of 'that' and Devadatta as related to present time which is the primary meaning of 'this', excluding the difference between the two; so in the *Tattvamasi* the relation of substance and attribute is between self characterised by mediacy, etc. which is the primary sense of *Tat* and self characterised by immediacy, etc. which is the primary sense of *Tvam* excluding the difference between the two. Thirdly, the relation of the implied and implying (*lakṣalakṣaṇa*) is between the words that (*saḥ*) or between their meaning and the identical Devadatta, divested of conflicting attributes, viz., being related to past and present time; so in the *Tattvamasi* also the relation of the implied and the implying is between the terms *tat* and *tvam* or their meaning and the identical self, bereft of conflicting attributes such as mediacy and immediacy etc.

Ānandabodha maintains that one has to understand the sentence *Mahāvākya Tattvamasi* in the same way as the sentence 'This is that Devadatta', e.g. two persons have seen one Devadatta at some place and time and that later the same two people have come across the same Devadatta at another place and time. Of the two, one may reconise him to be Devadatta, while the other may not. Then the first would tell the second, 'This is that Devadatta'. Here the informer does not mean that the two places and times are the same, nor does he means that the two Devadattas under those two conditions are not in some respects different.

Devadatta when previously seen may have been very stout while Devadatta as seen later might be lean. The statement does not mean that the stout Devadatta is in all respects the same as the lean Devadatta; but what is recognised by stoutness or leanness. So when it is said 'This is that Devadatta', no identity is posited between the leaness of Devadatta and the stoutness of Devadatta. Omitting these accidental qualities, viz. leanness, stoutness, etc., what is qualified by them is asserted to be the same, Similarly, when the individual self, the ego, to which agency and enjoyment belong, is distinguished from pure being, and the latter alone is asserted to be identical with *Brahman*. Thus one part of the usual meaning of Individual Self or 'Thou' is abandoned part of it is retained, while by 'That' also is not meant as usual the pure consciousness, which is remote (*parokṣa*). By 'That', pure consciousness alone is meant, and by 'Thou', the pure self, free from agency etc. is meant. So Ānandabodha assertes that the sentence expresses apposition (*sāmānādhikaraṇa*) between the two, *Brahman* and Individual Soul.

The meaning of the sentence is understood by means of *jahadajahallakṣaṇā* (exclusive-non-exclusive implication) which is defined as 'when part of the primary sense of a word is discarded and part of it accepted[1]. This type of implication is also called *'bhāgatyāga lakṣaṇā'*. In the above said sentence differences in the accidental qualities of Devadatta are ignored, and Devadatta in himself is taken as the referent. Ānandabodha employs the syllogism:

Tattvamasivākyamakhaṇḍārthaniṣṭham

akāryakāraṇadravyavarttitve sati

1. *Yatra vācyaikadeśatyāgenaikadeśānvayastatra jahadajahati lakṣaṇā.* Nyā. K. p.290.

sāmānādhikaraṇatvāt
soyam devadatta iti vākyavat
(NM. p.269; PM. p.19)

Ānandabodha further states that the statement *Tattvamasi* is to be interpreted in a different way unlike the statement *nīlamutpalam* and *mṛṇmayo ghaṭaḥ* since the former i.e. *nīlamutpalam* is a statement of a substance (*dravya*), characterised by the property of *utpalatva* and a quality characterised by the property of *nīlatva* (blue-ness).

The latter sentence i.e. *mṛṇmayam ghaṭaḥ* is having two sentences, i.e. *mṛt* and *ghaṭa* in *kāryakāraṇasambandha* (cause and effect relation). In the first sentence i.e. *nīlam utpalam* though *sāmānādhikaraṇyajñāna* (despite their difference in connotation they are intended to denote the same thing) and *viśeṣaṇaviśesyatājñāna* (the knowledge of a certain thing which while being characterised by *utpalatva* has also the characteristic of *nīlatva* viz. *nīlābhinnamutpalam* nevertheless the *Tattvamasi* cannot be interpreted in the similar way. In case of *nīlamutpalam*, the relation of the meanings of the two words as *viśeṣaṇa* and *viśeṣya* presents no logical difficulty but it does so in the case of *Tattvamasi*. For the primary meaning (*vācyārtha*) of *Tvam* is *aparokṣatvādiviśiṣṭacaitanya* and that of *Tat parokṣatvādiviśiṣṭacaitanya* which cannot be related in the *abhedasaṁsarga* on account of their inherent opposition. To avoid this logical impasse the *lakṣaṇā* is recoursed. In other words, the meaning of *abheda* (identity) being impossible taking the *vācyārtha*, the *lakṣārtha* viz. *aparokṣatvādyupalakṣitacaitanya* and *parokṣatvādyupalakṣitacaitanya* is accepted. This removes the contradiction and proves the identity conveyed by the proposition between these two. This stage is called as *lakṣalakṣaṇabhāvajñāna*, the *viśiṣṭa* being the *lakṣaka* and the *upalakṣita* the *lakṣa*. Thus, *abheda* is not a *saṁsarga* type as in *nīlamutpalam* which involves duality, but what is known as *svarupabheda*. In other words the ultimate logical significance of *Tattvamasi* is the Ultimate Reality which discards all adjectives or predicates as incompatible with its nature the *śuddhacaitanya*, not a *samsṛṣṭārtha* but an *akhaṇḍārtha*.

Secondly, in case of the statement *mṛṇmayam ghaṭaḥ* there is *kārya-kāraṇa* relation but the condition in the *Tattvamasi* is different as there is no cause and effect relation between *Tat* and *Tvam*. Hence *Tattvamasi* cannot be interpreted on par with the sentence *mṛṇmayam ghaṭaḥ*, maintains Ānandabodha.

4.3 The Pravartaka (Motivating force)

Śālikanātha in his *Prakaraṇapañcikā* (pp.428-433) to prove *kārya* (what ought to be done or work) as the *pravartaka*, (motivator) argues as follows :

I. The *kārya* (work or act) is *pravartaka* (motivating force) which includes all the orders and prescriptions in practical life urging a person to act. In the verbal expression, *kārya* is regarded as the *pravartaka* which repeats itself in *praiṣas* (an order, command or invitation) and the like. When an action is ordained by a senior to a junior it is called *praiṣa*, the action is called *āmantraṇa* when it is agreed by two equal people and it is named *adhyesana* when it is requested by a junior person (PP. p.430; NM. p.187).

II. *Kārya* (work) is the chief thing (*pradhāna*) to be achieved through various actions playing the role of motivating forces (*kṛtisādhyam pradhānam*). It is the *kārya* which is kept in view and with reference to which action is directed (NM. p.187). There are two factors in this definition of *kārya*, viz. *kṛti-pradhānatā* (the aim of that action) which is known by the mental cognition (*mānasāvaseya*) while *kṛti-sādhyatā* (the possibility of being accomplished through action) is realised by inference (*anumāna*). In this way the *kārya* is known by two *pramāṇas,* viz. mental cognition and inference (*anumāna*). There is no conflict between these two *pramāṇas* as found in case of the rice which is cognised directly but its cooking turning it into *odana* is initially inferred by a person. When the *kārya* is properly grasped then it motivates a person to accomplish it e.g. a child after knowing 'this is my *kārya* undertakes the activity which can accomplish it. The activity of a baby towards breast-feeding is also due to the grasping of *kārya* (PP. p.266; NM. p.187-188).

III. *Kāryatā* cannot be identical with the *iṣṭasādhanatā* since former is always of the nature of *kṛtisādhyatā* (possibility of achievement through the action). *Kāryatā* always takes the form of an incomplete action, involving a process and therefore it is seen neither in past, nor in present but always related to future. But *iṣṭasādhanatā* is instrumentality with regard to the desired result *(iṣṭa)* and hence can be realised in connection with the past and the present objects also (PP. p.428), e.g. a tired person considers the moon as the instrument (*sādhana*) of his delight but never thinks it as obtainable by his effort. Thus, in the moon there is *sādhanatā* but not *kāryatā* as both are distinctly different from each other like fire and ice, and therefore are not synonyms, and thus *kāryatā* cannot be defined as *iṣṭasādhanatā* (NM. p.188-189).

IV. In the practical life the command O, Chaitra, bring water (*caitra jalamānaya*) urges Chaitra to the activity of bringing water. All the words in such sentences, other than the injunctive 'affix (*vidhiliṅ*) express their own meanings. Then, by the process of inclusion and exclusion (*āvāpodhārābhyām*) the injunctive affix (*liṅ*) expresses this *kārya* (work) and the other words in the sentences express their own meanings as connected with this *kārya*. In the Vedic texts also, the injunctive sentences like *agnihotram juhuyāt svargakāmaḥ* express *kārya* (something to be brought about). The import of all words therefore should be *kārya* (PP. p.430; NM.p.190-191).

V. In the Vedic texts the injunctive affix (*liṅ*) in the verbal form *juhuyāt* on account of its relation to the word *svargakāma* in *agnihotram juhuyāt svargakāmaḥ* indicates the *apūrva* since the person for whom the directive is meant being qualified on account of his desire for heaven would not be enthusiastic to undertake the activity, the consequent impossibilty of its use towards the protection of reward (*phala*) which is everlasting. This element which is useful for the production of *phala* is to be determined by the law of presence and absence i.e. activity being present, the reward is produced and not otherwise. The *apūrva* created by the process of ritual leads a person to the attainment of heaven and merely the action which is in process (PP.441; NM. p.191).

VI. In the sentence *agnihotram juhuyāt svargakāmaḥ* the word *svargakāmaḥ* expresses neither the reward (*phala*) i.e. heaven nor the agent of that action, (*kartā*) but indicates the person, directed for that *kārya*. A person who recognises the *kārya* as his own is called *niyojya* who is enjoined to do that *kārya* (PP. p.433). A person becomes *niyojya* when *kārya* expressed by that sentence is realised by him as his own. This *kārya* is named as *niyoga* since it provides an incentive to that person, motivates him for leading to that activity (PP. p.441). It is *niyoga* that lasts till the *phala* takes place. Thus, *apūrva* is of a link between the action performed in the present and the *phala* obtained in the future.

Niyoga is related to *niyojya* (the person directed for that action) being the source of his desired object and is related to *phala* being the immediate cause of it (NM. p.193).

VII. Since *niyoga* is supposed to produce the result (*phala*) it is not regarded as subordinate to *phala*. *Niyoga* cannot be a true *niyoga* unless there is a *niyojya* (the person directed for that activity who in fact, undertakes the activity which is the source of his desired end (*phala*). *Niyoga* thus needs *phala* only as the end of the actions of the agent with whom it is directly connected. This relation between *niyoga* and *phala* can be compared to the relation between the master and the servant. Without the servant the master cannot be a true master and yet it is the master that is more important person of the two. Similarly *phalas* like *svarga* and others though oblige *niyoga* being the end of the action, *niyoga* is more important than *svarga* like the master (PP. p 443). *Niyoga* therefore is accepted as the import of the sentence as a whole (NM. p.190).

VIII. Following the practice in the wordly life, the *saṅgati* of the sentence is understood in *kārya*. When there is a doubt about the meanings of the words, they are settled from the context or from the words of sentences e.g. *Yavamayaḥ caruḥ*. In this sentence the meaning of the word *yava* is doubtful and is settled from the nearby sentences like *athānyā auṣadhayo mlāyante*. In the same way, the meaning of the injunctive affix in Vedic sentences like *agnihotram juhuyāt svargakāmaḥ* and others is settled from the words occuring nearby, viz. *svargakāma*. The word *svargakāma* has a double purpose as it indicates the person eligible to undertake the activity as well as the reward (*phala*) of that activity. Thus, it proves the existence of *apūrva* or *niyoga* which is the link joining the two ends i.e.

the activity and the *phala*. Thus, *apūrva* is accepted as the meaning of injunctive sentences in the Vedic texts.

Ānandabodha in his *Nyāyamakaranda* refutes the arguments of Śālikanātha as follows:-

I. Ānandabodha questions the significance of the word *prādhānya* in the definition of *kārya* viz. *kṛtisādhya pradhānam kāryam*. Ānandabodha argues that *prādhānya* with reference to *kṛti* would be applicable only to either *phala* (reward) or to its *sādhana* (instrument). The mind also does not grasp anything as *pradhāna* besides these two. If *pradhāna* would mean as being the cause of both *phala* and its *sādhana* then it would eventually result in the acceptance of *Iṣṭasādhanatā* as the *pravartaka* (NṂ. pp.203-205).

II. 'This is my *kārya*' is not at all a notion, but a desire to act. This is grasped by the mental cognition (*mānasāvaseya*) and therefore it is the object of the knower's cognition only. Being so, it does not establish any concrete object. Though the rise of the moon is desired for coolness still no activity is expected because the moon is not attainable by any effort. The desire to act (*cikirṣā*) is a desire and yet it is different from all other ordinary desires and therefore it has an unique import (NM. p.208).

III. *Kāryatā* over the above *iṣṭasādhanatā* is not realised as no one acts without understanding it as *iṣṭasādhana*. *Praiṣas* (command) lead to action only when it is realised that they are the means (*sādhana*) for the desired reward. (*phala*). Citing the words from the *Prakaraṇapañcikā* Ānandabodha proves that Śālikanātha himself does admit the necessity of *iṣṭasādhanatā* for creating the activity, when Śālikanātha says '*karma* which by itself is of a painful nature becomes a *kārya* (a thing to be done). The cause of this is the state of being an instrument for *phala* through which *kāryatā* is attained.

By their very nature, actions are the causes that produce misery, but the knowledge of their being an instrument for *phala* through which *kāryatā* is attained. By their very nature, actions are the causes that produce misery, but the knowledge of their being *kārya* (necessarily to be done) depends on the knowledge of their instrumentality towards *phala*. (PP.p.429). Bhavanātha (740 A.D.) also supports this view when he says in his *Nayaviveka* (p.38) that a rational being undertakes an activity thinking 'this is my *kārya*' only when he realises it to be the means of his desired end (p.39). Thus *iṣṭasādhanatā* includes *kāryatā* also and *kāryatā* is not different from *iṣṭasādhanatā*. (NM. p.205).

IV. *Kāryatā* cannot be accepted as the *pravartaka* for *kāryatā* by itself does not lead to any activity. If *kāryatā* were to mean the principal end of effort, it would result in being of the nature of *phala* and thus would not be *pravartaka*. If it be said that *kāryatā* related to *phala* creates the activity towards *sādhana*, then that would be absurd. *Kāryatā* meant for one objective cannot create (*kriyā*) for the different. Moreover, in the injunctive sentence there is no word which expresses this *kārya* and the *saṅgati* (synthesis) of all words in the injunctive sentence cannot denote *kārya* also. Thus the injunctive affix (*liṅ*) does not necessarily denote *kārya* (NM. p.210).

V. There is no possibility of the production of *apūrva* (not known before). Ānandabodha argues that the Mīmāṁsakas are making a very simple proposition unnecessarily very difficult and complicated. He takes up the illustration of *daśapūrṇamāsa* sacrifices which themselves consist of a number of subsidiary sacrifices. Ānandabodha points out that subordinate sacrifices performed earlier and on specific days, cannot be reasonably supposed to contribute to the *apūrva* created by the entire sacrifice. Thus, according to the Mīmāṁsakas also the *apūrva* generated by an action does not directly produce the *phalāpūrva* but instead produces only intermediate *apūrvas*, which later produce the *phalāpūrva*. In other words, this would mean that action releases a chain of *apūrvas* mutually connected with earlier and ultimately related to *phala* or final reward. According to Ānandabodha, it would be much easier, and reasonable also to understand *kārya* (action) itself directly related to reward by doing away with the hypothetical *apūrvas* (NM. p.221).

Ānandabodha further maintains that if *apūrvas* would be action it would be the object of other *pramāṇas* and therefore would lose the very nature of being *apūrva* (not known before). If *apūrva* is something beyond *kārya*, then it would be known through the statements, for, the *saṅgati* (synthesis) of sentences denotes only *kārya*. Without being the object of the other *prāmāṇas*, the relation of *apūrva* also could not be understood because, for the knowledge of relation, knowledge of the related is a necessary prerequisite. It cannot be said also that injunctive affix (*liṅ*) in the Vedic texts has a specific power by virtue of which it generates the *apūrva*. Even when its relations with other words are not understood it possesses knowledge about a unique subject. For it is not proper to do away with this expectancy of relation, which as a rule resides in words. (NM. p.217).

VI. The word *svargakāma* specifically mentions the person addressed and does not necessarily indicate *niyoga*. Ānandabodha asserts that it would be too narrrow a view to admit that a person only undertakes the activity which proves to be an instrument for his desired object, a person desiring to exclude others from the group utters the words *grāmakāmah bhuṅkte* where the word *grāmakāma* being qualification distinguishes the person from others. It is clear that the *bhojana* is by no means a *grāmasādhana*. The word *svargakāma* in the same manner distinguishes the person from the common people, by laying down a specific qualification of the desire for attainment (NM. p.217).

VII. The illustration of a master and a servant, given for proving the principal nature (*prādhānya*) of *niyoga* is not a suitable one. There are two kinds of efforts intimately related to a sentient subject. The master makes efforts for himself to oblige the servant because of his own ends. Similarly the *niyojya* performs actions to fulfil his own desires. His actions thus are guided by his desires and not by *niyoga*. *Niyoga* can be compared to a master in the said example but it is not *pravartaka* and consequently cannot be the *pradhāna*. Further, there is not any sentient person to play the role of a master, to whose interests the *pradhāna* would belong. Again, it is absurd to accept that *niyoga* itself refers to heaven (*svarga*) as its own meaning, for, the two are by their nature distinct from each other and a desired object of the effort of a sentient being refers to others as its instruments. In the present case the heaven is the desired object and aim of the efforts of a sentient person, who is desirous of heaven and the heaven refers to *niyoga* as its instrument. The heaven, therefore, which is the *phala* with reference to *niyoga* cannot be its instrument (*sādhana*) (NM. p.218).

VIII. The words like *yava* are used in practical life for *dīrghasūka* etc., (a kind of rice). When they occur in the Veda their meaning could be determined from the concluding portion of the sentence (*vākyaśeṣa*). The *apūrva* cannot be taken to be indicated by the injunctive affix (*liṅ*). If *apūrva* is accepted to be known by some other *pramāṇa* then the Vedic sentences would be *anuvādakas* only. Therefore though there is simultaneous utterence of the injunctive affix with the word *svargakāma* still the injunctive affix cannot be accepted as indicating the *apūrva* (something new not known before). Thus the *saṅgati* of the Vedic sentences should not be understood as the *apūrva* (NM. p.220).

Refuting completely Śālikanātha's view Ānandabodha maintains that *iṣṭasādhanatā* is the motivator (*pravartaka*). To substantiate his view Ānandabodha cites the words of Vācaspati Miśra who, in his commentary on Maṇḍana's *Vidhiviveka* observes: "The injunction conveys *iṣṭasādhanatā* as intimately connected with the prominent meaning of an action to be performed" (*karttavyatāye ekārthasamavāyinī samīhita sādhanatā vidhiḥ* (NM. p.197). Ānandabodha maintains that being the object of *kṛti* (*kṛtyuddeśyatā*) need not be accepted as something over and above *kṛtisādhyatā*. In the above said definition there are two factors, viz. *kṛtisādhyatā* and *akārthasamavāyitā*. The first one i.e. *kṛtisādhyatā* excludes the objects, already accomplished, e.g. the rain on a dry land, which is the result of *kārirīṣṭi* performed by the sacrificer, is also desirable to the farmers. But not to them who are not enjoined to perform the *iṣṭi* as it is not sure (*kṛtisādhya*) by them. The other word *ekārthasamavāyinī* (intimately connected with *karttavyatā*) limits the field of *iṣṭasādhanatā*, because the objects in future such as the final reward etc., are *kṛtisādhya* (obtainable by efforts) but they are not intimately connected with *karttavyatā*. Thus *iṣṭasādhanatā* is *pravartaka* (which prompts a person to act).

Ānandabodha further says that mere desire cannot be *pravartaka* for, desire is seen also with reference to the final reward (*phala*). This desire for *phala* is unable to urge anyone to any activity, if the knowledge of instrumentality is absent. Besides the desire for *phala* cannot be accepted as the cause of activity towards its *sādhana*, for then, the desire for anything, say a jar, would lead to activity towards any other thing like cloth and others, and therefore the result would be a chaos (NM. p.198). Hence mere desire, like the mere knowledge of *iṣṭasādhanatā* cannot become *pravartaka*. So, the knowledge of *iṣṭasādhanatā* should be accompanied by desire for act as a *pravartaka*.

SECTION II

4.4 The Problem of Avidyā :

Ānandabodha in his two works, viz., *Pramāṇamālā* (p.10-11) and *Nyāyamakaranda* (pp.114-126) expounds the nature of *avidyā* or *māyā* (nescience) as it is propounded in the *Prasthānatraya*[1] and in the texts of his predecessors.[2] . He maintains that *avidyā* cannot become the material cause of the illusion if it is understood as false knowledge (*mithyājñāna*) or the negation of knowledge (*vidyābhāva*). *Avidyā* being the material cause (*upādānakāraṇa*) of world-illusion is supposed to be a *dravya* (substance) and in neither of these two senses *avidyā* can be regarded as a substance. Further, *avidyā* is beginningless (*anādi*) and indefinable (*anirvacanīya*). According to Ānandabodha, the indefinable nature of *avidyā* is determined following the nature of the effects (*kārya*) of the *avidyā* which is not something (*apramāṇika*), because the occasional happening of an effect (*kārya*) necessarily requires the operation of a cause and without a material cause (*upādānakāraṇa*) no effect (*kārya*) can be produced merely by the instrumental cause (*nimittakāraṇa*). All effects (*kāryas*) except *dhvaṁsa*

1. Bṛh. Up. IV.3.20, IV.4.3; IV.4.10; Iśa.Up.10.11 Kaṭha, Up.2.4. 5; Muṇḍ Up. 1.2.8; 9; Swet. Up. 5.1.
2. BSŚB, I.4.3, II.2.2., I.2.23, IV.3.14, II.1.33, I.3.19; *Bhāmatī* I.2.7; PP. P.98.

(destruction) are produced by material cause (NM. p.122). An unreal effect cannot be a creation of a real material cause. The object which has no existence, and no efficacy (*śakti*) to produce *kāryas* cannot be a material cause also. As neither that which existent (*sat*) nor non-existent (*asat*) can be the substratum (*āśraya*) of the illusory object, a cause (*kāraṇa*), therefore, which is neither *sat* (existent) nor *asat* (non-existent) is to be admitted as the cause of illusion (*bhrama*) or world-appearance. The world-appearance is unreal, so it cannot be the effect of a real substance and it cannot also emerge out of an unreal substance which cannot be the cause of any existing thing. Hence the cause must be *avidyā* which is neither real (*sat*) nor unreal (*asat*) (NM. p.123; PM. p.10). In his *Pramāṇamālā* Ānandabodha rightly quotes from Vācaspati's *Brahmatattvasamīkṣā* which is a commentary on the *Brahmasiddhi* of Maṇḍana Miśra (670-720 A.D) that *avidyā* is called *anirvacanīya* because it is a hypothetical category which cannot be described as real, unreal, both or neither and is therefore indescribable (*anirvacanīya*) (*ata eva uktam ācārya Vācaspatinā Brahmatattvasamīkṣāyām sadsadubhayānubhayādi prakārairanirvacanīyatvamevahyavidyānāmavidyātvamiti* (PM. p.10). Thus, by the nature of its effects, viz., illusion as *anirvācya* or *anirvacanīya* the nature of *avidyā* as *anirvācya* is determined. *Āvidyā* is regarded to be *anādi* (beginningless) because if some other cause of *avidyā* is admitted it will lead to the fault of infinite regress (*anavasthā*) (NM. p.123-124). In this way the beginningless and indescribable *avidyā* is the cause of the wordly illusion. (*yat tat anādi anirvācyam rajatādi upādāna sa eva saṁkaram avidyā siddhyanti* (NM. p.124).

According to Ānandabodha the acceptance of such a category is merely the logical consequence of indicating some possible cause for the illusion of the world. For, considering the nature of the illusion as it is existent, its cause can only be something which is neither real or unreal. It cannot be specified. Hence it is indefinable (*anirvacanīya*) (PM. p.10).

Ānandabodha points out that *avidyā* is proved through *arthāpatti* (presumption). Without *avidyā* there would not be an appearance of the utterly non-existent objects like horn of a human being; and there would not be sublation (*bādha*) of the real objects.

4.5 The locus of Avidyā

Only in the *Nyāyamakaranda* Ānandabodha has elaborately dealt with the problem of the locus of *avidyā* but not in his other works, viz., *Pramāṇamālā*, *Nyāyadīpāvali* and *Nyāyadīpikā*. The two theories viz. *Brahmāśrita avidyāvāda* (the theory upholding *Brahman* as the locus of *avidyā*) and *Jīvāśrita avidyāvāda* (the theory which upholds *jīvātman*) as the locus of *avidyā* which are evolved and developed by pre-Ānandabodha Advaita philosphers are systematically analysed and examined by Ānandabodha. That the *Brahman* is the locus advocated by Śaṅkara,[1] Sureśvara[2] and his followers but Maṇḍana and his follower Vācaspati propound the theory of *Jīvāśrita avidyā* in their celebrated works like *Brahmasūtra Śāṅkarabhāṣya, Naiṣkarmyasiddhi, Brahmasiddhi*[3] and *Bhāmatī*[4] respectively. The upholders of the theory, viz., *Jīvāśritāvidyā* advocate that the *Brahman* cannot be the locus of *avidyā* for the following reasons.

Firstly, *Brahman* is pure consciousness (*viśuddhacit*), self-luminous (*svayaṁ prakāśa*) and of the nature of *light*

1. BSŚB, 1.4.3, *Parameśvarāśrayā māyāmayī mahāsuptiḥi*.
2. N'SK. PP.105-106, Bṛhad. Var.Part I, PP.55 to 58, verses 175 to 182; Part II, p.675 to 677, verses 1215-1227.
3. BS. pp.10-11, Part I.
4. *Bhāmatī, Adhyāsabhāmatī*, I.1.4, 1.2.1, 1.4.1, 1.4.6.

(*prakāśasvabhāva*) whereas *avidyā* is of the nature of darkness (*aprakāśa*). Hence there is contrariety between *Brahman* and *avidyā* like light and darkness. Because of the contradictory nature *avidyā* cannot exist in the *Brahman* (NM. p.309).

Secondly, the *Brahman* being omniscient (*sarvajña*) is completely devoid of *avidyā*. It will cease to be omniscient if it would be considered as endowed with *avidyā*. The existence of *avidyā*, therefore, is not logically possible in the *Brahman* (NM. p.313).

Thirdly, the *Brahman* cannot be the locus of *avidyā*, for, in that case the system of bondage and emancipation (*bandhamokṣavyavasthā*) cannot be logically explained; bondage, according to the Vedānta, is *avidyā* itself and *mokṣa* is nothing but the absolute cessation of *avidyā* which veils the *Ātman* and projects it as something else and the realisation of one's own essential nature. One cannot achieve emancipation as long as *avidyā* is not completely perished. Hence by providing *Brahman* as the locus of *avidyā* the whole system of bondage and salvation will colapse since *avidyā* will be located eternally in the *Brahman* and consequently *mokṣa* would not be achieved. (NM. p.314.).

Fourthly, there cannot be the order of the teacher and taught if the *Brahman* is accepted to be the locus of *avidyā*. As he becomes a teacher who is completely devoid of *avidyā* as it is said *brahmaveda brahmaiva bhavati* (Muṇd. Up.III.2.9) and a taught has to remain always with *avidyā*. If *avidyā* exists in the *Brahman* no such teacher and taught relation is possible.

Ānandabodha refutes all these arguments of the *pūrvapakṣa* advanced against *Brahmāśrita avidyāvāda* as follows :-

Firstly, Ānandabodha argues that *Brahman* can be the locus of *avidyā* since the opposition between the *Brahman* and *avidyā* because of their nature of light and darkness respectively as pointed out by the *Pūrvapakṣa* is baseless. There is no such opposition between *Brahman* and *avidyā*, since *avidyā* is not negative (*abhāvarūpa*) like darkness. It is not the absence of light (*prakāśa*), but indefinable (*anirvacanīya*) as it is not *sat* (real) nor *asat* (unreal) nor both *sadasat* (real-cum-unreal) nor something else different from *sat*, *asat*, and *sadasatbhinna*. Hence there is no harm, says Ānandabodha, in considering *Brahman* to be the locus of *avidyā*.

According to Ānandabodha, an object which is not of the nature of light (*prakāśa*) is not inert (*jaḍa*) and therefore would not be opposed to any entity whose nature is light. For insentient worldly objects are cognised by light and the entire non-sentient world is illumined by the supreme consciousness (*cit*) identified with the self-luminous *Brahman*[1] itself. Therefore the relation of the location and the object located (*āśrayāśrayībhāva*) between the *Brahman* and *avidyā* is logically tenable (NM. pp.318-328).

It cannot be argued that if *avidyā* which is of the nature of darkness, would be located in the *Brahman* whose nature is *prakāśa*, then there would not be any other light to remove *avidyā* because the transformation of mind (*antaḥkaraṇapariṇatibhedarūpam prakāśāntaram*) caused by the constant practice of *śravaṇa* (hearing), *manana* (reflection) and *nididhyāsana*[2] (contemplation) taking the form of intuitive supreme light dispels *avidyā*

---

1. Kaṭha Up. V.15; Śwet. Up.6.14; Muṇḍ, Up.2.2.10 Bṛh. Up. IV.3.9.
2. Bṛh. Up. III.4.5; IV.5.6

in toto, says Ānandabodha. He illustrates the point by giving the following examples. As the sun-rays fallen on the glass mirror (*darpaṇa*) are capable of burning the grassblades similarly the supreme light arising out of constant meditation on the self destroys *avidyā* (*dṛśyate hi darpaṇasahakṛtārkaprabhayā dagdhṛtvam* NM. p.321). Just as the *katakaraja* (the dust or powder made of *kataka* plant) planted in muddy water causes the mud to settle down therby cleaning the water like crystal (*yathā khalu katakarajaḥ prakṣiptam pāthasi rajontarāvile rajontarāṇi samharan svayamapi samhṛyamāṇamanāvilam pāthaḥ kurute*) similarly the constant meditation on the Supreme Self destroys all the impurities like *avidyā* etc., residing in mind. Further, as the bamboo fire destroys itself without any support in the similar way *antaḥkaraṇapariṇati* (mental transformation) destroys all the aspects of *avidyā* (*evamiyam aikātmyavidyapyaśeṣa pramātrādi bhedanivartaka nirāśrayā sati sāmyati* (NM. p.322) and finally vanishes with its effects.

Secondly, about the objection, viz. as the *Brahman* is omniscient (*sarvajña*) *avidyā* cannot exist in the *Brahman*, Ānandabodha argues that *Brahman*, though omniscient (*sarvajña*) can be the locus of *avidyā* since the omniscience (*sarvajñatva*) which is admitted to be its cause (*avidyāvatttayā eva sarvajñatva iti brumaḥ*, NM. p.323) Omniscience of the *Brahman* is possible in three ways I) valid means of knowledge (*pramāṇa*) II) through illusion (*bhrānti*) or III) innate intelligence (*svabhāvasiddhayā vā prajñayā*). Firstly, since all the valid means of knowledge belong to the world of *bheda* (difference) they cannot express the Supreme Reality and its omniscience in a valid manner.

Secondly, the illusion cannot exist for one who does not have *avidyā*. Thirdly, even innate intelligence (*savbhāvasidhi* or *prajñā*) cannot know the whole of the universe without *avidyā,* for the *puruṣa* or the *Ātman* by nature, has neither attachment nor any relation based on *avidyā* with worldly objects. In this way *avidyā* implies *Paramātman* and does not negate it (NM. p.324).

Fourthly, as to the prima facie arguments regarding the impossiblity of the existence of bondage and emancipation (*bandamokṣavyavasthānupaptti*), Ānanda-bodha points out that these two conditions caused by *avidyā* are on par with the objects seen in a dream. When *avidyā* itself is removed, these conditions of bondage and emancipation are neither expected nor logically desirable in the *Brahman* and these two conditions cannot properly be explained also (NM. p.325).

Fifthly, Ānandabodha counteracts the arguments, viz. impossiblity of the teacher and taught relation of *Pūrvapakṣa* that arrangements of teacher and taught (*guruśiṣyavyavasthā*) is possible because the difference between teacher and the taught takes place only in the realm of *avidyā* and would cease to exist on its removal (*guruśiṣyavyavasthāpi samānayogakṣamaiva*) (NM. p.325).

Ānandabodha refutes the theory known as *Jīvāśrita avidyāvāda* upheld by Maṇḍana Miśra and his follower Vācaspati Miśra in their works *Brahmasiddhi* and *Bhāmatī* respectively.

Ānandabodha argues that *Jīvātman* (individual self) cannot be the locus of *avidyā* since *Jīvātman* is not a separate entity. The unity of *Brahman* and *Jīvātman* is proclaimed by the Upaniṣadic authority i.e. *anena jīvena ātmanā anupraveśa* (Chā. Up. 6.3.7; 2.3). Those who advocate *Jivāśritāvidyāvāda* argue that *Brahman* cannot be the locus of *avidyā* for it is of the nature of light and *avidyā* is of the nature of darkness and therefore both *avidyā* and *Brahman* are opposed to each other. This logic is also applicable in case of *Jīvāśrita avidyāvāda*. As *jīvātman* is not separate from the self-luminous *Brahman* and *avidyā* is of the nature of darkness. Thus the opposition which is supposed in case of *Brahman* is unavoidable in the case of *Jīvātman* as the locus of *avidyā*. (NM. p.309).

It cannot be said that though unity of *Brahman* and *Jīvātman* is real (*tāttvika*) still the difference (*bheda*) between *Brahman* and *Jīvātman* is the creation of *avidyā* and hence it does not go against the authority of the *śruti* (scripture), and thus *Jīvātman* can be considered to be the locus (*āśraya)* of *avidyā*. According to Ānandabodha this view is baseless since it leads to *parasparāśraya* (interdependence). *Jīvātman* would depend on *avidyā* for its difference and *avidyā* would depend on *Jīvātman* for its locus (*āśraya*).

It is argued that there is nothing illogical in case of *avidyā* and it can possibly reside in a liberated person. Ānandabodha rejects this view since as long as *avidyā* is not fully dispelled one cannot be a *mukta* or liberated person.

Thus, according to Ānandabodha a person gets bound to this illusory world due to his *avidyā* and dispelling the same completely he attains the *mokṣa* i.e. the Supreme *Brahman*.

4.6 Theories of Error (Khyātivāda):

The concept of *bhrahma* (illusion) or *viparyaya* (error) has been accepted as a form of invalid knowledge (*apramā*) by almost all schools of Indian philosophy.[1] Moreover, error is an erroneous cognition of one thing as another thing or an illusory perception of one thing as another. Valid knowledge (*pramā*) is the apprehension of an object as it is while error is the cognition of an

1. Singh, B.N, *Indian logic*, p.26.

object as it is not. The Sanskrit term for error is *'khyāti'* (cognition) derived from the root *khyā* meaning. 'to perceive' or 'to manifest'. Among the Indian philosophers the ways of explaining error widely differ as they advocate a theory of error suited to their respective metaphysical views.

There are five prominent theories of *bhrama* (error) propounded by the schools of Indian philosophy, viz., the theory of self- apprehension (*ātmakhyāti*), the theory of non being's apprehension (*asatkhyāti*), the theory of non-apprehension (*akhyāti*), the theory of misapprehension (*anyathākhyāti*) and the theory of indefinable's apprehension (*anirvacanīyakhyāti*)[1]. All these theories of error have been classified into two groups viz, *satkhyāti* and *asatkhyāti*. According to the former, an error is the cognition of the existent (*sat*). There are three theories under *satkhyāti*, viz. *anyathākhyāti*, *ātmakhyāti* and *akhyāti*. According to the theory of *asatkhyāti*, an error is non-existent. Ānandabodha explains all these theories in his three works - *Pramāṇamālā*, *Nyāyadīpāvali* and *Nyāyamakaranda*. Apart from the *anirvacanīyakhyāti* advocated by the Advaitins Ānandabodha like Śaṅkara[2] refutes all these theories pointing out duly the logical fallacies and finally establishes the validity of the Advaita theory called *anirvacanīyakhyāti*.

Ātmakhyāti (Self-apprehension) :

The theory of error called *ātmakhyāti* (self-apprehension) is advocated by the Yogācāra school of Buddhist philosophy otherwise known as *Vijnānavādins*. Error, according to this school, is the external manifestation of the internal cognition (*jñānakārasyeva vahiravabhāsa*) (NM. p.99). The Yogācāra idealist school

1. Sastri, S.Kuppuswami, *A Primer of Indian logic*, p.123.
2. BSŚB, *Adhyāsabhāṣya*.

advocates that the entire world is an illusion, a reflex or a thought-image. Nothing is real except consciousness (*vijñaptimātra*) or mind (*cittamātra*). Just as a man with defective eyesight sees the vision of double moon, or floating hairtuft before his eyes, or a moving circle in a firebrand, or the fatamorgana in a desert, or takes bubbles for crystals, in the same way the ignorant man who has not attained the absolute wisdom (*samyak-jñāna*) sees the vision of direct colours and forms and acts on the presumption that they are real. They are the projections of the mind[1] and appear as something external.[2]

The diversity of things and the plurality of innumerable persons, in short, the whole universe and its inhabitants are creation of the mind.[3] In the nacre-silver illusion the subjective silver-form of cognition appears as the form of an external object. The silver (*rajata*) is not absolutely unreal. It is real as the form of the internal cognition, but the mistake consists in taking it to be the form of an external object. The silver (*rajata*)' is a mental fact whereas in the illusion it is taken for an extramental fact. The Yogācāra school does not recognise any cogniser other than the momentary idea. So, according to this school, in illusion a momentary idea cognises itself as external. An utterly non-existent object like ether-lotus (*ākāśapadma*) does not appear, there must be a vitiation of the general rule, viz. 'It is, as it appears' (*yad yathā pratibhāsate tat tathā*

1. *Vijñaptimātramevaitad asadarthāvabhāsanāt. yathā taimirikasyāsat keśacandrādi darśanam. Viṁśatikā* of Dharmakīrti.
2. *Yadantarjñeyarūpam tu bhirvadavabhāsate/Ālambanaparīkṣā* 6.
3. *Dṛśyam na vidyate bāhyam - cittam citram hi dṛśyate. dehabhogapratiṣṭānam cittamātra vadāmyaham. Laṅkavatārasūtra/cittamātra of* Dharmakīrti, *verse* 23.

eva iti autsargika anyathātvam),(NM. p.99). The cognition, viz. 'this is not silver' must be accepted as sublating 'thisness'. It involves the flaw of *gaurava* (prolixity) in assuming the denial of both silver, the locus (*āśraya*), and 'thisness' can be sublated being external. The silver, thus remains internal as of the nature of cognition. The Yogācāra school also argues that the sublation (*bādha*) of thisness negates the existence of silver in front as well as anywhere at distance, perception being impossible of a thing at a long distance. Thus, one has to accept that the silver is identical with perception (NM. p.100).

Ānandabodha sets aside the view of Yogācāra by arguing that when the silver aspect is accepted as internal, the appearance of externality, though unreal, has to be accepted. Besides, if objects are accepted as internal then in the case of the superimposition of fire on a heap of *gunjas* (a small shrub of that name bearing a red black berry) there would be the possibility of perceiver's body being on flame (PM. 9). If that existence in cognition also is unreal, then the superimposed thing would be completely non-existent or indescribable. It cannot be said that the thing existing in cognition is not unreal, but only does not create any effect (PM. p.10), since there would not be any action of a person, desirous of fire towards that object. To avoid this contingency, the Yogācāra school has to admit that the objects though actually existing internally appear as external, and thus external appearance causes the activity of a person. Ānandabodha maintains that the object itself externally causes the action and it is needless to imagine any internal object which is incapable of creating any effect externally (PM. p.10). The fallacy of *gaurava* (prolixity) is a defect only in presumption. Here the sublative cognition is not imagined, by any one but it is a self-evident experience of all. So the acceptance of internality of the external object is untenable, maintains Ānandabodha.

Asatkhyāti (Theory of Non-being's Apprehension):

The theory of error called *asatkhyāti* is advocated by the Mādhyamika school of the Buddhist philosophy. According to this school, error is the cognition of an absolute non-existent object (*atyanta asantamartham avabhāsayanti samvid eva vibhrama*) (NM. p.102). This school advocates that an absolute non-existent object (*atyanta asat padārtha*) appears in error, for instance, in shell-silver illusion, an absolute non- existent object in illusion is proved by the sublating cognition i.e. 'this is not silver' after understanding the error, 'this is silver'. When the sublating cognition (*bādhakadhi*) i.e. 'this is not silver' arises, the silver which appears in illusion gets negated and thus, the non-existent nature of silver is proved. Since the object of error i.e. silver is sublated it is not *sat* (existent object) but only *asat* (non-existent) object which can appear in an illusion. Cognition itself has special illuminating power acquired by its previous cognition, which is called nescience (*avidyā*). In the place where shell-silver error occurs, there is no silver and consequently there is no sense-object contact, still there arises the silver-cognition because of internally differentiated residual impressions (*saṁskāravāsanā*) (NM. p.110; PM.8; ND. p.5).

If further argued that if there is no appearance of the absolute non-existent object in error there cannot be the sublating cognition, i.e. "this is not silver" after its real cognition. The object of the sublative cognition, for instance. 'this is not silver', is the non-existent object. The non-existent object appears by its own nature, not as real (NM. p.111).

The sublative cognition shows the unreal nature of the silver that appears as real in error. As the existence of objects is to be accepted as they appear, and there is conflict between the illusory cognition and the sublative cognition, it is sound to admit the appearance of non-existent object in illusory cognition.

Ānandabodha refutes all these above said arguments. He criticises the view by arguing that the sublating cognition (*bādhakadhi*) which negates the illusory cognition "this is silver," does not prove the non-existent object supposed to appear as object of illusory cognition. Even if the illusory cognition becomes devoid of object, there is no harm since there is one type of cognition known as *vikalpa* which is also devoid of object. It is said by Patañjali in his *Yogasūtra* (*śabdajñānānupāti vastūśūnyo vikalpaḥ*) (YS. 1.9; NM. p.109). An illusory cognition is objectless similarly *vikalpa* cognition is objectless. Hence there is no validity of admitting appearance of a non-existent object in illusory cognition for the suppliment of an object to the sublative cognitions. Secondly, the so-called 'appearance of *asat*' never becomes an object of immediate cognition.

Ānandabodha illustrates this point quoting from the *Iṣṭasiddhi* of Vimuktātman i.e. *na hi nari śṛṅgam bhāti gaviva*. According to Ānandabodha, an *asat* (non-existent object) cannot be an object of direct cognition as a horn is not seen in case of a man as in case of a cow.

Further, Ānandabodha questions the object of the capacity. If the object of the capacity (*sāmarthya*) is said to be non-existent, is it then produced (*kārya*) by the capacity or indicated (*jñāpya*) ? The non-existent object cannot be a *kārya* (produced). Again, if the capacity of a cognition produces it who else will be there to manifest it? It also cannot be indicated by the capacity (*jñānasāmarthya*). Thus, the view of Mādhyamika is untenable.

Akhyāti (The theory of non-apprehension)

Ānandabodha in his *Pramāṇamālā, Nyayadīpāvali* and *Nyāyamakaranda* thoroughly criticises the theory of non-apprehension (*akhyāti*) propounded by the Prābhākara school of Pūrva-Mīmāṁsā in the following way.

The followers of the Prābhākara school propagate the doctrine of the self-validity (*svataḥ prāmāṇya*) of *samvid* (knowledge)[1] and reduces all error and doubt to simply an absence of knowledge. All knowledge, according to this school, is valid[2] which prompts us to activity. According to this school, what is called error or illusion (*viparyaya*) is not false knowledge. If all cognition is self-luminous (*svaprakāśa*) and therefore true (*yathārtha*), the consciousness expressed in the judgement "this is silver" cannot be erroneous. When one mistakes a piece of shell for silver, the error is due to the failure to distinguish the two different elements in it, i.e. the idea of silver and impression of "this". One mixes up the perceived and the remembered elements in one single psychosis. The object of a cognition is the thing which is presented to consciousness. In "this is silver" what is presented to consciousness is "silver" and not "shell". One does not cognise the shell as silver, for the shell never enters into consciousness. The idea which is remembered does not agree with the fact, since the judgement "this is silver" is superseded by the judgement "this is only a piece of shell" when the

1. *Kiñca svata eva yadupapadyate----mitau ca kacidanupapattanar stiti svayamprakāsaiya yuktā*, PP. p.173
2. *Yathārtha sarvamebeha vijñanamitisiddhaye. prābhākara gurobhāva ssamiunah pracakṣate.* PP.V.53, p.4.

knower picks up the piece. The error is due to *akhyāti* or non-apprehension of the difference between the given and the remembered elements. The perceived element, "this", and the remembered element, "silver", are true; only there is non-discrimination (*akhyāti*) of the two factors as distinct. This non-discrimination is due to certain defects of the sense-organs and the suggestion of similarity between shell and silver, which rouses the mental residum (*saṁskāra*) of the silver previously cognised.

This unconsciousness of the distinction between the given and the remembered elements leads to action. In actual experience there is no difference between the valid and the invalid cognitions of silver, since both give rise to the same kind of activity on the part of the agent. Thus, an error is not a unitary cognition but a composite of two cognitions whose distinction is not apprehended. It is not the positive misapprehension but a negative non- apprehension.

According to the Prābhākaras, the recollective nature of the cognition of silver is proved by *pariśeṣa*[1] (elimination) or remainder (NM. p.58). The cognition of silver arises by means of a direct contact between silver and the eyes. The shell (*sukti*) cannot be accepted by the content (*ālambana*) of the silver cognition because that which appears in the cognition can be only its content, and it goes against the experience. Due to non-discrimination the illusory cognition of silver appears as similar to the cognition of a real silver, and this prompts some practical activity which is similar to that prompted by the real silver. Consequently one bends down to pick the 'silver' and is disappointed to find merely a piece of shell. Then it is realised that

1. Śālikanātha, *Prakaraṇapañcikā*, pp.51-52.

'this' is not silver. The Prābhākara sets forth the syllogism as follows:-

Idam smaraṇam

anākalita rajatasyānutpadyamānatvāt

yadittham tattathā

yathobhayavādyavivādāspadam rajatasmaraṇaṁ.

(NM. p.62)

(The silver-cognition is memory, because it does not arise in a person who has not seen silver earlier, which is like this, is like that :- the cognition which does not arise in a person who has not seen the object before is memory - like the common cognition of silver.)

In a dream the memory of the past experience is revived by some unseen agency (*adṛṣṭakāraṇa*) and appears like cognition because that which is recollected is forgotten.

In the error of the yellow conch (*pitaśankhaḥ*) there are really two cognitions, one apprehending the yellowness of the bile, and the other apprehending the substance of the counch without apprehending its whiteness. Then, because the substance and a quality always stand in a mutual expectancy (*ākāṅkṣā*), the two apprehensions cannot remain unrelated, and consequently the manifestation appears as similar to the manifestation of a real yellow conch. In the illusion of the double moon the rays issuing from the two eyes give rise to two different cognitions of the moon which is one and the illusion persists inspite of the fact that the oneness of the moon is not forgotten. This is not a case of memory-obstruction. Here as in the 'yellow conch', illusion there is a non-discrimination between two cognitions and not between one cognition and one memory image as in the shell-silver illusion. In all these illusions the non-discrimination is caused by defects.

Defects simply disturb the normal functioning of a cause; they cannot give rise to a different effect. A defective seed of wheat results in a deficient growth or no growth, but it cannot produce a barley plant. Similarly, the defect of the sense produces either an incomplete cognition of the nacre or no cognition, but it cannot produce the cognition of an entirely different object, viz. the silver.

Ānandabodha sets aside the theory of *akhyāti* as follows:

The Prābhākara defines error as *vivekāgraha* (non-cognition of difference between cognitions and their objects).

Ānandabodha asks a question: what does the term *vivekāgraha* denote? In the *Nyāyadīpāvali* (p.9) Ānandabodha suggests four possible alternative answers and dicards them viz. *bhedāgraha* (non-cognition of difference), *bhedakāgraha* (non-cognition of the maker of difference), *parasparābhāvāgraha* (mutual non-cognition) and *asaṁsargāgraha*. *Bhedāgraha* means non-cognition of difference either between the two cognitions or between the cognition and the object. The difference between the cognitions cannot be said to be non-cognised, as cognitions are self-luminous (*svayaṁprakāsa*). The objects also are manifested through this cognition. Moreover, difference is accepted by the Prābhākaras as the very nature of objects. Hence the words conveying non-cognition (*vivekāgraha*) cannot be producer of difference when objects are manifested. Two contardictory attributes i.e. the appearance of nature (*svapratibhāsa*) and the non-appearance of difference (*sva svabhāvabhūta-bhedapratibhāsa*) cannot be accepted to be residing in one object.

Secondly, the word *bhedaka* in the *bhedakāgraha* would either mean *bhedotpādaka* (producer of the difference) or *bhedajñāpaka* (indicator of difference). As difference is nothing but the object itself, producer of difference would mean producer of object. Thus, the word *bhedakāgraha* would imply that without understanding the jar-maker (*ghaṭakartā*) one cannot know the jar (*ghaṭa*) which is not tenable. The other alternative i.e. *bhedajñāpaka* is similarly absurd, as the word *bhedaka* cannot mean any sense and without the awareness of sense, activities are seen to be undertaken (ND. p.9). By the indicator of difference one cannot take differentiating qualities or special qualities of the object (*bhedyaḥ dharmaḥ*). If they are known, difference also would be known; if they are unknown, there would not be any activity. If it is said that some of the qualities are known and some like shellness etc. are unknown, then the person desiring silver may proceed towards a stone whose stoneness is not known. The cognition of similarity also cannot be accepted as the cause of activity as activity is seen in the case of yellow conch (*pitaḥ śaṅkhaḥ*) though it is not similar to the white one.

Thirdly, *parasparābhāvāgraha* means non-apprehension of the absence of one into or from the other is also untenable. When the word 'this' (*idam*) denotes the object in front and one 'silver' (*rajata*) is remembered both the objects are known and the difference which is of the nature of either of them also must be known. There is no non-apprehension of difference. When difference (*bheda*) is accepted as the nature of positive entity (*bhāvarūpa*) non-apprehension of difference becomes impossible.

Fourthly, *asaṁsargāgraha* is the *a-tādātmyasya a-samavayasyāgraha*. The non-association implies absence of association which, ultimately would not be different from the objects appearing either as 'this' or as 'silver'. As absense of a jar is not different from the ground (*bhūtala*) so also the absense of association is not different from that which is related to 'this' (*idam*) or 'silver'. Therefore, non-association (*atādātmya*) should be accepted as non-different from the positive entities *bhāvapadārthas* which appear in the cognition.

In the shell-silver illusion, the silver (*rajata*) cannot be accepted as an object of memory since the cogniser can point out the object in front by finger as silver (NM. p.75). and the defects in the sense organs cannot also prevent the capacity of producing effect as there are some cases of defects where altogether a new effect results.

It is untenable to say that the untrustworthy nature is because of inconsistency of cognitions with their objects because self-validity of cognitions is due to their being cognitions and not because of being non-contradictory (*avyabhicāreṇa*). (NM. p.75).

The inference put forth to prove the recollective nature of silver-cognition is illogical since the perceptive nature of the silver-cognition is proved.

In the instance "conch is yellow" ; (*pitaḥ śaṅkhaḥ*) non- cognition of non-relation cannot be accepted when yellowness and conch are cognised. It is unnecessary also since the case can be well explained by superimposition as in the case of shell-silver.

The theory of *akhyāti* fails to explain the activity of a person desirous of silver towards the object in front. The activity of the sentient is produced only by cognition and never by a non-cognition. The cognition of similarity is present there in the non-cognition accepted by Prābhākara but it is contradictory to the experience. The cognition '*gavaya* is similar to cow (*go sadrśo gavayaḥ*) cannot be the cause of the activity towards a *gavaya* of a person desirous of a cow. Besides, the non-cognition of non-silver may result in negligence. The activity of a person desiring silver towards 'this' is reasonably due to desire of that object (silver), otherwise there would be mutual conflict as a person desires one and acts towards another (NM. p.71). The silver cognition has for its content the object in front as it invariably causes the effort for a person desirous of that.

The sublative nature of 'this is not silver' does not lie in the non-cognition of difference. The statement i.e. all cognitions are true does not stand to reason. So the theory of *akhyāti* is untenable, maintains Ānandabodha.

Anyathākhyāti (Theory of Misapprehension)

Ānandabodha also criticises the Bhāṭṭa theory of error and pointing out logical flaws adequately sets aside it in his works. Theory of error which is known as *anyathākhyāti* or *viparitakhyāti* has been propounded by the Bhāṭṭa school of the Pūrva-Mīmāṁsā. However, the theory of error postulated by the term *anyathākhyāti* of the Naiyāyikas slitely differs from that of Bhāṭṭas.

According to the Bhāṭṭa school error is an appearance of an object in the form of another, for instance, in shell-silver, shell *(śukti)* appears in the form of silver (*rajata*) which is an apprehension of another object i.e. shell, Hence illusory cognition arises in the form - This is silver (*iyam śukti*) in the substratum of real shell. An error manifests a real object in the form, of a different object which too is real.[1]. In all cases of illusory perception it is only the relation between the

1. *Tatraśuktikārajatādijñānam śuktikākhyam bhavam śuktikārūpeṇa sadrūpam bhāvāntarasya rajatasya yat sadrūpam rajatarūpam tena rūpeṇa grunhan bhrāntam bhavati.* NR or *SV, Nirālambana* p.117.

subjects and predicate elements, e.g. 'this' and 'silver', which is unreal and appears to be real. The related objects however are always real.

Accordingly an illusion is a positive mis-apprehension in which the mistake consists in identifying two unrelated real objects under the influence of vicious subjective and objective conditions.

The Bhāṭṭas argue that an absolute non-existent entity cannot appear in error and also an existent object cannot appear in error. The sublating cognition arising in the form of 'this is not silver' after the error, proves that since the object of erroneous perception i.e. silver (*rajata*) gets sublated by the object of real cognition i.e. of shell, it is not *sat* (existent) because *sat padārtha* cannot have sublation (*bādha*). The object of erroneous perception, is not *asat* (unreal) for its appaerance (*atyantāsataḥ arthasya pratibhāsāsambhavāt* NM. p.81). Thus, the object of error not being *asat* and not being *sat* (real), is to be accepted as appearing in form of another object, for instance, it is the piece of shell that appears as silver. The term *anyathā* (otherwise) in the term *anyathākhyāti*, according to Bhāṭṭas, refers to the appearance of the object, i.e. it is a cognition (*khyāti*) of an object as what it is not (*anyathā*). As the silver witnessed in the locus of shell is not absolutely unreal, for the sublating cognition which cancels it in the form of 'this' is not silver' proves its reality for the time being. The sublating cognition only sublates the identity of silver with the object in front i.e. shell, and implies the existence of silver in another place or some other place, but not absolute non-existence of silver (*anyathāvabhāsahidam-kārāspada tādātmyaniṣedhātmā* NM. p.82.).

The Bhāṭṭas uphold the view that *abhāva* or *asat* (non-existence) is not complete absence like sky-flower (*ākaśakusuma*), but absence of another positive entity.

Hence, Kumārila, the propounder of the Bhāṭṭa school of Mīmāṁsā philosophy contends in his celebrated work *Ślokavārttika*[1] that *Abhāva* is another positive entity, in respect of other objects, and not something else as that which is impossible to be explained.

Absolute non-existent object (*atyanta asat padārtha*) cannot be an object of cognition, but the non-existent object, which is expressible in the form of an existent object, can become the object of cognition, for instance, in shell-silver illusion, since shell, though non-existent, being expressible in the form of existent object becomes the object of erroneous cognition "this is silver". And shell invaribly becomes the object of effort of a person desirous of silver. This proves that shell *(śukti)* itself appears in the form of silver (*rajata*). Further, the *pratyabhijñā* (recognition) in the form of "this appeared as silver so far" that takes place after the rise of the sublating cognition (*bādhakadhi*) proves that shell appears otherwise i.e. in the form of silver.

Ānandabodha criticises the Bhāṭṭa theory of *anyathākhyāti* as follows:

He argues that a cognition cannot arise without a corresponding object. If in the shell-silver illusion, silver is supposed to be existing elsewhere then the cognition of silver cannot take place.

As Bhāṭṭas contend that non-existent object cannot have appearance in perception, Ānandabodha questions the appearance of an object denoted by "this" as silver. As a matter of fact, shell exists in its own nature, but the nature identical with silver, is not real, by which it can become the object of cognition, the silver cannot be real, for, the sublating cognition would not have any

1. *Bhāvāntaramabhāvonyo na kaścidanirupaṇāt*. SV, 3.23; NM. p.83.

object (*bādhadhiyaḥ nirālambanapātāt*) (NM. p.85) as a real cannot be sublated. The validity of the sublation "this is not silver" is an all accepted truth. The assertion of the reality of silver would reverse it and would make the first cognition i.e. "this is silver" as valid. Even though the non-existence of silver does not resemble the sky-lotus, silver being existent elsewhere still the silver existing elsewhere cannot be the cognition. The existence of one object, i.e. of shell cannot deny the absolute non-existence of the other objects. The relation of identity of silver with shell does not explain the cognition because, if the so-called identity is present here it cannot be sublated, and if absent it cannot be the object of cognition. This mutual identity should either be real (*sat*) or unreal (*asat*). It can not be a third category. The two objects, which are regarded as of the nature of mutual negation (*anyonyābhāva*), are accepted as acquiring the forms of each other. But according to Ānandabodha, this acquirness of the form of each other is inexplicable. If it is the same as the object denoted by 'this', then, there would not be cognition of 'silver'. If it is of silver only, it would be cognised at any place as on the wrist of a beloved, and not here as 'this' (*idam*). If it is a third entity like a jar, transcending both the *idam* and the *rajata* then the cognition as 'silver' would certainly be impossible. So this explicability, contends Ānandabodha, is the same as indescribability of the object of error.

Apart from this, the non-existence (*asat*) is common to both the silver and its identity. Hence there is no harm in admitting the non-existence of silver itself, though a non-existent object cannot be an object of illusory cognition the existence of silver can be accepted as the shell itself. It would not be opposite to the experience (*anubhava*), since the opposition cannot be proved. There cannot be opposition between two cognitions since cognitions can have the objects like colour, taste etc. The opposition (*virodha*) cannot be of nature of conflict between existence (*bhāva*) and non-existence (*abhāva*) in one positive entity as these two aspects are not seen in one entity. It cannot be argued that as an eunuch, where two *bhāva* and *abhāva* are seen, there can be existence and non-existence in one positive entity, for, above said example of eunuch is not an appropriate one on the strength of which there would be contigency of appearing both the shell and the silver together. Thus, silver existing elsewhere cannot be logically proved by the Bhāṭṭas, contends Ānandabodha.

Anirvacanīyakhyāti (the theory of indefinable apprehension)

The Advaita school expounds the view that so long as the illusion of a snake or silver lasts there comes into being the corresponding object which is logically indefinable. The Advaita school maintains that in the rope-snake illusion the snake must be present where it is seen, though it enjoys merely a temporary existence so long as the illusion lasts, and because it can be neither absolutely real, nor absolutely unreal, nor both together, it must be indefinable.

Ānandabodha maintains that the term *anirvacanīya* is used in order to explain that the object of error is not existent (*sat*), or non-existent (*asat*) or existent cum non-existent (*sadasat*). However, *anirvacanīyatā* (inexplicability) does not mean inability of expression at all since there would be a contingency of keeping mum. (NM. p.119).

The term *anirvacanīyatā* means *sadasadvilakṣaṇatā* (distinct from existent and non-existent). Ānandabodha defines *sadasadvilakṣaṇatā* as distinction from both the aspects defined by distinction of every aspect (*ekaikaprakāravailakṣaṇyāvacchinnobhayaprakārvailakṣaṇam lakṣaṇamāśriyate* (NM. p.112). To prove this, Ānandabodha in his *Pramāṇamālā* employs the syllogism as follows :

Vibādapadamanirvācyam

bhādhyatvāt

yaduktasādhyamah na bhavati na taduktasādhanam

yathā ātmā.

Further, in *Nyāyamakaranda* Ānandabodha points out that the object of illusory cognition like silver is *sadasadvilakṣaṇa*. It is proved by the means of knowledge (*pramāṇa*) called *arthāpatti* (presumption).

The object of error is not verifiable and may therefore appear to be unreal but its knowledge without a corresponding object is conceivable. Hence the reality with which knowledge acquaints us is not always of the same kind, and that the objects of error is of a type which is ontologically different from that of the common objects. The cognitions of the objects of error can be explained only by admitting their distinct nature from both the existent and the non-existent.

They being distinct from *asat* are perceived and being distinct from *sat* are sublated (NM. p.113).

In this connection Ānandabodha puts forth the view of Prakāśātman who in his *Pañcapādikāvivaraṇa* defines *anirvācya* as distinct from the absolute and the empirical reality. According to him sublation (*bādha*) is a negation on account of the *upādhi* (adjunct) of the subject. *Anirvācya* (indefinability) therefore is defined as that which becomes the subject matter of the cognition of sublation and which arises on account of the cognition that sublates (NM. p.126). Vivaraṇakārā accepts three types of reality (*sattā*) viz., the absolute reality of the

Brahman, the empirical reality of ether etc. *(ākāśādi)* which is characterised by the adjunct of *māyā* and the phenomenal reality of silver etc., characterised by the adjunct of *avidyā*. Thus, there is no contradiction between the former cognition i.e. 'this is silver' and the latter one i.e. 'this is not silver'. Silver experienced in the former cognition is produced by *avidyā* and latter cognition gives the absence of the absolute and the empirical reality and proves the unreality of silver (*rajata*).

Ānandabodha maintains that as in the view of *anyathākhyāti* silver existing in some other place appears as being in front similarly in the view of *anirvacanīyakhyāti* silver (*rajata*) though distinct from existent object appears as existent. In the later cognition also, the existence of silver never appears, on the contrary, it sublates it. Thus, there is contradiction in the experience by accepting silver as distinct from both the existent and non-existent. The latter cognition sublates the empirical reality of silver, since the silver is created by the *avidyā* which is sublated when its substratum i.e. the shell is realised. The silver in illusion which is unreal appears as empirically real. It is the appearance which is sublated by the later congition, since what is cognised there cannot be refuted there only. Otherwise the shell would also be refuted like the silver. One cognition in this way cannot sublate the other one, it can only indicate its otherwiseness (*anyathābhāva*). Thus, the sublation would take the form as 'upto this time it appeared as silver, not now'. And the sublation cannot be admitted in the same phase as it would be contradictory to the previous cognition. Further, one cognition cannot disprove the content of other cognition so far as cognitions are limited to their own contents (NM. p.121). To admit a contentless cognition would mean to accept the Mādhyamika Buddhist's view, which negates the external existence of contents (NM. p.121).

Ānandabodha in his *Nyāyamakaranda* puts forth the definition of *anirvācya* as *jñananivartyatva* (that which can be sublated by knowledge) from the *Iṣṭasiddhi* (p.3) of Vimuktātman (NM. p.124). Ānandabodha proves that the definition of Vimuktātman is not inconsistent since the desirable *Ātman* is never sublated and the sublative silver etc. are indescribable. But the nature of sublation cannot be proved since cognitions restricted to their contents cannot sublate the content of other cognitions. Ānandabodha supports the definition of *anirvācyatā* as the objectivity of sublation which means the complete cessation of *avidyā* along with its effects (*savilāsaavidyā nivṛttireva bādhaḥ tadgocaratā anirvācyatā* (NM. p.25). Thus the theory of *anirvacanīyakhyāti* is logically sound, maintains Ānandabodha.

Further, Ānandabodha examines the interpretation of the term *anyathā* given by the Bhāṭṭas. He refutes the concept of *anyathā* by arguing that this another (*anyathā*) can exist neither in the substratum of shell-silver cognition, nor any where else. For its existence elsewhere cannot be proved neither by *anubhava* (experience) nor by *anupapatti* (impossibility of otherwise explanation). Three kinds of cognitions which arise in connection with shell-silver illusion are (a) cognition of silver itself (b) cognition of sublation of silver (c) recognition of silver. These cognitions cannot prove the existence of silver elsewhere (*anyatra*). The cognition of silver shows silver as an aspect of "this". The cognition of sublation determines the absence of silver in front. Thus Ānandabodha points out that the object of erroneous cognition cannot be anywhere else like that of eating ether in dream (*svapne nabhobhakṣaṇa*) the existence elsewhere of the object of erroneous cognition cannot be proved by *anupapatti* (impossibility of otherwise explanation).

Ānandabodha examines the nature of sublation (*bādhadhī*) i.e. this is not silver. According to him, the sublating cognition does not consist in the denial of identity (*tādātmya*); it recounts the silver on the object 'this' and denies that aspect alone and not all the identities. After the denial of the cognition of two different objects between which identity (*tādātmya*) is supposed to be existing arises as the two trees appear identical from a long distance, but when the identity is denied, there is no appearance of the two trees distinct from each other. The sublating cognition "this is not silver" denies the nature of silver but not the identity of silver with shell.

CHAPTER V

SOTERIOLOGICAL VIEWS

This chapter embodies comprehensive and critical analysis of Ānandabodha's soteriological views i.e. nature of *mokṣa* (emancipation) and means of *mokṣa* expounded in his work, viz. *Pramāṇamālā* and *Nyāyamakaranda*.

In the *Nyāyamakaranda* apart from the Advaita Vedānta theory Āṇandabodha sets forth other seven theories of *mokṣa* as his *pūrvapakṣa*. These are propounded by the heterodox and orthodox philosophical schools of the Jaina, Mādhyamika, Yogācāra, Sāṁkhya-Yoga, Nyāya-Vaiśeṣika and the Prābhākara of Pūrva-Mīmāṁsā. Ānandabodha repudiates all these aforementioned theories adducing counter arguments and finally proves logical validity of the Advaita view expoused by the *Prasthānatraya* and the Advaitic texts of his predecessors. However, no direct reference to these above said schools has been given by Ānandabodha but Citsukhācārya in his commentary on *Nyāyamakaranda* identifies most of them. In the other works of Ānandabodha no such refutation of the antagonistic theories on the nature of the final beatitude has been made.

5.1 THE HETERODOX SCHOOLS:

(A) The Jaina Theory

According to the heterodox Jaina school *mokṣa* is the continuous rising up of the self being devoid of all limiting adjuncts, like the body, the senses and their activities (*pralīna nikhilopādheḥ kṣetrajñasya satatordhvagati.* NM. p.270).

In the *Tattvārthasūtra*[1] Umāsvati gives the account of *mokṣa,* viz. when the actions (*karma*) eight in number are destroyed, pure knowledge (*kevalajñāna*) appears and the *Jīva* becomes pure (*śuddha*), conscious (*buddha*), free from all defects (*nirāmaya*), omniscient (*sarvajña*), all perceiving (*sarvadarśin*) endowed with pure knowledge *(kevalin)* and self-restraint *(jina)*. This stage of *mokṣa* is called *jīvanmukti* (emancipation in embodied state). The liberated *(kevalin)* at this stage acquires four infinites - infinite knowledge (*anantajñāna*), infinite perception (*anantadarśana*), infinite power (*anantavīrya*), and infinite bliss (*anantasukha*). After this stage, the seeker of *mokṣa* gets rid of the remaining four kinds of actions *(karmas)* viz. *āyuṣya, nāma, gotra and antarāya* and gets completely liberated. When all these actions are destroyed the soul goes upwards.

In the liberated state, the body, senses and mind remain absent since there does not remain any adjunct (*upādhi*) in the form of actions (*karma*). Hence the liberated soul enjoys eternal, un-obstructed and transcendental bliss. Mādhavācārya explains[2] the Jaina view by saying that at the time of the attainment of *mokṣa* all future actions get dissolved since all the causes of bondage like false perception etc., are destroyed and

---

1. *Tadanantaramūrdhvam gachatyālokāntāt. Tattvārthasūtra,* X.1; *Sarva-Darśana Saṅgraha of Mādhavāchārya,* p.77.
2. Ibid.

all past actions get abolished in the presence of the causes of *nirjara*,. There arises the absolute release from all actions and the soul rises upwards not returning to his mental world afterwards. So *mokṣa* is said to be eternal upward movement. In liberation the soul goes upwards, because of the momentum due to its previous activity, the non-existence of the relation to the elements which kept it down, breaking of the bondage, and its natural tendency to go upwards.

Ānandabodha very briefly sets aside the Jaina view. The constant upward going of *Jīva* is impossible since the *Jīva* is, in reality, all-pervasive (*vibhu*) and omnipresent. Because of eternal and all-pervasive nature of *Brahman* the characterisation of the upward going or movement does not hold good. This theory simply causes labour or striving (*āyāsa*) and hence does not stand to reason, says Ānandabodha.

(B) The Mādhyamika Theory

Ānandabodha criticises the theory of *mokṣa* postulated by the Mādhyamika, a Buddhist heterodox idealistic school propounded by Nāgārjuna (200 A.D.) and his followers like Candrakīrti and others. This school propagates *mokṣa* (emancipation) as the annihilation of uninterrupted stream of cognition (*vijñāna*) defiled by the defects like the incessant birth and affilictions like passion, malice and delusion (*uttarādhārabhāvena nirantarotpādakleśādidoṣadūṣitabodha santativicchedalakṣṇo mokṣa*, NM. p.270)

Quoting from the Buddhist texts *Prasannapādavyākhyā* on *Mādhyamikaśāstram* of Nāgārjuna, Ānandabodha explains that according to Mādhyamika, *mokṣa* is the absolute annihilation of the stream of cognitions like the extinction of a lamp (*pradīpa*).

In the Mādhyamika literature such as *Mādhyamikaśāstra*, also called *Mūlamādhyamikakārikā*, and the commentary thereon called *Prasannapādavyākhyā*, *mokṣa*[1] is termed *nirvāṇa*. It consists of the annihilation of all cognitions of the flow of the stream of *kleśa, karma, janma* etc. As long as the stream of *vijñānas* continues, *nirvāṇa* is unattainable, since it results after the cessation of all cognitions (NM. p.270).

Ānandabodha refutes this view by arguing that the annihilation of the streams of cognitions as *mokṣa* cannot be the highest goal of human beings. If it is supposed to be the highest goal (*paramapuruṣārtha*) then it is with reference to whom? asks Ānandabodha. Only two alternatives are possible. Either it may be in case of men who have the stream of cognitions or in the case of the stream of cognitions themselves (*santāninām pūruṣārtha kiṁ vā santānasya*). The first alternative is unsound since those who have the stream of cognitions (*bodhasantati*) are, according to Mādhyamika school, momentary selves continuously perishing and arising, and hence there cannot be any relation between these fleeting selves and *nirvāṇa* (*na tāvat santāninām, teṣām svarasaparinirvāṇena mokṣaphalasambandhābhāvād*). Neither second alternative is correct, for the stream of cognitions (*vijñānasantati or bodhasantati*), according to this school, is of the nature of self. Thus, the annihilation of the stream of cognitions will amount to the destruction of the dearest self *(Ātman)*. One's destruction or self-destruction cannot be one's highest goal. It is not proper to accept the stream of cognitions other than the persons, having the stream of cognition to whom *bandha* and *mokṣa* can be attributed. Secondly, in that case there

1. *Tatra niravaśeṣasyāvidyārāgādikasya kleśagaṇasya prahāṇātsopadhiśeṣam nirbāṇamiṣyate. Prasannapāda* Commentary on MK. p.519.

does not remain any enjoyer of the fruit i.e. *mokṣa*. Without him there cannot be any reward i.e. *mokṣa* at all, says Ānandabodha (NM. pp.271-274).

(C) The Yogācāra Theory

The Yogācāra school of Buddhism propounded by Aśvaghoṣa and his followers maintain that *mokṣa* or *nirvāṇa* is the origination of the stream of pure cognitions devoid of the obstacles in the form of objects and acquired by the intensity of concentration (NM. p.270). The intrinsic *vijñāna* which is said to be the absolute reality becomes impure by the dispositions of the actions (*anādikarmavāsanā*) and appears in the form of external objects that have no real existence; when the *anādikarmavāsanās* cease by the intensity of concentration (*bhāvanāprakarṣa*), the pure cognition (*viśuddhavijñāna*) arises and the appearance of externality (*bāhyarūpa*) disappears. This origination of pure cognition, according to the Yogācāra system, is *mokṣa* otherwise called *nirvāṇa*. The Yogācāra account of *mokṣa* is unacceptable according to Ānandabodha. For *vijñāna* (consciousness) according to this school, is not permanent. Since the cognitions or consciousness (*pūrvaparavijñānas*) arise and perish, the transitoriness of the *vijñānas* is proved. Hence it cannot be the highest goal of the human beings. Secondly, the stream of pure consciousness cannot be itself the human goal (*puruṣārtha*) as it amounts to the denial of *puruṣārtha* for a man who endeavours to acheive it. If the stream of cognitions (*cittasantati*) would be said to be *puruṣārtha* (highest goal) and also existent at the time of *mokṣa* then, the existence of miseries (*duḥkha*) is to be accepted in the state of *mokṣa* since misery originates because of the dispositions of attachments (*rāgādivāsanā*) caused by the impressions of the transmigratory world (*saṁsāravāsanā*). As long as the transmigratory impression (*saṁsāravāsanā*) does not cease in entirety there cannot be absolute annihilation of the *rāgādivāsanā* (dispositions of attachment) etc. As a result of the presence of *saṁsāravāsanā*, *rāgādivāsanā* will continue and it will further lead to the transmigratory world *(saṁsāra)*, and consequently, *mokṣa* would be impossible, contends Ānandabodha (NM. p.274).

5.2 Orthodox Schools

A) The Sāṁkhya Theory

The classical Sāṁkhya system expounds the theory of *mokṣa* as the existence of *puruṣa* in its pure form after the discrimination. (NM. p .270). According to this system, *mokṣa* is only phenomenal, since bondage does not belong to *puruṣa*. Bondage and release refer to the conjunction and the disjunction of *puruṣa* and *prakṛti* resulting from non-discrimination (*viveka*). *Prakṛti* does not bind the *puruṣa* but itself in various ways (SK. 62). *Puruṣa* is entirely free from the opposition of merits and demerits. While bondage is the activity of *prakṛti* towards one not possesing discrimination, *mokṣa* is its inactivity towards one possesing discrimination (SK. 61). On release the *puruṣa* unmoved and self-collected as a spectator contemplates *prakṛti*. But *viparyaya* is said to be *dharma* of *buddhi*, attribute of intellect, the first evolute of *prakṛti* (primordial nature) which has two forms, viz., *sāttvika* and *tāmasika;* the former consists of *dharma, jñāna, vairāgya* and *aiśvarya* and the latter comprises of *adharma, ajñānā* or *viparyaya, rāga, and anaiśvarya.*

The Sāṁkhya view is not tenable, asserts Ānandabodha for the following reasons :-

This view of the Sāṁkhya is not logical. For *mokṣa* should be the cessation of the bondage of a person who is bound by *viparyaya* etc. A person who has no bondage and is totally free cannot attain *mokṣa* for other *puruṣa* who is in bondage. If it would happen it would lead to contradiction which is found in the Sāṁkhya theory of *mokṣa*. The Sāṁkhya holds *viparyaya* or *ajñāna* as the cause of bondage which is a *dharma* of *buddhi,* not *dharma* of *puruṣa* (NM. p.282).

The existence of *puruṣa* in its pure nature is bereft of the experience of the supreme bliss (*paramānandānubhuti*). There cannot be manifestation of the supreme bliss in the state of *mokṣa* since *puruṣa* has been characterised as witness, indifferent and neutral. The final beatitude being devoid of the experience of bliss cannot be the highest goal of human beings (NM. p.282).

According to the Sāṁkhya, *viparyaya* (false knowledge or non-discrimination) between *Puruṣa* and *Prakṛti* is the cause of bondage. Iśvarakṛṣṇa iṇ his *Sāṁkhyakārikā* quoted by Ānandabodha, contends that *viparyāyāt iṣyate bandhaḥ* (one undergoes *bandha* because of *viparyaya*). *Viparyaya* is said to be *dharma* of *buddhi* (attributes of intellect), the first evolute of *prakṛti* (primordial nature) which has two forms-*sāttvika* and *tāmasika,* the former consists of *dharma, jñāa, vairāgya* and *aiśvarya* and the latter comprises of *adharma, ajñāna* or *viparyaya, rāga, and anaiśvarya* (NM.pp.282-283).

It is illogical, for *mokṣa* should be the cessation of the bondage of a person who is bound by *avidyā* etc. A person who has no bondage is totally free cannot get *mokṣa* for other *puruṣa* who is in bondage. If it would happen, it will lead to contradiction which is found in the Sāṁkhya account of *mokṣa*. The Sāṁkhya holds *viparyaya,* or *ajñāna,* as cause of bondage, which is a *dharma* of *buddhi,* since it is pure by nature. Hence *puruṣa* cannot have *bandha* and *mokṣa* by *viparyaya,* on the contrary, *buddhi* should have *bandha* and *mokṣa*. To advocate *puruṣa's bandha* because of *viparyaya* considering it as *dharma* of *buddhi* is contradictory, since it amounts to imprisonment of a saint corresponding to *buddhi* and release of a theif i.e. *buddhi* for the merit of a saint i.e. *puruṣa*.

The Sāṁkhya system upholds that *baṇdha* and *mokṣa* are attributed to *puruṣa* figuratively (*upacārāt*) but these two in reality belong to *prakṛti*. The *puruṣa* does not undergo bondage and *mokṣa* but it is *prakṛti* which is bound and gets liberated.

Ānandabodha quotes the *Sāṁkhyakārikā* of Iśvarakṛṣṇa who advocates *aupacārikabandha* and *mokṣa* of *puruṣa*, and rejects this view of the Sāṁkhya by arguing that false attribution of *bandha* and *mokṣa* is illogical since there is no occasioning reason (*nimittakāraṇa*) for this *upacāra*. The relation between *puruṣa* and *prakṛti* called *svasvāmibhāva* (*puruṣa* being the lord of *prakṛti*) cannot be the cause (*nimitta*) of this false attribution since *puruṣa* has been characterised by the Sāṁkhya as indifferent (*udāsīna*). No such example is available wherein a throughly indifferent person becomes the lord, (*svāmi*), on the other hand, it is found that kings who are the lords of their servants are not *udāsīna* but quite active and interested in controlling their subordinates. The *puruṣa* in the Sāṁkhya being indifferent cannot be the lord of *prakṛti* who renders her sevices as a servant for the experience of joy and sorrow of *puruṣa* and causes to act for *puruṣa* in *mokṣa*. And in case of the relation master and servant, the servants become helpful, but according to the Sāṁkhya system *buddhi* cannot render any help to *puruṣa* who is intrinsically pure (*nirmala*) by nature (NM. p.289).

Moreover, the Sāṁkhya system compares *prakṛti* with a dancer (*nartakī*). This comparision of *prakṛti* with *nartakī* is not logical, says Ānandabodha. For a dancer exhibits her performances on the stage in dramatic representations and makes her performances attractive by display of love and other passions and in this way creates pleasure in the minds of spectators. But *buddhi* i.e. *prakṛti* of the Sāṁkhya does not do any such kinds of things for *puruṣa* since the latter does not need any such thing (*anupakāryatvāt*) (NM. p.284). A dancer also cannot give happiness to a person who does not take interest to see her performance (*adidṛkṣu*). On the other hand those who are in need of happiness look at dancer and do all kinds of efforts for happiness, and hence are not *udāsīna* (indifferent) like the *puruṣa* of the Sāṁkhya system.

Further, *prakṛti* is not fit (*yogya*) to be seen by *puruṣa* because if seen by the latter then he must see it perenially (NM. p.285). It cannot be argued that only the *puruṣa* in the *saṁsāra* (migratory state) sees the *prakṛti* while the liberated ones do not, since the same blue object cannot be said to be fit being seen by others. Moreover, without accepting some sort of difference in the *puruṣa* the difference in their fitness (*yogyatā*) cannot be granted. Above all *yogyatā* (fitness) is the power of action. In case of the *Sāṁkhyapuruṣa* who is intrinsically pure is incapable of any addition (*anādyatiśaya*), even the action of observing something is impossible in his case (NM. p.206).

Thus, *prakṛti* cannot be the object and fit for observation of the *puruṣa*. Hence *prakṛti* cannot be compared with the *nartakī* who performs on the stage and is perceived by spectactors. It is, therefore, reasonable to say that *prakṛti* is in no way helpful (*upakāriṇī*) to *puruṣa* and the relation of a master and a servant cannot exist between the *prakṛti* and the *puruṣa* (NM. p.286).

Ānandabodha further asks if there would be any relation existing between *prakṛti* and *puruṣa* then whether it is different from these two i.e. *puruṣa* and *prakṛti*, or identical with them? It cannot be said to be different from them since the Sāṁkhya accepts only two basic eternal principles, *prakṛti* and *puruṣa* and this relation would be third principle. If the relation between *prakṛti* and *puruṣa* is said to be identical, it would exist as long as both the *prakṛti* and the *puruṣa* would exist and as a result, *mokṣa* would be impossible. The Sāṁkhya view,viz., *prakṛti* acts for the enjoyment *(upabhoga)* and emancipation *(apavarga)* of the *puruṣa* is absurd since there are only two positions possible; either the *prakṛti* would act only once, supply the objects of sense organs like sound and the like to the *puruṣa* and afterwards it would be inactive. If it goes on acting, there would be no end for her activity. In both the cases *mokṣa* cannot take place. Hence it cannot be said that the activity of the *prakṛti* has for its purpose only the enjoyment as well as *mokṣa* of *puruṣa*.

The Sāṁkhya further says that as grass and water consumed by the cow become transformed into milk and nourish the calf and as these cease to function after the nourishment of the calf so does the *prakṛti* functions for the *mokṣa* of the *puruṣa* (SK 57; NM. p.287). Ānandabodha like Bādarayāṇa counteracts this view by saying that *prakṛti* being insentient (*jaḍa*) cannot make any distinction between a liberated person and other; nor can she supply objects for the enjoyment to the *puruṣa* or secure *mokṣa* for the *puruṣa* (SK 57; NM.p.287).

(B) The Nyāya-Vaiśeṣika Theory

According to the Nyāya-Vaiśeṣika school *mokṣa* consists in the existence of the individual self (*Ātman)* in its essential nature after the cessation of all special qualities *(navānām ātmaguṇānām buddhisukhaduḥkh- ecchā-dveṣaprayatnadharmādharmasaṁskārāṇām nirmūlocche-dopavargaḥ*. NM. p.508; VS. V.2.18.) like consciouness (*buddhi*), *sukha* (pleasure) etc. (NM. p.270). Gautama (400

A.D.) expounds the nature of *mokṣa* in his *sūtra, tadatyantavimokṣo'pavargaḥ* (NS. 1.1.22), (*mokṣa* is absolute cessation of misery). While commenting on the *sūtra* Vātsyāyana (600 A.D.) defines *mokṣa* as the condition of immortality, free from fear and imperishable. Jayanta referring to the above said *sūtra* in his *Nyāyamañjarī* opines that pronoun "*tat*" (that) in the *sūtra* denotes pain as well as all the nine special qualities of the soul and the adverb *atyanta* (absolute) conveys the sense of absolute cessation of these qualities. In the statement of Jayanta Bhaṭṭa one can see the synthesis of the Nyāya-Vaiśeṣika view about the nature of *mokṣa*.

The Nyāya-Vaiśeṣika view is not reasonable, asserts Ānandabodha, for, in the state of *mokṣa*, the absolute annihilation of all the special qualities like *buddhi* (consciousness) etc., is advocated by the Nyāya-Vaiśeṣika school. Because of the annihilation of all the qualities of the *Ātman, sukha* (delight), which is the quality of the *Ātman* also gets destroyed. This is actually not the real highest goal since every person strives for the attainment of highest *sukha* (joy) only in the attainment of *mokṣa*. (NM. pp.275-276).

Secondly, since the fruit of *mokṣa* is not the experience of the supreme bliss and one experiences misery in its achievement, Nyāya-Vaiśeṣika concept of *mokṣa* cannot be the object of endeavour of human beings. An intelligent person, says Ānandabodha, should not endeavour to achieve such a goal which ends with unhappiness. No person acts for the cessation of misery but for the experience of bliss, for example, the action for the removal of the pain with regard to the piercing of thorn is for the experience of the delight of relief from pain (NM. p.276).

Thirdly, the cessation of misery cannot be cognised because of the annihilation of *buddhi*, attribute of *Ātman*.

Hence the state of *mokṣa* not being cognised is identical with unconscious state (*murcchāvasthā)* (NM. p.277).

It is unsound to hold the view that *duḥkhābhāva* (absence of misery), not being cognised, can be *mokṣa* like the *duḥkhābhāva* at the time of dreamless sleep (*suṣupti*), for, there is no means of knowledge *(pramāṇa)* to cognise the absence of cognition in the time of dreamless sleep. The absence of anything is cognised by cognition, but the absence of cognition cannot be cognised by cognition itself. If the absence of cognition (*samvedanābhāva*) is said to be cognised by cognition, then it cannot be said that there is the absence of all cognitions. Further, the connection or relation of the *(liṅga)* with the absence of all cognitions cannot be cognised. Therefore in the time of dreamless sleep the absence of all cognitions cannot be determined by inference (*anumāna*). Moreover, the recollection *(smṛti)* determines the cognition of happiness in the dreamless state (NM. p.277-278).

Thus, the Nyāya concept of *mokṣa* viz., absence of the experience of delight (*ānanda*) is like the annihilation of one's own self. Hence Nyāya-Vaiśeṣika account of *mokṣa* does not stand to reason.

(C) The Vaiṣṇava Theory

Ānandabodha sets forth the Vaiṣṇava theory of *mokṣa*. According to this theory, *mokṣa* is the acquisition of an imperishable body (*akṣayaśarīralābha*) (NM. p.271).

Ānandabodha sets aside this view by arguing that the ultimate goal of human being has been characterised as a non-eternal state (*anityāvasthā*). The acquisition of imperishable body (*akṣayaśarīra*) is non-eternal and would be destroyed for being an effect (*kārya*) as that of physical bodies of human beings. And, no alternative means can be adopted to save the unavoidable destruction of the physical body. Hence this kind of *mokṣa* cannot be the highest goal of life as it is perishable by nature (NM. p.281).

(D) The Prābhākara Theory

According to the Prābhākara school, *mokṣa* consists in the disappearance of all merits and demerits resulting from actions. It is on account of merit and demerit accruing to the soul, it is born in the physical body; consequently when all merits and demerits disappear, there remains nothing that could lead the soul to be born again in a body; and when the soul ceases to have connection with the bodies, and hence also with the sense organs, etc. all its metapsychic troubles end and it is free and liberated.[1] As to how all this comes about, the following explanation have been provided. First of all the man becomes disgusted with the troubles that he has to undergo during his life on the earth; finding the pleasures of the world also to be invariably accompanied by some sort of pain, he comes to lose all interest in and longing for pleasures also; he thereupon turns his attention towards *mokṣa;* he ceases to perform such acts which are prohibited and which lead to trouble and also those that are prescribed as leading to some sort of happiness here or hereafter, he all previously acquired from them; he destroys the sole receptacle or abode of his experience by the knowledge of the soul, as sided by qualities as contenment, self-control and so forth, all of which are laid down in the scriptures as tending to put a stop to the further return of the soul into this mortal world; it is only

1. *Ātyantikastu dehocchedo niḥśeṣadharmādharma parikṣayanibandhano mokṣaḥ. Tayorekāntocchede pyapagatadehendriyasambandhaḥ samutkhātanikhilasāṁsārika-duḥkhabandhano mukta ityucyate.* PP.156.

when all this has come to an end the soul becomes liberated.

Ānandabodha sets aside this view by saying that absolute destruction of the physical body is not possible unless *avidyā* completely ceases with its effects. The complete destruction of the body cannot take place after the absolute annihilation of merit and demerit (*dharma* and *adharma*) which is impossible without the realisation of non-dual *Ātman*. Unless there is complete destruction of the storage of the actions (*karmāśaya*) the cycle of birth and death would not come to an end since the *karma* will be effective in the future in the relevant time. The cessation of the cycle of birth and death is impossible because while a person is enjoying the fruit of the past *karmas* the other actions will be performed by him and thus it has no end i.e. *reduct ad absurdum*. Moreover, even if a person desirous of *mokṣa* will not perform the *kāmyakarmas* (obligatory works) still these actions are unavoidable and when these actions will be destroyed by the enjoyment of their fruits other actions would rise up at that time. As a result, the process will continue infinitely. Thus it involves the fault of infinite regress (*anavasthā*) (NM. p.307).

(E) Ānandabodha's Theory

Ānandabodha in his two works, viz., *Pramāṇamālā* and *Nyāyamakaranda* (pp.288-289), after making a thorough criticism and refutation of the opponents' views as discussed above, defines the essential nature of *mokṣa*, the supreme ideal of life (*paramapuruṣārtha*). Like Śaṅkara[1] and his successors (Bṛ. Up. BV I. 4. 303. II. 1. 1., II.4.88; *Naiṣkarmyasiddhi*, I.7. *ekātmyapratipattiryā svātmānubhavasaṁśrayā sāvidyā samṛtebījam tannāśo*

1. *Brahmabhāvaśca mokṣaḥ*, BSŚB I.1.4; *Phalam ca mokṣo'vidyā nivṛttirvā*, Bṛh. Up ŚB on I.1.7.

muktirātmaḥ). He puts forth the view that mokṣa (emancipation) is the manifestation of eternal, supreme, unsurpassed noumenon bliss and the elimination of all pains along with complete cessation of effects of *avidyā*[1].

When the *Jīvātman* realises his real blissful nature, the manifestation of the eternal, pure and Supreme Bliss takes place and three kinds of sorrows, (PM. p.20) viz. *ādhyātmika, ādhibhautika,* ānd *ādhidaivika,* completely perish. The *Jīvātam* (individual soul) becomes the *Brahman* and remains in his true nature i.e. the nature of transempirical bliss as stated in the Upaniṣadic texts[2]. Hence Ānandabodha maintains that *mokṣa* consists of the realisation of the non-dual *Brahman,* or the intuition of one supreme intelligence that is beyond all duality and misery.

Quoting from the *Brahmasiddhi*[3] of Maṇḍana Miśra Ānandabodha aptly points out that *mokṣa* (emancipation) in the Advaita philosophy is nothing but the absolute removal of nescience or ignorance *(avidyānivṛtti) (aśeṣa avidyānivṛttirniśśreyasamiti*) NM. p.289). As one, non-dual, without a second *Brahman* whose essential nature is self-luminous (*svayaṁprakāśa*) and unsurpassed supreme bliss (*anatiśayānanda*) appears as dual (*sadvītiyamiva*), individuated, by worldly objects (*sāṁsārikadharmakaluṣitamiva*) with the appellation of *Jīva* (individual soul) through the agency of the beginningless nescience (NM. p.288). Thus, the beginningless nes-

---

1. *Nityaniratiśayasukhābhivyaktirniḥśeṣa duḥkhac-chedalaksaṇo mokṣaḥ sa āvidyāstamayaḥ,* NM. p.288, 289, PM. p.20.
2. *Brahmaveda Brahmaiva bhavati. Muṇḍ* Up.III.2.9; Iśa Up.7 BS.V.20; XIII.30; *ānando Brahmeti vyajānāt,* Tai, Up.3.6.
3. *Avidyāstamayo mokṣaḥ sa saṁsāra udāhṛtā / vidyaiva cādvayāśānta tadastamaya ucyate // Brahmasiddhi, Niyogakāṇḍa,* Verse, 106, p.119; NM.p.271, 289; PM.p.20.21.

cience or ignorance is itself mundane existence (*saṁsāra*) and *mokṣa* is the extinction of *avidyā* brought out by the dawn of the highest knowledge of the Supreme Self called *Paramātman* or *Brahman* (NM. p.289).

Ānandabodha explaining the point more clearly says that the sorrows or misery (*duḥkhas*) are not natural to the *Ātman* (PM. p.20) but the effects (*kāryas*) of *avidyā,* the material cause of the world-illusion. Unless and until the cause of misery i.e. *avidyā* is not completely dispelled, there cannot be annihilation of misery and manifestation of eternal supreme bliss. Hence the cessation of nescience (*avidyānivṛtti*) is the manifestation of the highest bliss, (*tasmāt avidyānivṛttirevānatiśaya-sukhābhivyaktiraśeṣānarthanirvṛttiśceti gīyate* PM. p.20).

Thus, Ānandabodha repudiates the prima facie theories of *mokṣa* put forward by the heterodox and orthodox schools, Jaina, Buddhist Mādhyamika, Yogācāra and Sāṁkhya, Nyāyā-Vaiśeṣika, Vaiṣṇava, and the Prābhākara of Pūrva-Mīmāṁsā.

He establishes the Advaita theory of *mokṣa* as postulated by the renowned Advaita preceptors like Maṇḍana with the help of scriptural statements and valid logical reasoning.

5.3 The means of Mokṣa

Like Śaṅkara[1] and his followers[2] Ānandabodha in his *Pramāṇamālā* and *Nyāyamakaranda* upholds the view that the path to *mokṣa* lies in and through knowledge, (*jñāna*) i.e. the final immediate intuition of the non-difference of the individual soul from the Supreme soul, *Brahman.* Since *mokṣa* has been stated as a state of

1. *Īśvarasvarūpāparijñānād bandhastatsvarūpaparijñānāttu mokṣaḥ / tatha ca śrutiḥ - jñātvā deve sarvapāsāpahāniḥ* ....BSŚB III.2.5; III.4.1,
2. *Bhāmatī,* III.3.34; III.4.6

avidyānivṛtti (cessation of nescience), only way to the attainment of his highest goal (*paramapuruṣārtha*) is the *Brahman* intuition (PM. p.20, NM.pp.288- 89) as the *avidyā* (ignorance) which is the root of all the imperfections and ills of the world can be destroyed only by knowledge (*jñāna*), not by any other means.

Ānandabodha further maintains that *mokṣa* which is the goal to be reached by the *ātmavidyā* or *ātmajnāna* is not directly or indirectly connected with *karma* or *kriyā*. The fruit of *karma* (action) is *dharma* which could be secured by following faithfully the injunctions of the śāstras and by avoiding *adharma* (demerit) as described in the scriptures. The fruit of *karma* (action) admits of increase, decrease or excess. The fruit of *ātmajñāna* is only the removal of obstacles in the way of the acquisition of *mokṣa* which is always the same, partless and changeless etc. There is no question about excess, refinement, special form of worship in the case of *mokṣa* which is just the *Jīva's* own nature when the screen put up by *avidyā* is removed with its effects.

Thus, *mokṣa* being the cessation of nescience (*avidyānivṛtti*) *karma* has no role to play directly in its achievement[1] (NM. p.336; PM. p.21). Ānandabodha proves this fact by the following example. As in the worldly state the perception of the reality of a piece of shell does not dispel the illusion of silver in its substratum and in dispelling illusions requires the help of some other thing similarly without the intuition of the ultimate reality nescience or illusory notions existing in the minds of individual souls regarding the nature of the *Brahman*, the Supreme self, is not destroyed by *karma* (actions). Thus, following the worldly occurences

---

1. *Avidyāstamayo mokṣa iti tāvat samarthitam/ tena mokṣabhupā yatvam vidyayā na tu karmaṇām//* NM. p.336; PM p.21.

it is proper to say, according to Ānandabodha, *Brahman*-intuition *(brahmāvagati)* is the cause of the removal of the *avidyā* which is beginningless *(anādi)* and indefinable *(anirvacanīya)*. Ānandabodha quotes numerous texts[1] from the *Upaniṣads* and *smṛti* texts for providing the validity of his view, i.e. knowledge *(jñāna)* as the sole means to final beatitude. Ānandabodha further maintains that the *smṛti* texts which apparently go against the assertions made by the scriptural statements should somehow be interpreted in accordance with the scriptural texts. If these texts are unable to be interpreted accordingly they are to be rejected because they cannot be opposed to the scripture. (NM. pp.351-352). Thus, Ānandabodha proves by the scripture and logical reasoning that intuition of non-duality is the only means to release and not again an iota of action (*tasmāt jñānamevaikam mokṣasādhanam, na punaḥ karma leśopiti siddham* (NM. p.352).

Ānandabodha refuting the validity of *karma* as a means of *mokṣa* in the way mentioned above proceeds to set aside the doctrine of *Jñāna-karma samuccaya* (combination of the knowledge with action). In the history of the philosophical literature the doctrine of *samuccaya* (combination of the knowledge and action as a means) is famous and accepted by some outstanding pre-Śaṅkara Advaita philosophers like Brahamadatta[2], Bhartṛprapañca[3] and Maṇḍana Miśra[4] respectively.

Śaṅkara was the strongest opponent to this doctrine of *samuccaya* and in his commentaries on the

1. *Na karmṇā na prajayā dhanena/ etāvadare khalaamṛtatvam/ Kaivalyopaniṣad,* p.3; Iśa. p.10 NM.p.337
2. Pandeya Murlidhara, *Śrīśaṅkarātprāgadvaitavāda,* p.279.
3. *Ibid*. p.165.
4. *Brahamasiddhi,* p.245, 248.

Prasthānatraya succintly repudiates this philosophical tenet by means of tenable logical arguments. Like Śaṅkara Ānandabodha does not favour this doctrine of *samuccaya* and hence attempts its refutation in his words, by presenting the *pūrvapakṣa* view as follows:

Though in the *śruti* and *smṛti* texts action (*karma*) as the means of *mokṣa* has been refuted still the *samuccaya* (conjunction) of *jñana* (knowledge) and *karma* (action) has been favoured or sanctioned. For example, the text of the *Iśāvāṣyopaniṣad* i.e. *jñānādeva ca kaivalyam prāpyate yena mucyate/ karmaṇā badhyate janturvidyayā ca vimucyate,* says that action in conjunction with knowledge is the cause of *mokṣa* (NM. p.338). The other texts of the *Upaniṣads* also support the said text,[1] i.e. both knowledge and action on account of their different effects are useful for *mokṣa*. As *mokṣa* is the cessation of transmigration and the attainment of *Brahman,* there is utility of *karma* (action) for the cessation of transmigration and the utility of knowledge lies in the removal of *avidyā*. As *Brahman* being *jīvātman* is always attained but it is hidden by *avidyā* alone like the ornament round the neck (NM. p.339). There are other texts which clearly advocate this view. Thus, scriptural statements which refute validity of action refer to action alone, not action without collaboration of knowledge. And the sentences mentioning conjunction mean that one of them is the direct cause and the other indirect like the plough and the food for the satisfaction i.e. food is the direct cause of satisfaction and the plough is the indirect cause. In the same way knowledge is the direct cause of *mokṣa* and *karma* is indirect cause for the acquisition of knowledge through the removal of sins (NM. p.341).

---

1. *BG. V.II; 10; Manusmṛti XII, 104.*

Ānandabodha refutes this by saying that if *mokṣa* is to be achieved by action, it would be non-eternal like any other worldly object. The collaboration between the knower of *Brahman* and the doer of virtuous actions is only on the path of attainment. Ānandabodha quotes that *Brahmasūtra*[1]. to substantiate his view that the individual souls are led to *saguṇabrahman* for it occupies a place to which souls may go but not to *nirguṇabrahman* since it is all-pervading. With the highest *Brahman* the ideas of one who goes or the object of going or act of going cannot be connected for that *Brahman* is present everywhere and is the inner-self of all. This view has been expounded by Bādari, a pre-Śaṅkara Advaitin. Thus Ānandabodha proves that *karma* is useful only on the way of preparation for the attainment of the Supreme beatitude, but the efficacy of ritualistic actions is not for the removal of nescience which is the highest goal of human being. It is only highest intuition (*brahmāvagati* or *brahamasākṣātkāra*) which is able to eradicate the binding and blinding *avidyā* and by that way illuminating the essential nature of noumenal Reality.

1. *Kāryam Bādharirasya gatyupapatteḥ/* BS. IV. 3.7.

CHAPTER VI

PREDECESSORS AND SUCCESSORS

This chapter contains the discussion of predecessors and successors of Ānandabodha. It has been shown how Ānandabodha quotes from the prominent texts of his predecessors and how he borrows their arguments in favour of his defence and refutation. In the same way Ānandabodha's influence on his sucessors, both Advaitin as well as non-Advaitin has been discussed in this chapter.

Ānandabodha's outstanding works, viz., *Nyāyadīpikā*, *Nyāyadīpāvali*, *Pramāṇamālā* and *Nyāyamakaranda* bear ample evidence to his thorough knowledge with the vast field of Sanskrit literature. He was well-versed in the Vedic texts, Upaniṣads, *Bhagavad Gītā*, *Brahamasūtra* of Bādarāyaṇa and the texts of his prominent predecesors like Gauḍapāda, Śaṅkara etc., as well as the *Nyāyabhaṣya* of Vātsyāyana, *Yogasūtra* of Patañjali and many other celebrated works. In his works Ānandabodha mainly quotes the statements of *Prasthānatraya* and *Smṛti* texts in order to prove the logical validity of the Advaitic doctrines propounded by his predecessors like Śaṅkarācārya, Maṇḍanācārya and others. To eradicate the philosophical theories postulated by the antagonistic schools like Jaina, Buddhist,

Sāṅkhya-Yoga, Nyāya-Vaiśeṣika Prābhākara and Bhāṭṭa Mīmāṁsā schools.

Jaina

Ānandabodha refers to two main doctrines advocated by the Jaina schools. These are: the size or dimension of the soul as that of the physical body and the upward movement of the soul as the conception of *mokṣa*.

Buddhism

Ānandabodha has also refutes the tenets of the Buddhist thinkers, mainly, the propounders of the two prominent schools, viz., Mādhyamika and Yogācāra (nihilism and uncompromising idealism) of the Mahāyāna stream of Buddhism. He puts forth as his *pūrvapakṣa* the well-known doctrines, viz., the doctrine of momentariness (*kṣaṇikavijñānavāda*), the doctrine of error known as *ātmakhyāti* and the doctrine of *nirvāṇa* advocated by the Yogācāra school whose main expounders are Aśvaghoṣa (100 A.D.) and his followers like Asaṅga (400 A.D.), the author of the celebrated work *Mahāyānasūtrālaṁkāra*. But in his work *Nyāyamakaranda* Ānandabodha does not directly or indirectly indicate the name of the text nor the author to whom he refers. Since the tenets are very well-known in the philosophical domain they are easily identified as those of the *Buddhist* philosophers as it is done by Citsukhācārya in his commentary. Similarly Ānandabodha criticises the main doctrines of Mādhymika which are: the *asatkhyātivāda* (the theory of non-beings apprehension) and the *nirvāṇa* (emancipation). Apart from these, Ānandabodha also quotes from the Buddhist works, viz., *Mūlamādhyamika Kārikā* of Nāgārjuna and *Pramaṇavārttika* of Dhrmakīrti. Though Ānandabodha criticises their doctrines from the Advaitic point of view nevertheless he faithfully and accurately sets them forth in his *Nyāyamakaranda*.

Sāṁkhya School

In his work *Nyāyamakaranda* Ānandabodha like Śaṅkara takes up the Sāṁkhya system as his *pradhānamalla* and devotes a number of pages to refute its two main doctrines, viz., the diversity of *puruṣa* (souls) and the nature of final emancipation (*mokṣa*). The views set forth and refuted by Ānandabodha seems to be of the classical Sāṁkhya propounded by Īśvarakṛṣṇa, author of the locus classicus *Sāṁkhyakārikā* from which a number of verses are quoted by Ānandabodha.

Nyāya-Vaiśeṣika School

Ānandabodha is also indebted to the Nyāya-Vaiśeṣika thinkers like Vātsyāyana, Jayanta Bhaṭṭa and Śrīdhara. In his *Nyāyamakaranda* and *Pramāṇamālā* Ānandabodha criticises the Nyāya-Vaiśeṣika views, viz., the diversity of the *Ātman* (individual self), the doctrine of extrinsic validity of knowledge (*parataḥprāmāṇyavāda*) and the doctrine of *mokṣa* (emancipation). These views have been faithfully presented and aptly refuted from Advaitic point of view by Ānandabodha. To substantiate his own Advaitic position he quotes from Vātsyāyana's *Nyāyabhāṣya* on the *Nyāyasūtra* of Gautama. He also quotes the Nyāya and Vaiśeṣika *sūtras* while he puts forth the Nyāya-Vaiśeṣika views as his *pūrvapakṣa*.

Though Ānandabodha does not quote directly in some cases from the works of Gauḍapāda and Śaṅkara it is clearly evinced that he has adopted their philosophical tenets. In this connection it is significant to note that *Nyāyadīpāvali* is an important independent work dealing with the unreality of the world in support of which Ānandabodha has quoted the syllogism of Śaṅkara on *Kārikā* of Gauḍapāda (II.4).

Ānandabodha is also highly indebted to Maṇḍana Miśra who, according to outstanding scholars like Hiriyanna, Sangamlal Pandey, is different from Sureśvarācārya, the immediate follower of Śaṅkarācārya. Ānandabodha profusely quotes from the *Brahmasiddhi* of Maṇḍana, designated by him Ācārya in his works. Besides, Ānandabodha in his *Nyāyamakaranda* makes serious efforts in defending Maṇḍana's views and to defend them which are refuted by Śālikanātha in his *Prakaraṇapañcikā*. Sangamlal Pandey in his book has beautifully noted this fact. Unlike his predecessors mainly Sarvajñātman, Prakāśātman, and Vimuktātman, Ānandabodha not only rejects some views of Maṇḍana but he also acclaims some of his prominent theories as discussed in the aforegoing chapters.

Ānandabodha is also indebted to the immediate disciples as Śaṅkarācārya, viz., Padmapāda and Sureśvara. The definition of *mithyātva* (falsity) stated by Padmapāda in his *Pañcapādikā* is stated by Ānandabodha in *Nyāyamakaranda*. Ānandabodha in *Nyāyamakaranda* also indirectly supports the views of Sureśvarācārya who has expounded the theories regarding the *Brahman* as the locus and object of *avidyā*.

Ānandabodha is indebted to Maṇḍana's follower Vācaspati Miśra, whom he quotes thrice from his work, *Brahmatattvasamīkṣā*, a commentary on Maṇḍana's *Brahmasiddhi*. Besides, we also find some similar passages in the *Bhāmatī* and *Nyāyamakaranda*. But Ānandabodha refutes Vācaspati's view upholding the individual soul (*Jīva*) as the substratum of *avidyā*.

Apart from this Ānandabodha is also indebted to Vimuktātman and respectfully calls him as *Guru* in the *Nyāyamakaranda*. Ānandabodha also quotes in his

Nyāyamakaranda from the *Vivaraṇa* of Prakāśātman whom he follows faithfully. He has also written a commentary *Śābdanirṇayadīpikā* alias *Nyāyadīpikā* on the *Śābdanirṇaya* of Prakāśātman.

SUCCESSORS

Ānandabodha has exercised considerable influence on his successors. His influence is evident from the reference made to him and his works. The Advaitic authors who came after Ānandabodha had borrowed his arguments to vindicate their positions. The dialectic method, erudite style and forceful logical arguments are the main factors which have influenced his successors to a great extent.

The works of Madhusūdana Sarasvatī reveal that he was highly influenced by Ānandabodha who is very much esteemed by the former who has imitated the style of *Nyāyadīpāvali* of Ānandabodha in writing his *Advaitasiddhi*. Madhusūdana also in the *Advaitasiddhi* (pp.316, 384, 696, 845) refers to numerous arguments from the *Pramāṇamālā* (pp.4-7) and the *Nyāyamakaranda* (p.260) and amplifies them. He also quotes from Ānandabodha's works either to explain or to establish a theory like *Mithyātva* (falsity of the world) or to refute his *pañcamaprakārāvidyānivṛtti vāda* in his *Advaitasiddhi*.

Similarly, Appayya Dīkṣita was highly influenced by Ānandabodha whose doctrine of *Pañcamaprakāra avidyānivṛtti* has been discussed and favoured in his *Siddhāntaleśasaṁgraha*.

Bhāratitīrtha Vidyāraṇya also has borrowed some valuable views regarding the self-luminosity of the *Ātman* from the *Nyāyamakaranda* of Ānandabodha. In his *Vivaraṇaprameyasaṁgraha* (p.85) Vidyāraṇya borrows verbatim a syllogism i.e. *saṁveditā na saṁvidadhīnaprakāśaḥ saṁvitkarmaṇāmantareṇa aparokṣatvāt saṁvedanavat* (NM. p.135).

Likewise Cāndupaṇḍita in his commentary on the *Naiṣadhīyacarıta* has put forth a passage borrowed from the *Nyāyamakaranda*. This indicates that he is very much indebted and influenced by our author. Further, the followers of Rāmānuja's Viśiṣṭādvaita school like Vedānta Deśika in his *Tattvaṭīkā* on *Śrībhāṣya* (p.489) and *Satadūṣanī* refutes the views of Ānandabodha. Sudarshana Bhaṭṭāraka in his *Śrutaprakāśikā* and Rangarāmānujamuni in his *Bhāvaprakāśikā*, the commentators of the *Śrībhāṣya* have also referred and criticised Ānandabodha's views.

Similarly, Vyāsa Tīrtha, the author of *Nyāyāmṛta* and Jaya Tīrtha, ardent advocates of the Dvaita school of Madhva have criticised the views of Ānandabodha with reference to the theory of *mithyātva*, and also borrowed some significant arguments for the refutation of Advaitic view points. These are clear indications regarding the impact of Ānandabodha on his successors.

CHAPTER VII

ĀNANDABODHA'S PHILOSOPHY: A CRITIQUE

This chapter incorporates a critique of Ānandabodha's philosophy.

7.1 Prasthānatraya

Ānandabodha being an Advaita philosopher and a strict follower of Śaṅkara bases his advaitism on the tenets of the *Prasthānatraya,* mainly the principal Upaniṣads which contain some germs of the Advaitism. Idealistic monism adumbrated in the philosophical Upaniṣads and considerably developed as a philosophical system by Śaṅkara was further elaborated by his eminent successors like Ānandabodha and others. The principal doctrines of the *Prasthānatraya* discussed by Ānandabodha are as follows:

The Upaniṣads speak of *parabrahman* which is infinite, eternal,[1] omnipresent, omniscient and one[2] pure spirit as the Ultimate Reality. The *Brahman* is transcendental, non-phenomenal (*nisprapañca*) and being (*sat*), consciousness (*cit*), and bliss (*ānanda*)[3]. The *Brahman* transcends the spatio-temporal order governed by causality. The *Brahman* is the *Ātman*[4] pure universal

1. *Nityam vibhum sarvagatam susūkṣmaṁ.* Muṇḍ, Up. I.1.6.
2. Chā. Up. VI. 2.1; Kaṭh. Up.ii.1.11
3. *Satyaṁ jñānamanantam brahma. Tai.* Up., II.1.1
4. *Ayamātmā sarvānubhuḥ.* Bṛh. Up. II. 5.19.

consciousness, which is the foundation of reality in the Individual selves and the ultimate ground of the universe. It is the pure self-luminous consciousness; the phenomenal world being illumined and manifested by its light. It is the supreme bliss[1] which transcends all the empirical limitations, which are due to the intercourse of the senses and their respective objects. On the whole there is no difference of opinion regarding the nature of the *Brahman* in the texts of *Bhagavadgītā* and *Brahmasūtra*. According to both God is immanent and transcendental Reality which is the source of creation, preservation as well as dissolution of the universe and attaining which there is no return to this mortal world (BG. IV.9.V.17, VIII.15, BS IV.4.22, 1.1.19.).

The Individual Soul (Jīvātman) :

The Individual soul (*Jīvātman*) is different from the body, the sense-organs, *manas* and *buddhi* (intellect). It is the knower (*jñātā*), enjoyer (*bhoktā*) and active agent (*kartā*)[2] and experiences joys and sorrows which are the fruits of its actions. The Individual self with an uncontrolled and impure mind and devoid of discrimination enters into bondage, and as a result undergoes birth and death. When the Individual Self knows it by meditative trance and purges off all its impurities and knows the Supreme Reality it becomes itself *Brahman*.[3]

The Phenomenal World

The *Brahman* is the cause of names and forms of determinate objects. The world which existed in an unmanifest condition in *Brahman* before creation was

1. *Ānandam brahma*. Tai. Up. II.6.1. *Vijñānamānandam brahma*. Bṛh Up. III.9.28; III.7. *Muṇḍ*. III.2.8.
2. Bṛh. Up. III. 1.28 Chā. Up. IV.II.23.
3. Muṇḍa. Up. III.2.9.

made manifest by the latter. The world is permeated by the *Brahman* which is the divine spirit. All creatures[1] come from the *Brahman* as sparks come out from fire, as plants shoot forth on the earth, as hairs spring from a living body, or as threads come out from the body of a spider. The *Brahman* ejects the world out of itself and withdraws it into itself even as a spider ejects out thread out of its own body and withdraws it.[2] The temporal, spatial and causality-bound world is the manifestation of this infinite and eternal spirit.

The Sūtrakāra maintains[3] that the *Brahman* alone with its intrinsic creative power is the material and instrumental cause of the universe. Even as milk turns into curd without any extraneous help so the *Brahman* transforms itself into manifold effects in the world. The universe thus created by him having transcendental reality is empirically real and not illusory or false like the one seen in a dream.[4] *Mokṣa* is freedom from bondage *avidyā* or *māyā*. It is intuitive realisation of infinite, eternal and universal spirit, *Brahman*. *Mokṣa* is becoming *Brahman* (*brahmabhāva*), state of identity (*sāmya or ekatva*) of the Individual Self with the Supreme Self, *Brahman*, a state of eternal peace and indefinable supreme bliss.

Knowledge or *Vidyā* is the supreme means of liberation.[5] One who knows *Brahman* becomes *Brahman*[6] and attains the supreme goal. The *Ātman* or *Brahman*

---

1. Sinha, Jadunatha, HIP. Vol.I. p.11
2. Ibid.
3. BS. I.I.2, 18, II.1.9, II.1.24.
4. BG. II. 2.28, 29.
5. Īśa Up., 9-11; Bṛh Up., IV.4.10; Kaṭh. Up., I.1.6.,I.2.4,5.
6. *Brahmavidāpnoti param.* Tai. Up., II.1. *Sa yo brahma veda brahmaiva bhavati,* Muṇḍ. Up. III.2.9; Bṛh. Up. II.4.5; 4.15; IV. 5.6.

should be seen, heard, reflected and meditated on, because it is the dearest of all and by knowing it the whole world is known. The ontological, epistemological, soteriological and ethical views of the *Prasthānatraya* are duly and fully discussed in the works of Ānandabodha. Though the texts of the *Prasthānatraya* give scope to diverse philosophical doctrines like polytheism, henotheism, monotheism and monism which are considered to be containing the germs of all the orthodox schools of Indian philosophy, Ānandabodha interprets some Upaniṣadic texts keeping in view the monistic idealism of Śaṅkara. Ānandabodha therefore maintains in his works that the *Brahman* is the only transcendental Reality which is one, non-dual, and having the nature of pure consciousness and positive supreme bliss (*paramānanda*). The Individual Self (*Jīvātman*) is not a real entity and hence it has no distinct existence because of being a reflection (*pratibiṁba*) of *Brahman* as that of the moon in the water. *Avidyā or Māyā* is the material cause of the world-illusion. The plurality of the Individual Selves is an illusion which vanishes after the true realisation of the essential nature of the *Brahman*, the Supreme Self. The world has phenomenal Reality only and hence from the point of view of the *Brahman* which has ultimate transcendental Reality it is false (*mithyā*) as the appearance of the objects seen in the state of dream. Since *avidyā* which is indefinable and beginningless in nature is the cause of *Jīvabhāva* of the *Brahman* and the world- illusion, the absolute cessation of nescience (*avidyānivṛtti*) is the supreme goal (*paramapuruṣārtha*) i.e. *mokṣa*. As *mokṣa* is the complete cessation of nescience (*Avidyā*) with its miraculous effects and consequently there takes place realisation of pure supreme bliss. *Karma* (ritualistic action) has utility in purifying the mind of an aspirant of *mokṣa* Thus *karma* is an indirect cause of the supreme beatitude.

These monistic tenets of Ānandabodha are at par with those of the thoughts of the *Prasthānatraya.* He is completely faithful to these texts of the *Prasthānatraya* in interpreting and analysing the monistic observations and expounding the philosophy of Advaita. From this point of view, Ānandabodha's discussion is quite faithful and reasonable.

Ānandabodha, however, in his *Pramāṇamālā* (p.20) identifies the God Viṣṇu with the *Brahman,* the supreme Reality. This is a distinctive feature in the philosophy of Ānandabodha who seems following the BG in this respect. Further, Ānandabodha adds some tenets to his philosophy which are completely new in his thought and not expounded by either the Upaniṣadic thinkers nor the *Gītākāra* nor the *Brahmasūtrakāra,* e.g.*avidyā* as the material cause of the world-illusion, the locus of *avidyā,* the doctrine of *avidyānivṛtti.* In addition to it Ānandabodha also does not discuss some of the important concepts like *Jīvanmukti, Brahmaloka* and the nature of enlightened soul.

7.2 Heterodox Systems

(A) Jaina School

The concept of final liberation (*mokṣa*) and the popular dimension of the *Ātman* upheld by the Jainas are rightly set aside by Ānandabodha in his *Nyāyamakaranda.* Ānandabodha mentions that the dimension of *Jiva* is not possible which is essentially not different from all pervasive *Brahman,* the Supreme Reality.

Secondly, Ānandabodha presents Jaina theory of *mokṣa* as the continuous upward movement of the Soul (*Ātmanaḥ satatordhvagati*). But Ānandabodha does not present this view of Jaina school accurately and faithfully. It seems that perhaps for the purpose of refutation he has twisted and so misrepresented the original Jaina view. Ānandabodha puts forth the Jaina view that *mukti* consists in the everlasting upward movement of the Soul, which the Jainas have never said, and which is a misrepresentation of how the Jainas conceive of the condition of the Soul in the moments immediately following death in the universe, is held in the middle of the *āloka*, in the form of the trunk of the man, with *siddhaśīla* at the top, the place where the head should be. This *siddhaśila* is the abode of the omniscient souls, and maybe called the spiritual eye of the universe. So *mokṣa* is said to be eternal upward movement. On liberation the soul goes upward, because of the momentum due to its previous activity, the non-existence of the relation to the elements which kept it down, breaking of the bondage, and its natural tendency to go upwards.

7.3 Buddhist Schools

Ānandabodha in his *Nyāyamakaranda* refutes the view points of the Yogācāra and Mādhyamika schools. The Yogācāra school propounds that *vijñāna* (consciousness) being transitory arises and perishes continuously. Ānandabodha criticises this tenet of Yogācāra by saying that since *vijñāna* (consciousness) is identical with the *Brahman* or the *Ātman*, it is eternal and not transitory.

Secondly, Ānandabodha criticises the doctrines of *mokṣa* expounded by the Yogācāra school i.e. *mokṣa* is the origination of the stream of pure cognition (*śuddha-citta-santānam*) free from the dirt of object-forms (*viṣayākārādyupaplava-śūnyoḥ*) obtained by the intensity of emotion (*bhāvanāprakarṣa*).

According to Ānandabodha, this kind of *mokṣa* is not possible since the cessation of previous impure stream is presupposed in this view. Further, *vijñāna* is produced by desire, which itself actually is destroyed by the contemplation of truth. If this real cognition does not destroy the desire then worldly life will continue to exist even in the state of *mokṣa* and this kind of *mokṣa* is not desired by anyone. Ānandabodha in presenting this view does not make any injustice to the school. His presentation goes in accordance with the original texts of the Buddhist school.

Ānandabodha has also refuted the theory of illusion, *ātmakhyāti* of the Yogācāra school, by arguing that even when the silver aspect is accepted as internal, the appearance of externality, though unreal, has to be accepted. Besides, if objects are accepted as internal then in the case of the superimposition of fire on a heap of *Gunjas,* there would be the possibility of perceiver's body being on flame. The acceptance of internal nature of object is both unnecessary and also impossible to maintain. In presenting this view, Ānandabodha is also faithful to the original Buddhist texts.

Ānandabodha has refuted the Mādhyamika theory of illusion, *asatkhyāti* according to which, an *asat* (unreal object) is experienced in the cognition. Since this theory directly permits the cognition (*khyāti*) of an unreal object (*asat*), it is known as *asatkhyāti*. Ānandabodha criticises this theory on the ground that the sublative cognition does not indicate the non-existence or unreality of the object.

Ānandabodha also refutes the Mādhyamika view of *mokṣa* i.e. the cessation of the stream of cognition (*bodhasantati*) pulled by the defects like *kleśas* etc. that continuously arise with different intensity. He argues that since the cognition that are momentary, perish of their own accord and then they would not have any relation with the effect (*phala*) like salvation. Again, this *mokṣa* is like the cessation of one's own self. In presenting the views of Mādhyamika Ānandabodha is very mush faithful to the original Buddhist texts.

7.4 The Sāṁkhya School

Ānandabodha in his *Nyāyamakaranda* discusses two main theories of the classical Sāṁkhya system expounded mainly by Iśvarakṛṣṇa, viz., the theory which advocates the plurality of *puruṣa* or *Ātman* and the theory of *mokṣa* or *kaivalya*. In the *Nyāyamakaranda* (pp.18-19) Ānandabodha says that birth, and death etc. related to the physical body cannnot prove plurality of the *Ātman* (*kiṁca jananādayaḥ kṣetrasamavāyinaḥ kṣetrajñasya bhedaḥ prasādhyataḥ iti kim kena saṁgatam*). Since Ānandabodha has argued at length for the refutation of the doctrine of plurality advocated by the Nyāya-Vaiśeṣika school, he simply says : *etenedamapi parāstam* (by this, Sāṁkhya view is refuted). His argument is very brief for the refutation of the Sāṁkhya view. According to the Sāṁkhya school, the diversity of *puruṣa* is real, which is proved by the birth, death etc. But Ānandabodha rejects this view by saying that these phenomena like birth, death etc., belonging to the physical body and not to the *Ātman* cannot prove the plurality of the *Ātman* which is identified with the *Brahman*.

It is true that Ānandabodha has faithfully presented the Sāṁkhya notion of *mokṣa* which means *puruṣa's* isolation (*kaivalya*) from *prakṛti*. Describing the nature of *kaivalya*, the SK 65 contends that *puruṣa* perceives the *prakṛti* whch has ceased to produce effects like intellect, ego and the rest and stopped from assuming the seven forms since *prakṛti* has fulfilled both the purposes of bondage and release of the *puruṣa*. On account of the destruction of all the previous impressions (*saṁskāras*) generated by *dharma* and the rest after obtaining the separation from body and the purpose being fulfilled the cessation of the *prakṛti* being effected, the *puruṣa* acquires liberation (*kaivalya*). Secondly, Ānandabodha has argued that the Sāṁkhya is wrong in advocating *mokṣa* as a state of *puruṣa*'s remaining in his natural form of *svarūpāvasthāna* after *vivekadarśana* or realisation of true nature of *prakṛti* and *puruṣa* because this *kaivalya* is bereft of direct manifestation of bliss (*ānanda*) the Sāṁkhya system does not hold the manifestation of *ānanda* in the state of *mokṣa* nor *puruṣa*'s nature as that of *ānanda* by which there could be direct experience of supreme bliss. Hence the Sāṁkhya conception of highest goal being devoid of *ānanda* cannot be taken into account since the highest *puruṣārtha* should be endowed with supreme bliss.

The Sāṁkhya denies *puruṣa*'s blissful nature and hence there is no scope of experiencing *ānanda* in *mokṣa*. Thus, Ānandabodha has very rightly put forth the Sāṁkhya view. The extant Sāṁkhya texts neither expound the experience of *ānanda* in the state of *mokṣa* nor the blissful nature of the *Ātman*. According to the SK and SS, *Puruṣa* is neutral, witness, pure and indifferent. Dasgupta rightly remarks: "the Sāṁkhya view differs from the Vedānta, firstly in this that it does not consider the soul to be of the nature of pure intelligence and bliss *(ānanda)*. Bliss with Sāṁkhya is but another name for pleasure and as such belongs to *Prakṛti* and does not constitute the nature of soul."[1]

From the above analysis, it is evidently clear that Ānandabodha's presentation and discussion of the Sāṁkhya view are very much faithful to the original

1. Dasgupta, S.N. HIS. Vol.I, p.238.

Sāṁkhya texts. He imposes the view of Advaita on the Sāṁkhya. As an ardent advocate of Advaita Ānandabodha holds that *mokṣa* should be equated with direct manifestation of *ānanda*. For Advaita Vedānta, it is reasonable, as this school considers *mokṣa* to be identical with the *Brahman* endowed with pure bliss. Ānandabodhas, argument with reference to the notion of bondage is not tenable. He has argued that *mokṣa* should be absence of bondage of the one which is bound; bondage is caused by *ajñāna* and *rāga* which are the attributes of the *buddhi*. Hence *Puruṣa* should be neither bound nor released rather it is *buddhi* which should be bound and liberated. Ānandabodha has also quoted two *kārikās* 62 and 63 of Īśvarakṛṣṇa to point out the flaw of the Sāṁkhya. It is right that Sāṁkhya views *ajñāna* and *rāga* as the attributes of *tāmasikabuddhi* and the cause of bondage but SK also contends that *prakṛti* binds herself through the seven forms - *dharma, vairāgya, aiśvarya, adharma, ajñāna, avairāgya* and *anaiśvarya* but frees herself for the specific purpose, viz., release of the *puruṣa*. Ānandabodha argues that *bandha* and *mokṣa* cannot be falsely attributed to *puruṣa* because of absence of *nimittakāraṇa* (occasioning cause). The relation between *prakṛti* and *puruṣa* as that of *svasvāmibhāva* cannot be *nimitta* for such figurative attribution as *puruṣa,* according to Sāṁkhya, is *udāsīna*. *Buddhi* cannot render any help to *puruṣa,* a *svabhāvanirmala* entity.

The Sāṁkhya system figuratively attributes bondage and *mokṣa* to *puruṣa* and admits the relation of *svasvāmibhāva* between the *prakṛti* and the *puruṣa* as *nimittakāraṇa*. Ānandabodha criticises that *nimittābhāvād upacārānupatti,* due to absence of occasoning cause figurative attribution is not possible but the Sāṁkhya holds that the want of discrimination is the cause of bondage and emancipation. Thus, while according to the Sāṁkhya *bandha* and *mokṣa* of *puruṣa* are to be figuratively taken due to the *aviveka* Ānandabodha asserts that the relation of *svasvāmibhāva* between *puruṣa* and *prakṛti* is not possible. Secondly the *bandha* and *mokṣa* of *puruṣa* is real, *ipso facto*, and not an attribution (*upacāra*).

Further, Ānandabodha denies the service of *buddhi* to *puruṣa* on account of his being *svabhāvanirmala* or pure by nature. This goes against the Sāṁkhya view as the Sāṁkhya holds that *buddhi* accomplishes *puruṣa*'s experiences, and discriminates the subtle difference between *prakṛti* and *puruṣa*. Thus, the Sāṁkhya admits the *upakāra* (service) of *buddhi* to *puruṣa*. Ānandabodha wrongly identifies *buddhi* with *prakṛti* not found in the extant Sāṁkhya texts.

Ānandabodha argues that *buddhi* like a dancing lady, by means of her self-exposition cannot be a helper (*upakāriṇī*) of *puruṣa*. This argument does not seem in accordance with the original text of the Sāṁkhya system as the extant texts advocate the service of *prakṛti* and *puruṣa* in spite of *puruṣa*'s neutral and pure nature.

Ānandabodha has argued that a dancing girl in the form of *Prakṛti* cannot show herself to an indifferent person, and hence cannot be *dṛśyopakārikā* for *puruṣa* and the relation of *svasvāmibhāva* does not hold good. Thus the service of *prakṛti* to *puruṣa* is not determinable. We have already seen that the Sāṁkhya system proves the authenticity of *svasvāmibhāva sambandha*. Hence it is not reasonable to speak of the indeterminability of the said relation, as pointed out by Ānandabodha.

7.5 The Nyāya School

In his work, *Nyāyamakaranda* and *Pramāṇamālā* Ānandabodha puts forth some ontological, epistomological and soteriological doctrines of the Nyāya school. By means of pointing out logical defects inherent in the Nyāya tenets and duly exposing the logical validity of the Advaitic doctrines Ānandabodha has evidently proved the superiority of the Advaitic standpoints.

Ānandabodha refutes the Nyāya doctrine of diversity[1] of the *Ātman* by arguing that the diversity of the Individual souls is an erroneous conception created by *avidyā* because the Individual Soul is essentially the same as the *Brahman,* one without a second.

Secondly, Ānandabodha criticises the Nyāya doctrine of extrinsic validity of the knowledge[2] (*parataḥ prāmāṇyavāda*). The Nyāya school advocates that the knowledge or cognition (*jñāna*) which is a special attribute of the *Ātman* is not self-luminous and it needs another type of cognition or knowledge for its manifestation otherwise their would not arise any doubt about the cognition of an object. Ānandabodha sets aside this Nyāya view by saying that the knowledge or consciousness (*vijñāna* or *samvid*) is identical with the self-luminous supreme Reality called *Brahman* and hence it is self-luminous as it is said in the *Upaniṣads.*

Thirdly, Ānandabodha refutes the Nyāya doctrine which expounds the mental perception[3] (*mānasapratyakṣa*) of the *Ātman*. He argues that the *Ātman* being *Brahman* is self-evident and self-illuminating. The perception (*pratyakṣa*) which is valid in the sphere of the phenominal world cannot cognise the transcendental Reality *Brahman.*

---

1. Vide. chapter III.
2. Vide. chapter. III.
3. Ibid

Fourthly, Ānandabodha criticises the Nyāya view of *mokṣa*[1] i.e. acquirement of the natural state (*svarūpāvasthāna*) of the consciousness after the destruction of all special qualities (*viṣeṣaguṇa*) like knowledge and others. He refutes this view by saying that in this salvation, which is nothing but the natural state, acquired after the destruction of all special qualities happiness also would be destroyed being a special quality. Ānandabodha seems to be very much faithful to the original Nyāya texts. Though he does not mention the name of the author or the Nyāya texts which he criticises still these are clearly identified as those of the Nyāya school represented by Jayanta Bhaṭṭa and Śrīdhara.

The realism of the Nyāya and illusionism (*māyāvāda*) of the Advaita are diametrically opposite doctrine. While the Nyāya school advocates the diversity of the selves on the basis of perception (*pratyakṣa*) Ānandabodha's Advaita negates it completely on the basis of *Avidyā* or *Māyā*. Taking into consideration these main points we can very well say that Ānandabodha, an Advaitin is justified in critcising duly the Nyāya views and has not made any textual misrepresentation in expounding their doctrines.

7.6 The Pūrva Mīmāṁsa School

Ānandabodha in his two works, *Nyāyamakaranda* and *Pramāṇamālā* devotes a considerable number of pages in discussing and refuting the principal viewpoints of the two prominent Pūrva-Mīmāṁsā schools i.e. Prābhākara Mīmāṁsā and Bhāṭṭa Mīmāṁsā. The main standpoints of the Prābhākara Mīmāṁsā criticised by Ānandabodha are as follows:

1. Vide chapter. V.

The Prābhākara school advocates that the *Ātman* (self) is distinct from the body, the sense-organs and the intellect or cognitions. It is eternal, ubiquitous and manifold as there is a distinct self in each body and manifested in all cognitions of objects[1]. The Prābhākara school regards the self as a substance, which is not of the nature of consciousness, but a substrate of consciousness.

Ānandabodha in the *Nyāyamakaranda* criticises the doctrine of plurality of the *Ātman* advocated by the Prābhākaras. Keeping in view the monistic tenet of identity of the Absolute *Brahman* with the Individual Self Ānandabodha refutes this doctrine of Prābhākara. Since the diversity what appears in the illusory world created by *Māyā* or *Avidyā* is an appearance and hence lacks reality, there is no diversity of the Individual souls in the transmigratory world[2].

Secondly, the Prābhākara school does not regard the self as an object of consciousness or mental perception, because the same self cannot be the knower and the known. The knowing self can never be the known object. So the Prābhākara school maintains that the self is known as the subject of all cognitions of object; that there is no 'I'-consciousness in addition to consciousness of objects. Cognition manifets themselves, their objects (*viṣaya*) and the self as the knower (*jñātā*), or substrate (*āśraya*).[3]

Ānandabodha criticises this doctrine of the Prābhākara school which denies self-luminosity nature of the *Ātman*. According to Ānandabodha, since the self-luminous *Brahman*, the transcendental Supreme

1. PP. p.141
2. Vide Chapter III.
3. PP. p.153.

Reality is the *Ātman* and there is no iota of difference, the *Ātman* like *Brahman* is self-illuminating and does not require any other worldly light for its manifestation rather the whole world is manifested by this supreme light of the *Brahman.*[1]

Thirdly, the Prābhākara school advocates the theory of *Akhyāti* or *Vivekakhyāti*. In the illusion 'this is silver' 'this' is perceived, and 'silver' is remembered; there is non-discrimination (*aviveka*) of the two psychoses from each other. Non-dicrimination is non-apprehension (*akhyāti*) of distinction (*viveka*). It is non-cognition of difference (*bhedāgraha*). The distinction between the perceived element 'this' and the remembered element 'silver' is not apprehended. Non-apprehension of the distinction leads to the illusion 'this' is silver[2]

Ānandabodha critcises this *akhyātivāda* of the Prābhākaras and holds that the object of error is indescribable (*anirvacanīya*) and hence *anirvacanīyakhyāti* is only logically sound.[3]

Fourthly, the Prābhākara school advocates that the *kārya* or *niyoga* is the urging factor to act (*pravartaka*) in an injunctive sentence. The Prābhākara school regards *niyoga* conveyed by the injunctive affix is the cause of activity. As action enjoys an important position in the Mīmāṁsā philosophy, the Prābhākaras accept *kārya* as the *Pravartaka*[4]

Ānandabodha refutes this view of the Prābhākaras and holds that the *pravartaka* of an injunctive sentence

1. NM. p.57
2. PP. 208
3. NM. 107
4. PP. p.431, 441.

consists in *iṣṭasādhanatā,* the instrumentality with reference to desired object.[1]

Ānandabodha also refutes the views of the Jaratprābhākaras, the elder followers of the Prābhākara school who slightly differ from the modern Prābhākaras in their opinions about the nature of *niyoga*. They regard *niyoga* as the locus (*āśraya*) of the *pravartanā,* incentive to activity which is defined as the opposition to the absence of activity (*pravṛtyabhāvavirodha*).

This is produced by the *liṅ* - injuctive affix. *Niyoga* is a special variety of meaning of the nature of *kārya*.

Ānandabodha refutes[2] this by saying that *pravartanā* which is defined as antogonistic to the absence of activity is never seen to be a *pravartaka* since *pravartanā* is possible only in case of the absence of activity.

Ānandabodha also criticises the Prābhākara view of *mokṣa*. The Prābhākara school defines release (*mokṣa*) as the absolute cessation of merits and demerits and the consequent total destruction of the body.[3] It is absolute cessation of the suffering of empirical life consequent on the complete destruction of the self's contact with the body and the sense-organs, which are destroyed by the complete dissapperance of merits and demerits.[4] Prābhākara school regards consciousness as an accidental quality of the Self, due to its conjunction with mind and a body. When mind, the body and the sense-organs are completely destroyed on the destruction of merits and demerits, the self is divested of cognition, pleasure, pain, desire, aversion, violation,

1. NM. p. 199.
2. NM. p.235.
3. PP. p.156.
4. PP. p.156.

impression, and consciousness. *Mokṣa* is absolute cessation of merit and demerit and the consequent pleasure and pain. It is negative in character, and consists in the complete destruction of the specific qualities of the self.

Ānandabodha criticises this view by saying that since there is no experience of pure and transcendental bliss no intelligent man would strive for the attainment of this kind of *mokṣa*.

Ānandabodha in his *Nyāyamakaranda* also criticises the theory of error known as *anyathākhyātivāda*[1] of the Bhāṭṭa Mīmāṁsakas. According to the Bhāṭṭa school an error or illusion is a false perception or misperception of one object as another (*anyathā* or *viparita*). In the illusion 'this is silver', 'this' or the brightness of a nacre, which it has in common with silver is perceived owing to its contact with the visual organ, then 'silver' is remembered owing to the revival of the impression (*saṁskāra*) of silver.

Ānandabodha criticises this *anythākhyātivāda* of the Bhāṭṭa Mīmāṁsakas and logically establishes the *anirvacanīyakhyāti* propounded by the Advaitins.

These above mentioned viewpoints of the Prābhākara and the Bhāṭṭa school of Mīmāṁsā are critically evaluated by Ānandabodha in his works. He, by means of his ardent logical acumen has selected the weak viewpoints from the works of the above said schools and rebutted them in his works. As far as the presentation or exposition of the Mīmāṁsaka views is concerned Ānandabodha is very much faithfull to the original Mīmāṁsā texts. He, for the purpose of refutation of an opponent view does not make any deliberate attempt like twisting or misrepresenting the viewpoints

1. Vide. Chapter. IV

of the Mīmāṁsakas. Hence Ānandabodha's presentation does not bear any stamp of textual misrepresentation.

Secondly, Ānandabodha criticises all these from Advaitic point of view and pointing out exact lacune existing in their thoughts, proves the logical validity of the Advaita Vedānta. Though the central points of his Advaita philosophy are not originally different from the views propounded by his predecessors still on some issues Ānandabodha is quite original and explained very clearly like the fifth definition of *mithyātva* (illusoriness) of the world, and the theory of *avidyānivṛtti* (cessation of nescience) as *pañcamaprakāra* (fifth kind). He also exhibits his unique originality in refuting the views of the outstanding Advaitins like Maṇḍana and Vācaspati. Ānandabodha does not agree with Maṇḍana and Vācaspati on the point of *Jīvātman* as the substratum of *Avidyā* and *śabdajñāna* arising from the Upaniṣadic texts like *Tattvamasi* etc. as an indirect means for the intuition of the *Brahman*.

According to Ānandabodha the *Brahman* is the locus of *Avidyā*. He also does not make any categorical difference between the locus (*āśraya*) and object (*viṣaya*) of *Avidyā* as done by Maṇḍana in the *Brahmasiddhi* and later on followed by Vācaspati. He does not discuss at all the object of *Avidyā* and neglects the issue completely. However, from his dissussion we may grasp, though not clearly that he, like Sureśvara and Prakāśātman, holds *Brahman* as the object of *Avidyā* and does not recognise any difference between the *āśraya* and *viṣaya* of *Avidyā*. Ānandabodha also speaks *śabdajñāna* as the direct means of *mokṣa*. He also very correctly and faithfully puts forth their views in his work *Nyāyamakaranda* and does not make any textual misrepresentation. It is significant to note that Ānandabodha also favours some of the views of Maṇḍana like bliss as a positive entity and the doctrine of *sattādvaita* (ens-monism)[1] etc. and respectfully quotes from his works. This reflects Ānandabodha's independence of thought, logical acumen and indirectly proves that he neither blindy follows of the great Advaitins nor he simply refers to their concepts in his works. Ānandabodha's thorough and systematic disscussion bear the stamp of his deep understanding of their prominent viewpoints.

1. Shastri, Kuppusvāmi, op.cit.

CHAPTER VIII

ĀNANDABODHA'S DISTINCTIVE CONTRIBUTIONS

In ranking philosophical writers according to their substantial contribution to the Indian philosophical literature in general and Advaita Vedānta in particular one should give a very high place to Ānandabodha. He occupies a unique place in the history of Advaita in that he had the courage to advocate his original and independent views at the time when some critical issues of Advaita Vedānta were sharply criticised by the Naiyāyikas like Jayanta Bhaṭṭa and Udayanācārya and Mīmāṁsakas like Śālikanātha. With a notable attempt to prove the logical validity of the important tenets of Advaita Vedānta Ānandabodha has made valuable contribution to Indian philosophy in general and Advaita Vedānta in particular. In the following pages his contribution has been discussed.

8.1 Ontology

Ānandabodha asserts that the supreme bliss which is identified with *Brahman* is not only an absence of misery but it is a positive state of joy or delight. He argues that the transcendental bliss of which the empirical pleasure is only a fragment should be concieved positively and not negatively; for a positive category admits of specification and determination. The comparative degree, more and less are possible only in the case of a positive category. *Brahman* or the self is bliss, because it is the seat of supreme love (*paramapremāspadatayā*). There is not only the authority of scripture to show that the self is of the nature of bliss, but there is also the evidence of practical experience in the life of almost every person viz., in case of all the creatures the *Ātman* is dearest of all as it is stated by Bṛh. Up.II.4.5.

Thus, Ānandabodha has explained the blissful nature of the Supreme Reality.

Ānandabodha in a brilliant critique shows how the reality of the concept of difference (*bheda*) cannot be maintained with the help of any of the recognised means of valid knowledge.[1] He has successfully established the *mithyātva* (illusoriness) of the phenomenal world (*jagat*) which has no absolute reality. Employing appropriate logical syllogism in support of the *mithyātva* of the world he has made his position free from some logical fallacies[2] like *Viruddha, Satpratipakṣa, Asiddha, Savyabhicāra* etc. Though *mithyātva* of the world is one of the central tenets expounded by Śaṅkara and others still Ānandabodha's explicit discussion on this point is conspicuously marked by logical arguments and pertinent syllogisms which are generally not found in the earlier Advaita texts.

In the *Nyāyamakaranda* and *Pramāṇamālā* Ānandabodha has explained the theories of *avacchedavāda* and *pratibimbavāda* which, according to him, are distinctly different from each other like water tight compartments. Though all the Advaitins admit that the *Jīva* is essentially non-different from *Brahman*, the post-Śaṅkara Advaitins hold different views with regard

1. Vide Chapter, III.
2. *Ibid.*

to the way in which the *Jīva* is to be regarded. The reflection-theory (*pratibimbavāda*) is favoured by Prakāśātman, the author of the *Pañcapādikāvivaraṇa*[1]. According to this theory, the *Jīva* is essentially not different from *Brahman*. On the contrary, Vācaspati Miśra advocates the limitation theory (*avacchedavāda*)[2]. According to this theory, the *Jīva* is consciousness limited by *avidyā* even as pot-ether (*ghaṭākāśa*) is the ether (*mahākāśa*) limited by the pot. Though the same ether is both in and outside the pot imposes an apparent limitation with the result that we talk about the pot-ether (*ghaṭākāśa*). Similarly, though the *Jīva* (Individual Self) is really non-different from *Brahman*, it appears to be different due to *avidyā* which limits its original nature. In the *Nyāyamakaranda* and *Pramāṇamālā* Ānandabodha has furnished illustrations to prove the identity of the *Brahman* with the *Jīvātman*. Since Ānandabodha employs the illustrations for both the theories of *pratibimba and avaccheda* for expounding the central doctrine of the non-difference of *Jīva* and *Brahman* he shows his originality in not following blindly any particular sub-school.

Ānandabodha has also strongly refuted the views advocated by both heterodox and orthodox schools of Indian philosophy. According to him, the *Brahman* is absolute bliss, one without a second and esoterically it is identified with the Individual Self.

8.2 Epistemology

Ānandabodha's contribution to the epistemology is as valuable as his contribution to the Advaitic ontology. He has thoroughly examined and refuted in his *Nyāyamakaranda, Pramāṇamālā and Nyāyadipāvali* im-

1. Vide Chapter, I,
2. Vide Chapter, I,

portant theories of erroneous cognition, viz., (a) the *ātmakhyāti* of the Yogācāra school of Buddhism, (b) the *asatkhyāti* of the Mādhyamika school of Buddhism, (c) the *akhyāti* of the Prābhākaras, and (d) the *anyathākhyāti* of the Bhāṭṭas.

The doctrine of *avidyā* or *māyā* plays an important part in the metaphysics of Advaita Vedānta. According to Ānandabodha, *avidyā* alias *māyā* is the material cause of the empirical illusion and is the root cause of the diversity of the selves. *Avidyā*, according to Ānandabodha, is beginningless (*anādi*) and *anirvācya* i.e. distinct from both *sat* and *asat*. The term *avidyā* cannot mean either absence of knowledge (*vidyābhāva*) or false knowledge (*mithyājñāna*). Such a thing cannot be supposed to be a material cause of something. The nature of *avidyā* is determined by the nature of its effects, the illusion. It is regarded as beginningless since there will be an infinite regress if some other cause of this *avidyā* is accepted, for, the cause of that case also will have to be admitted. Without accepting *avidyā* there would not be any possibility of the appearance of absolutely non-existent objects like horn of a human being and there would not be sublation of the real objects.

Ānandabodha does not make any distinction between two terms *avidyā* and *māyā* which according to him are synonymous.

There are different views regarding the locus of *avidyā* among his predecessors.

According to Sureśvara and his follower Prakāśātman, the *Brahman* is the locus of *avidyā*. This is an important point of difference between the Bhāmatī school and the Viraraṇa school. It should be pointed out here that the source of Sureśvara's view is found in Śaṅkara's *Bṛhadāraṇaka Upaniÿṣad bhāṣya*. In the same way Vācaspati's view is to be traced in Maṇḍana's *Brahmasiddhi*. Ānandabodha in his *Nyāyamakaranda* puts forth the views of Maṇḍana and his followers like Vācaspati, refutes this by forceful arguments and finally supports the view of Sureśvara and Prakāśātman. He establishes that the *Brahman* is the locus (*āśraya*) of *avidyā*. Thus his contribution lies in offering valid arguments against the *Jīvāśrita avidyāvāda* and making a thorough discussion of the said issue which is not found in the prominent works of his predecessors.

Ānandabodha in his *Nyāyamakranda* takes up the doctrine of *sattādvaita* or *bhāvādvaita*[1] expounded by Maṇḍana. In Advaita literature, there is a well-established tradition which recognises two ways of viewing the Advaita doctrine; one of them is generally known as *bhāvādvaita* or *sattādvaita* (ens- monism). According to this view, there is only one absolute reality of a positive kind, viz., *Brahman;* all the non-dualistic Upaniṣadic texts like *Advitīyam, Asthūlam, anaṇu, Aharsvam* and *Neti Neti* teach the negation of the world (*prapaṇcābhāva*). The realisation of *Brahman* as the only absolute reality brings about the removal of nescience, which being negative in nature does not conflict with the absolute monism of Advaita. It excludes only a second positive reality (*bhāva*). The Advaita philosophy taught by the Vedāntic texts reduces itself in this manner to the accommodating type of Advaita known as *bhāvādvaita* or *sattādvaita*. Ānandabodha has adopted this doctrine from Maṇḍana in a slightly different way. As Ānandabodha has admitted both positive and negative reality i.e. positive reality (*bhāvarūpasattā*) of the *Brahman* and negative reality (*abhāvarūpasattā*) of the *avidyānivṛtti*,

1. Sastri, S.K. *Brahmasiddhi of Maṇḍanamiśra with Śaṇkhapāṇi's Commentary*, Intro. p. xxv.

he has accommodated the doctrine of *bhāvādvaita* and presented it in a little different way.

In the *Nyāyamakaranda* Ānandabodha maintains by an elaborate process of reasoning superiority of the scriptural texts (*śrutipramāṇa*) over other means of knowledge like perception.[1] He exposes fully the hallowness of the Prābhākara concept of *niyoga* or *kārya* and shows that this concept would turn out to be a meaningless shibbleth. *Iṣṭasādhanatā* (contributoriness to a desired end) and explains fully by saying that it is a vain attempt to bring *Brahman*-realisation directly within the scope of any kind of injunction (*vidhi*) as it is pointed out by Śaṅkara in his *bhāṣya*.[2]

Further, Ānandabodha is renowned in the history of Advaita philosophy as an expounder of specification or definition of *mithyātva* or falsity of the world. This definition has been maintained by Madhusūdana Sarasvatī in his outstanding work *Advaitasiddhi*. But Gauḍa Brahmānanda in his commentary on *Advaitasiddhi* entitled *Laghucandrikā* has very clearly referred to Ānandabodha i.e. *ādyam syāt pañcapādyuktam tato vivaraṇodite/citsukhīyam caturtham syāt antyamānandabodha jam*[3].

Ānandabodha like Śaṅkara maintains that the knowledge which one aspirant gets from the Upaniṣadic texts is direct (*aparokṣa*) and immediate. This is a very significant contribution to the Advaitic thought. In expounding the above said view he evidently differs from Maṇḍana who maintains in his *Brahmasiddhi* that the knowledge which we get from the Upaniṣadic texts

1. Vide, Chapter, IV
2. BSŚB. I. I. 4.
3. Gauḍa Brahmānanda, *Laghucandrikā* on the *Advaitasiddhi*, p. 206.

is indirect and mediate (*parokṣa*) and necessarily involves relation in some manner like any other cognition arising from a valid verbal testimony (*śabdapramāṇa*). Meditation upon the content of the verbal cognition is necessary in order to transform the indirect and mediate knowledge into direct and immediate experience. So, according to Maṇḍana, the direct intuition of *Brahman* springs from *prasaṅkhyāna* or repeated contemplation on the true import of the Upaniṣadic texts (*mahāvākyas*).

8.3 Soteriology

Ānandabodha has a noteworthy contribution to the Advaita soteriology also. Following Śaṅkara he has explained the Advaitic concept of *bandha* and *mokṣa* and means thereof in very clear terms. According to him, the *paramapuruṣārtha* (supreme beatitude) is the removal of *avidyā* and the manifestation of the supreme bliss identified with *Brahman*. Since *avidyā* is the root cause of all suffering which an individual experiences because of his misunderstanding of original nature of *Brahman*, *avidyā* is bondage and its absolute removal is *mokṣa*. The removal of *avidyā* takes place, when there is the realisation of the Self as the Absolute reality.

According to Ānandabodha, *jñāna* (realisation or intuitive experience) is the only means to *mokṣa*, the highest beatitude. Like Śaṅkara, he advocates that since the removal of *avidyā* is the blinding and the binding tree of *avidyā*, the ritualistic action has only secondary importance in that it removes the sins, purifies the mind of a *mumukṣu* and thus helps him in attaining the true knowledge of the self. In this matter Ānandabodha does not agree with Maṇḍana who contends that *karma* and *jñāna* are related as means (*upāya*) and end (*upeya*). He does not accept the contention that *karma* and *jñāna* being diametrically opposed to each other could not be brought into relation of means and the objectives. Maṇḍana further holds that verbal cognition which arises from the Upaniṣads should be supplemented by certain aids, (*sādhana*) like contemplation (*dhyāna*) in order to attain *Brahman*-intuition (*Brahmasākṣātkāra*). As a result of the repeated contemplation (*dhyānābhyāsa*) the impressions of the knowledge of the non-dual self obtained from the Upaniṣads grow and develop in such a way that they are able to remove the impressions of the beginningless illusion and thereby bring about the final manifestation of the real nature of the self. Since *karmas* are prescribed by scripture, they are also useful in attaining *mokṣa*. Ānandabodha does not subscribe to this view as according to him, *karma* has no utility for the attainment of *mokṣa*. He also does not favour the combination of *jñāna* and *karma* (*jñānakarmasammuccayavāda*).

Vācaspati Miśra follows Maṇḍana's view and holds that verbal testimony can generate only mediate knowledge having a relational content. It is *prasaṅkhyāna* or continued meditation which brings about the intuitive experience of *Brahman*. But this verbal testimony is capable of generating immediate knowledge. He is bold to reject the views of the great Advaitins like Maṇḍana and Vācaspati. Ānandabodha has also made a significant contribution in clearly explaining the concept of *avidyānivṛtti* (cessation of nescience). He has fully refuted the view of Maṇḍana who identifies *avidyānivṛtti* with the *Ātman* itself in his *Brahmasiddhi*. According to Ānandabodha *avidyānivṛtti* is of fifth kind of reality (*sattā*), i.e. *pañcamaprakāra* since it cannot be either *sat* or *asat* or *sadasadubhaya* or *anirvacanīya* like *avidyā*. *Avidyānivṛtti* cannot be regarded as 'real', for then the doctrine of monism fails, since both the *avidyānivṛtti* and *Brahman* would be real and that would be duality; it cannot be regarded as unreal in the sense of absolute nought or non-existent, for then, how could it be removed by right knowledge; it cannot be both existent or non-existent in the same sense, for that would be self-contradictory; it cannot be contended that there is no reason why it should not then exist even after emancipation or why it could after all be removable by true knowledge. It is therefore to be regarded as being of a unique nature different from all these four possible kinds, viz *sat, asat, sadasadubhaya,* and *sadasadanubhaya,* a fifth and distinct kind of entity. Because of this reason, the well-known scholar Appayya Dīkṣita in his *Siddhāntaleśasaṅgraha* respectfully refers to Ānadabodha saying, *pañcamaprakārāvidyānivṛttiriti Ānandabodhācāryāḥ.*[1]

8.4 Methodology

Another significant contribution of Ānandabodha is his special approach to the several problems. In the early eleventh century there was a great dominance of Naiyāyikas. Therefore Ānandabodha thought it necessary to defend Advaitic philosophy by adopting the Nyāya methodology to some extent in his works. Apart from forceful, logical and dialectical arguments he has also employed a number of significant syllogisms to explain his points. Ānandabodha paved the way for the writing of the great dialectical works like *Citsukhī* of Citsukha and *Ādvaitasiddhi* of Madhusūdana Sarasvatī. The uniqueness of Ānandabodha's texts lies in the amalgamating the Advaitic as well as Naiyāyika methodology to explain the principal tenets of absolute monism.

The greatness of Ānandabodha is amply attested by the number of thinkers like Appayya Dīkṣita, Madhusūdana Sarasvatī. Cāndupaṇḍita, Vyāsa Tīrtha and others who have taken note of his prominent

1. Dīkṣita, Appayya, *Siddhāntaleśasaṅgraha,* p.539.

doctrines. His contribution to Advaita is of lasting importance and his prominent views still hold away over the minds of scholars even after a lapse of several centuries. Ānandabodha is one of the best known figures in the literature of Advaita Vedānta and one of the few teachers of great renown who have left the characteristic hallmark on their sucessors. A respected authority and a reputed preacher of Advaita, a doughty champion of the Upaniṣadic tradition and a master mind skilled in dailectical reasoning Ānandabodha occupies a unique place in the galaxy of Advaita philosophers.

CHAPTER IX

ESTIMATE AND CONCLUSION

From the comprehensive and critical study of Ānandabodha's remarkable Advaitic works as presented in the foregoing pages we can say that Ānandabodha is really one of the greatest thinkers of the post-Śaṅkara Advaita thought. His works are very much valuable for significant exposition of the major Advaitic tenets and forceful arguments in support of their validity. Ānandabodha is also a poet as he rightly introduces himself by the epithet, *Sukavi* in his works. He has composed a number of verses in several metres. Ānandabodha occupies a significant place in the history of Advaita Vedānta for his multifaceted encyclopedic scholarship. He is a metaphysician, a profound scholar, a poet, a honest critic, a distinguished prose writer and dialectician. The celebrated works of Ānandabodha make evidently clear all these aspects of his scholarship. He makes use of his scholarship in his works in a very skillful and successful manner.

In his works Ānandabodha has made the fullest possible use of logic that is in accordance with *Śruti* (scriptural authority). He has successfully employed the Nyāya terms, techniques, syllogisms and dialectic method for the refutation of the opponents' views and establishment of Advaitic tenets.

In giving an estimate of Ānandabodha it is significant to note that he is completely agreed with Śaṅkara in his unsparing criticism and outright dismissal of *jñānakarmasamuccayavāda*. Ānandabodha subscribes Śaṅkara's view, viz., *Śruti* as the supreme source of *brahmajñāna*, the *Brahman* which is *siddhavastu* as the purport of Upaniṣadic statements, and impartite sense of the Upaniṣadic statements. However, Ānandabodha seems to be in perfect sympathy with Maṇḍana in explicitly maintaining Maṇḍana's doctrine of *sattādvaita* (ens-monism). Following Maṇḍana Ānandabodha accepts the fifth kind of existence of cessation of nescience (*pañcamaprakāra avidyānivṛtti*.) Ānandabodha also has expressed his independent thinking by refuting Maṇḍana's view, viz., *Jīvātman* as the locus of *avidyā* and *avidyānivṛtti* as the nature of the *Ātman* or the *Brahman*. Acknowledging his honourific authority Ānandabodha quotes profusely from Maṇḍana's *Brahmasiddhi* in order to substantiate his Advaitic positions. Although Ānandabodha follows some doctrines upheld by Maṇḍana and Vācaspati still he does not blindly imitate them. On the contrary, he also rejects their standpoints by putting forth regorous logical arguments and quoting scriptural texts. Ānandabodha also shows similar attitude to Vācaspati Miśra, the follower of Maṇḍana Miśra. He quotes verbatim from the important work like *Brahmatattvasamīkṣā* of Vācaspati. He also refutes his views of the locus of *avidyā*.

In the works of Ānandabodha Śaṅkara's brief views on various theories of error get expounded in a greater detail. The technique of Ānandabodha's criticism of other theories of error is to be specially noted here. According to him, criticism consists in drawing out the implications of the view of the opponent, on the basis of the principles accepted by himself (the opponent), and then pointing to the self-contradictory character of that view through sharp logical scrutiny. Here Ānandabodha asserts that by his logical assumptions, the opponent's position gets itself reduced to an absurdity. Ānandabodha thus repudiates the view of the opponents and establishes his own Advaitic standpoints. Thus the credit of critically elaborating other theories of error such as *asatkhyāti, ātmakhyāti, akhyāti, anyathākhyāti* and their dismissal in favour of *anirvacanīyakhyāti* goes to him.

Another important fact explored in the foregoing pages is that Ānandabodha does not follow strictly any particular sub-school, viz., *Bhāmatī* School of Vācaspati Miśra, *Vārttika* school of Sureśvara and *Vivaraṇa* school of Prakāśātman. He profusely quotes and refers to the prominent doctrines of almost all schools. This is very much clear from the examples given by him regarding the identity of *Jīvātman* with *Brahman*. He follows both *avacchedavāda* of Vācaspati and *pratibimbavāda* of Prakāśātman.

It is shown succintly how Ānandabodha made valuable as well as distinctive contribution by explication, amplification and subtle analysis of the important Advaitic tenets and thereby enriched Advaita school by making forceful refutation of the antagonistic schools. Further, it has also been discussed that Ānandabodha both as a commentator and author of the independent works has inspired and influenced his sucessors like Citsukha, Appayya Dīkṣita etc. both Advaitins and non-Advaitins. Our comparative perspective has made it evidently clear in the above pages that though Ānandabodha has collected materials for the content of his works from his celebrated predecessors still he has not blindly incorporated them but has added a number of novel points. The most important feature of his contribution is that he has made a thorough survey of prominent Advaitic tenets and reviewed them in the light of scriptural authority and logical reasoning.

Above all, Ānandabodha's bold attempt to uphold, defend and strengthen the principal tenets of Absolute Monism propounded by the great Śaṅkara, Sureśvara and their successors, when it was the victim of the Naiyāyikas and other powerful philosophical schools is the most noteworthy aspect. He has successfully given the lasting blow to the opponent schools by adopting their methods and technical terms and brought out the prominence of Advaita Vedānta. He, therefore, would be revered and remembered by the men of virtue as long as our Vedāntic culture survives in this universe.

Sarvam Khalvidam Brahma

BIBLIOGRAPHY

I.Original Texts in Sanskrit.

(A) Manuscripts

Nyāyadīpikā or Śābdanirṇayadīpikā of Ānandabodha,a commentary on the Śābdanirṇaya of Prakāśātman, Madras Government Oriental Manuscript Library, R. No.2986.

Pramāṇamālā of Ānandabodha, The Oriental Institute, An Alphabetical List of Manuscripts in the Oriental Institute, Baroda, Vol.I, No.XCVII, Gaekwad's Oriental series, Compiled by R.N. Siromani, 1942, Serial no.198, Accession. No.32.

(B) Published Works

Advaitasiddhi of Madhusūdana Sarasvatī, Edited by Ananta Krishna Sastri, Published by Tukaram Jawaji, Bombay, 1917.

Bhagavadgītā, Edited by Belvalkar, S.K. Bilvakunja Publishing House, Poona, 1941.

Bṛhadāraṇyakabhāṣya Vārttika, Commentary of Sureśvara on Śankara's commentary on the Bṛhadāraṇyaka Upaniṣad, Vols.I & II. Anandasrama Sanskrit Series 116, 1892-1894.

Bṛhatī, Commentary of Prabhākara on Śābarabhāṣya, with Pañcikā by Śālikanāntha, Madras University Sanskrit Series No.3. 1934.

Bhāmatī, Edited with Brahmasūtra Śāṅkarabhāṣya, Kalpataru and Parimala by Anantakrishna Sastri, Nirnaya Sagar Press, Bombay, 1917.

Brahmasūtrabhāṣya of Śaṅkara, Edited by Acarya Ram Narayan, Nirnaya Sagar Press, Bombay, 1948.

Brahmasūtrabhāṣya of Śaṅkara with Commentaries Bhāmatī, Kalpataru and Parimala, Edited by Sastri Anantakrishna, Nirnaya Sagar Press, Bombay, 1917.

Brahmasiddhi of Maṇḍana Miśra with the Commentary Vyākhyā of Śaṅkhapāṇi, Edited by Sastri, K.S. Madras, Govt. Oriental Manuscripts Series No.4, 1937.

Gīrvānapadamañjarī and Gīrvāṇavāṅmañjarī, Edited by Shah, U.P. The M.S. University Oriental Series No.4.

Iṣṭasiddhi, Edited by M. Hiriyanna, Oriental Institute, Baroda, 1933.

Kāvyaprakāśa of Mammaṭa, Edited by Ganjendragadkar A.B. Popular Prakashan, Bombay-34, 1970.

Kāvyādarśa of Daṇḍi with the Commentary of Jibananda Vidyasagara Bhattacharya and an Introduction and an English Translation By V.N. Iyer, V. Ramaswamy Sastrath & Sons, Madras, 1952.

Naiṣadhcarita of Śrīharṣa, Edited by K.K. Handiqui, Deccan College Monograph Series 4, Poona, 1956.

Naiṣkarmyasiddhi of Sureśvara, Edited by Hiriyanna, M. Bhandarkar Oriental Research Institute, Poona, 1925.

Naiṣkarmyasiddhi of Śureśvara, Edited by Raghavachar S.S. University of Mysore, Mysore, 1965.

Nayaviveka of Bhavanātha Miśra, Edited by S.K. Ramanatha Sastri, Madras University Sanskrit Series, No.12, Madras, 1917.

Nyāyakusumāñjali of Udayana with Commentary by Uttamur T. Viraraghavacharya, Tirupati Vani Press, 1941.

Nyāyadīpāvali of Ānandabodha with Pramāṇamālā and Nyāyamakaranda with a Commentary by Citsukha Muni, Edited by N.S.N. Swami Balaram Udasina Mandalika, Chowkhamba Sanskrit Book Depot, Benares, 1907.

Nyāyamañjarī of Jayanta Bhaṭṭa, Vizianagaram Sanskrit Series, Lazarus and Co., Benares, 2 Vols.

Nyāyadarśana of Gautama, Edited by Swami D.S. Bharatiya Vidya Prakashana, Varanasi-1, 1966.

Nyāyadīpāvali and Pramāṇamālā, Edited with Anubhūtisvarūpācārya's Commentary and Sukhaprakāśa's Commentary and English summary, by S. Subramanya Sastri, Annals of Oriental Research, Madras, 14, 1957- 58, 43-72.

Nyāyamakaranda of Ānandabodha with Pramāṇamālā and Nyāyadīpāvali, with a Commentary by Citsukha, Edited by N.S.N. Swami Balaram Udasina Mandalika Chowkhamba Sanskrit Book Depot, Banares, 1907.

Pramāṇavārttika of Dharmakīrti, Edited by Swami Dwarikadas Sastri, Buddha Bharati, Varanasi, 1968.

Pūrvamīmāṁsā of Jaimini with Commentary of Sabarasvāmin in 2 Vols, Kasi Sanskrit Series, No.42.

Śabdanirṇaya of Prakāśātmayati, Edited by T. Ganapatisastri, Trivendrum Sanskrit Series No.411. Trivandrum, 1917.

Śatadūṣaṇī of Vedāntadeśika, Vedānta Deśika Granthamālā, Kanchi, 1940.

Siddhāntakaumudī of Bhaṭṭoji Dīkṣita with the Commentary Bālamanoramā in 4 Vols., Kasi Sanskrit Series.

The Saṃkṣepaśārīraka of Sarvajñātman, Veezhinathan, N., University of Madras, Madras, 1972.

Saṁkṣepaśārīraka of Sarvajñātman, Edited by Vajhe B.S. The Chowkhamba Sanskrit Series Office, Banaras, 1924.

The Sarvadarśanasaṅgraha, Translated into English by Cowell and Gough, Kegan Paul & Co., London, 1984.

Sarvadarśanasaṅgraha of Mādhavācārya, Edited by Sharma U.S. The Chowkhamba Vidyabhavan, Varanasi-1, 1964.

Sarvadarśanasaṅgraha of Mādhavācārya, Edited by Abhyankar V.S., The Bhandarkar Oriental Research Institute, Poona, 1951.

Sāhityadarpaṇa of Viśvanātha, Edited by Singh Satyavrat, Chowkhamba Vidyabhavan, Varanasi-1, 1970.

Sāṁkhyakārikā, Edited and Translated by S.S. Suryanarayana Sastri, University of Madras, 1935.

Siddhāntabindu of Madhusūdana with the Commentary of Purushottama. Eng. Trans. by Divanji, P.C. Gaekwad Oriental Series, Baroda, 1933.

Siddhāntaleśasaṁgraha, Edited with an English translation by S.S. Suryanarayana Sastri, Vol.1, University of Madras, Madras. 1935.

The Brahmasūtras, Translated into English by S. Radhakrishnan, George Allen and Unwin Ltd., London, 1966.

Tarkasaṁgraha of Ānandajnāna, Edited by T.M. Tripathi Gaekwad Oriental Series, No.III, Baroda, 1917.

Tattvapradīpikā of Citsukhācārya with Commentary Nayanaprasādinī and Tattvacandrikā in Hindi, Kasi Sanskrit Series, 242, Chawkhamba Sanskrit Sansthan, Varanasi, 1987.

The Bhāmatī Catussūtrī of Vācaspati Miśra, Edited with an Eng. Tr. by Sastri, Surnarayana. S.S. and C. Kunhan Raja, Theosophical Publishing House, Madras, 1933.

The Rasagaṅgādhara of Jagannātha Paṇḍita with the Commentary of Nāgeśa Bhaṭṭa, Edited by Pandit Durgāprasād and Kāsināth Pandurang Parab, The Nirnayasagara Press, Bombay, 1988.

Upaniṣat-Samgraha, Edited with Sanskrit Introduction by J.L. Shastri, Motilal Banarasidass, Delhi, 1970.

Vedāntasāra of Sadānanda, Edited with Introduction and Tr. by Hiriyanna, M. Oriental Book Agency, Poona, 1929.

Vedāntaparibhāṣā of Dharmarāja Adhvarīndra, Edited with an Eng. trans. by Sastri, Suryanarayana, S.S.

Vivaraṇaprameyasaṁgraha, Translated into English by S.S. Suryanarayana Sastri and Saileswara Sen, Andhra University Series, 1941.

Vivaraṇaprameyasaṁgraha of Vidyāraṇya, Edited by Shri Shrikṛṣṇapanta Sastri, Achyuta-granthamālā, No.8, Kashi.

Yogasūtras of Patañjali, Edited by Rama Prasad, Oriental Books Reprint Corporation, 54, Rani Jhanshi Road, New Delhi, 1978.

Yajñaparibhāṣāsūtra of Āpastamba with the Commentary of Dūrtaswāmi, Edited by S. Bhattacarya, Calcutta, 16-1 Ghoshe's Lane, 1948.

II. General Works

Abhedānanda, Shankarottara Advaita Vedānta Meṅ Mithyātva Nirūpaṇa, Rajastan Hindi Grantha Akademy, Jaipur, 1973.

Balasubramanian, R. A Study of the Brahmasiddhi of Maṇḍana Miśra, Chaukhamba Amrabharati Prakashan, Varanasi, 1st ed. 1983.

Belvalkar, S.K., Shree Gopal Basu Mallik Lectures on Vedānta Philosophy.

Belvalkar and Ranade, History of Indian Philosophy, Vol. II, Poona, 1927.

Bhattacharya, K.C., Studies in Vedāntism, University of Calcutta, 1909.

Bhattacharya, Vidhushekhara. The Āgamaśāstra of Gauḍapāda. Calcutta: University of Calcutta, 1943.

Chakraborty, N.B. The Advaita Concept of Falsity - A Critical Study. Calcutta : Sanskrit College, 1967.

Chaudhury, A.K.R., Self and Falsity in Advaita Vedānta, Progressive Publication, Calcutta, 1955.

Das, S.K., A Study of the Vedānta. Second Edition Calcutta, 1937.

Citrava Siddheshwarashastri, Bhāratavarṣiya Madhyayugīna Caritrakoṣa, Bhāratīya Caritrakoṣa Maṇḍala, Poona-2, 1937.

Das. R.V., The Essentials of Advaitism, Motilal Banarasidass, Delhi 1933.

Dasgupta, S.N., Philosophical Essays, University of Calcutta, Calcutta, 1941.

Dasgupta, S.N. A History of Indian Philosophy, Vol. I and II. Cambridge Univ. Press, London: 1966, 1968.

Date, V.H., Vedānta Explained, Bookseller's Publishing Co., Bombay, 1959.

Deshpande, Uma, The Glimpses of Indological Heritage, Good Companion, Baroda, 1989.

Deussen, Paul, The System of the Vedānta, Oriental Publishers, Delhi, 1972, Trans. by Charles Johnston.

Devaraja, N.K. An Introduction to Śaṅkara's Theory of Knowledge. Varanasi, Motilal Banarasidass, 1962.

Datta, D.M. The Six Ways of Knowing, George Allen & Unwin, London, 1932.

Ghate, V.S., The Vedānta, The Bhandarkar Oriental Research Institute, Poona, 1960.

Gode, P.K., Studies in Indian Literary History, Vol.I., Bharatiya Vidya Bhavan, Bombay, 1953.

Gupta Sanjukta, Studies in the Philosophy of Madhusūdana Sarasvatī, Sanskrit Pustak Bhandar, Calcutta, 1966.

Hasurkar, S.S.· Vācaspati Miśra on Advaita Vedānta, Darbhanga, Mithila Institute, 1958.

Hiriyanna, M. Essentials of Indian Philosophy, George Allen and Unwin, London, 1951.

Hiriyanna, M. Outlines of Indian Philosophy. London: George Allen and Unwin, 1964.

Iyer, M.K.V., Advaita Vedānta, Asia Publishing House, New York, 1964.

Ittuthuran, E. The Philosophy of Advaita with special reference to Ānandabodha, Unpublished M.Lit. dissertation, Madras University, 1959.

Jacob, G.A. A Concordance to the Principal Upaniṣads and Bhagvadgītā, Motilal Banarasidass, Delhi, 1963.

Jani, A.N. A Critical Study of Śrī Harṣa's Naiṣadhacaritam, M.S. University Research Series 2. Baroda 1957.

Joshi, Arvind, Gauḍapāda, Eka Samikṣātmaka Adhyayana, Dakṣiṇa Gujarat Prādhyāpaka Pustaka Prakāśana Sahakārī Maṇḍala Li. Surat, 1984.

Jha, Ganganath, The Prabhākara School of Pūrva Mīmāṁsā, Motilal Banarsidass, Delhi.

Jha, Ganganath, Pūrva Mīmāṁsā in its Sources, with a Critical Bibliography by Umesh Mishra, Banaras Hindu University, Varanasi.

Kar, B.N., Theories of Error in Indian Philosophy: Analytical Study, Ajanta Publications, Delhi, 1978.

Karmarkar R.D. Śaṅkara's Advaita, Karnataka University, Dharwar, 1966.

Kirtikar, Vasudeva J, Studies in Vedānta, D.B. Taraporevala Sons and Co., Bombay, 1924.

Mahadevan, T.M.P. Gauḍapāda : A Study in Early Advaita. Madras, University of Madras, 1960.

Mahadevan , T.M.P. The Philosophy of Advaita, Madras, Ganesh and Co., 1969.

Mahadevan, T.M.P., Word Index to the Brahmasūtra Bhāṣya of Śaṅkara, 2 parts, University of Madras, Madras, 1971.

Mainkar, T.G. The Making of the Vedānta, Ajanta Publications, Delhi. 1980.

Malkarni, G.R., Metaphysics of Advaita Vedānta, The Indian Institute of Philosophy, Amalner, 1961.

Max Muller, Three Lecturers on the Vedānta Philosophy, Long mans Green & Co., 1894.

Mehta, Narmadashankar Devashankar, Vedānta Siddhānta Bheda or An Account of Various Followers of Śaṅkarācārya, S.N. Publications, Delhi, 1985.

Monier-Williams, Sir Monier, A Sanskrit-English Dictionary, Oxford University Press, London, 1964.

Mukherjee, A.C., The Nature of Self, 2nd Edition, The Indian Press Ltd., Allahabad, 1943.

Mukherjee Sastri, Nalinimohan, A Study of Śaṅkara, The University of Calcutta, 1942.

Murthy, K.S. Revelation and Reason in Advaita Vedānta. Waltair, Andhra Univ., 1959.

Murti, T.R.V. The Central Philosophy of Buddhism. London, George Allen and Wstwin Ltd., 1960.

Nachane, S.A., A Survey of Post-Śaṅkara Advaita Vedānta, Unpublished Ph.D. Thesis, The University of Poona, 1953.

Narain, K.A., Critique of Madhva Refutation of the Śaṅkara School of Vedānta, Udayana Publications, Allahabad, 1964.

Pandey, S.L., Pre-Śaṅkara Advaita Philosophy, Darshan Peeth, Allahabad, 1974.

Potter, K.H., The Presuppositions of Indian Philosophies, Prentice Hall of India Pvt. Ltd., New Delhi, 1963.

Potter, Karl. H. The Encyclopedia of Indian Philosophies, Vol.II, Motilal Banarsidass, Delhi, 1971.

Prithipal, D. Advaita Vedānta, Bharatiya Vidya Prakasan, Varanasi, 1969.

Radhakrishnan, S., Trans. The Brahmasūtra. George Allen and Unwin, London, 1960.

Radhakrishnan, S., The Principal Upanishads. George Allen and Unwin, London, 1956.

Radhakrishnan, S. Indian Philosophy. 2. Vols. George Allen and Unwin, London, 1966.

Radhakrishnan and C.A. Moore. A Source Book in Indian Philosophy. New Jersy: Princenton University Press, 1967.

Raja, K.K. Indian Theories of Meaning. Adyar Library and Research Centre, Adyar, 1963.

Raju, P.T. The Idealistic Thought of India, Allen and Unwin, London, 1953.

Ranade, R.D. A Constructive Survey of Upanishadic Philosophy, Bharatiya Vidyā Bhavan, Bombay, 1968.

Ranade, R.D., Vedānta - The Culmination of Indian Thought, Bharatiya Vidyā Bhavan, Bombay, 1970.

Raval, C.V. Śrīmad Śaṅkarācāryanu Tattvajñāna, Philosophy of Śrī Śaṅkarācārya, University Book Production Board, Gujarat State, Ahmedabad, 1974.

Roy, S.S. The Heritage of Śaṅkara, Allahabad Publications, 1965.

Sahasrabudhe. M.T. A Survey of Pre-Śaṅkara Advaita Vedānta, University of Poona, Poona, 1968.

Sastri, A.B. Studies in Post-Śaṁkara Dialectics, Calcutta, 1936.

Sastri, Kokileswara, An Introduction to Advaita Philosophy, Bharatiya Publishing House, Varanasi, 1979.

Sharma, B.N.K., Lectures on Vedānta, Karnatak University, Dharwar, 1973.

Sharma, C.D., A Critical Survey of Indian Philosophy, London, 1960.

Sharma, Rama Murti, Advaita Itihāsa Tathā Siddhānta, (Hindi), National Publishing House, Delhi, 1972.

Sharma, Rama Murti, Some Aspects of Advaita Philosophy, Eastern Book Linkers, Delhi, 1985.

Sharma H.L. Wisdom of Vedānta, Godk Publications, Delhi, 1981.

Sharma, V.A. Citsukha's Contribution to Advaita, Kavyalaya Publishers, Mysore, 1974.

Sadhale, G.S. Upaniṣadvākyamahākoṣa, Vol. I & II. The Gujarati Printing Press, Fort, Bombay, 1940.

Shastri, P.D. The Doctrine of Māyā, London, Luzac and Co., 1911.

Sastri, S.K. Compromises in the History of Advaitic Thought. Kuppuswami Sastri Research Institute., Madras, 1946.

Shastri, Udayavira, Vedānta Darśanakā Itihāsa, Virajānanda Vaidika Saṁsthāna, Gajiyavada (Up.), 1970.

Sengupta, B.K. A Critique on the Vivaraṇa School. Calcutta, Firma K.L. Mukhopadhyay, 1959.

Singh, R.P., The Vedānta of Śaṅkara, A Metaphysic of Value, Jaipur, 1949.

Sinha, Isvara, Bhāmatī : Eka Adhyana, Manthan Publications, Rohatak, 1983.

Sinha, J.N. History of Indian Philosophy, Vol. I & II, Calcutta, 1956.

Sinha, Jadunatha, Problems of Post-Śaṅkara Advaita Vedānta , Sinha Publishing House, Pvt. Ltd., Calcutta, 1971.

Sircar, M.N., Comparative Studies in Vedāntism, Humphrey Milford Oxford University Press, Bombay, 1927.

Sircar, M.N. The System Vedāntic Thought and Culture, Oriental Books, New Delhi, 1975.

Solomon, E.A. Avidyā, A Problem of Truth and Reality, Gujarat University, Thesis Publications Series - 8, Ahmedabad - 9, 1969.

Srinivasachari, S.M., Advaita and Visiṣṭādvaita, Asia Publishing House, Bombay, 1961.

Sundaram, P.K. Advaita Epistemology with Special Reference to Iṣṭasiddhi, University of Madras, Madras, 1968.

Tiwari, Kapil, N. Dimensions of Renuciation in Advaita, Motilal Banarasidass, Delhi, 1977.

Tripathi, M.S. A Sketch of the Vedānta Philosophy, Asian Publication Services, New Delhi, 1982.

Upadhyaya, V.P. Lights on the Vedānta, Chowkhamba, Varanasi, 1959.

Vidyabhusana, S.C., A History of Indian Logic. Delhi: Motilal Banarasidass, 1971.

Warrier, A.S.K. The Concept of Mukti in Advaita Vedānta, Madras: University of Madras, 1961.

Whitney, W.D. Sanskrit Grammar, a Breitkopf and Hartel Leipzig, 1879.

Winternitz, M.A., History of Indian Literature, Vol.I, University of Calcutta, 1927.

ARTICLES

Balasubramanian, R., -- "On the Locus of Avidyā" Journal of the Madras University, Vol.XLVII, No.2, July, 1975.

---------------------------------"Avidyā and The Illusory World" Journal of the Madras University, Vol.XLVII, No.I, January, 1976.

---------------------------------"The Place of Karma in the Advaitic Scheme of Discipline", Prabuddha Bhārata, Vol.LXVIII, Oct.1963, Nov.1963 and Dec.1963, Calcutta.

---------------------------------"Sureśvara on the Locus and Content of Avidyā" The Voice of Śaṅkara, Vol.15, No.I, 1990.

---------------------------------"Sureśvara on the Nature and Means of Liberation:, The Voice of Śaṅkara, Vol.16, No.1., 1991.

Chatterjee, Tara "An Attempt to Understand Svataḥ Prāmāṇyāvāda in Advaita Vedānta. Journal of Indian Philosophy, Vol.19, No.3, 1991.

Chattopadhyaya, S.K., "The Concept of Adhyāsa and the Vedānta of Śaṅkara" Indian Philosophical Quarterly, Vol.VI, No.4, July 1979, University of Poona.

Dasgupta, S.N. Māyā of Śaṅkara and His Followers, Philosophical Essays, Motilal Banarasidass, Delhi, 1982.

Ingalls, Daniel, H.H. - "Śaṅkara on the Question: Whose Avidyā." Philosophy, East and West, University of Hawaii, Honolulu, U.S.A., Vol.III, No.1, 1953.

Mayeda, Sengaku, Śaṅkara's View of Ethics, Philosophy : East and West, Essays in Honour of Dr. T.M.P.

Mahadevan, Edited by H.D. Lewis, Blackie & Son Limited, Bombay, 1976.

Nampoothiry, E. Easwaran, "Contribution of Kerala to Advaita Literature, Visvesvarananda Indological Journal, Edited by Virendra Sharma, Vol.XXII, June-Dc.1984.

Revaṭhy, S. "The Doctrine of Māyā in Advaita Vedānta". The Voice of Śaṅkara, Vol.14. No.3. and 4, 1989, 1990.

Shastri, Y.S. - "Doctrine of Māyā - A Critical Study", Sambodhi, Dr. S. Radhakrishnan Birth Centenary Special Issue, Vol.16, 1991.

Upadhyaya, K.N. "Śaṅkara on Reason, Scriptural Authority and Self-Knowledge" Journal of Indian Philosophy, Vol.19. No.2, 1991.

Veezhinathan, N., - "The Nature and Destiny of the Individual Soul in Advaita", Journal of the Madras University, Vol.XLVII, No.1, Jan., 1975.

Veezhinathan, N., - "The Interpretation of the Great Saying (Mahāvākyas) of the Upaniṣads". The Voice of Śaṅkara, Vol.15, No.1, 1990.

Veezhinathan, N., - "The Preceptors of Advaita Vedānta", The Voice of Śaṅkara, Vol.15, No.1, 1990.

Venkata Rao, M.A., "Note on Nyāyamakaranda" The Quarterly Journal of Mythic Society 32, 1941.

PERIODICALS

Bulletin of the Ramakrishna Mission Institute of Culture, Golpark, Calcutta.

Indian Philosophical Quarterly, University of Poona, and Pratap Centre of Philosophy, Poona-7.

Journal of Indian Philosophy, Edited by B.K. Motilal, D. Reideal Publishing Company, Dordrecht, Holland, Boston.

Journal of Indian Council of Philosophical Research, Edited by Daya Krishna, Indian Council of Philosophical Research, Rajendra Bhavan, New Delhi.

Journal of the Asiatic Society of Bombay.

Philosophy East and West, Hawaii, University of Hawaii, Honolulu, U.S.A.

Prabuddha Bhārata, Mayavati, Almore, Himalayas.

The Quarterly Journal of the Mythic Society, Edited by Suryanath, U. Kamath Nripatunga Road, Banglore-2.

The Voice of Śaṅkara, Edited by N.C. Krishnan, Ādi Śaṅkara Advaita Research Centre, Madras.

The Vedānta Keśarī, Edited by Swami Smarananda, Sri Ramakrishna Math, Mylapore, Madras.

Brahmavidyā, The Adyar Library Bulletin, The Adyar Library and Research Centre, The Theosophical Society, Madras.

Sambodhi, Edited by Dr. Ramesh S. Betai and Yajneshwar S. Shastri, L.D. Institute of Indology, Ahmedabad, 1991.

APPENDIX A

NYĀYAS USED BY ĀNANDABODHA

(1) *Alābhe mattakāśinyā dṛṣṭā tiryakṣu kāmitā* PM. p.2

(2) *Āśāmodakatṛptanyāya* NDI. p.7

(3) *Bhikṣukapādaprasāraṇanyāya* NDI. p.7

(4) *Bijāṅkuranyāya* NM. p.312

(5) *Ekākinī pratijñā hi pratijñatam na sādhayet* NM.p.117

(6) *Gobalivardanyāya* NM. p.350

(7) *Gomayapāyasīyanyāya* NDI. p.7

(8) *Jalakatakareṇunyāya* NM. p.322

(9) *Kaṇṭhacāmikaranyāya* NM. p.339.

(10) *Koṣapānanyāya* NM. p.89.

(11) *Lāṅgalam Jīvanamnyāya* NM. p.341.

(12) *Maṇiprabhāmaṇimatinyāya* NM.p.148.

(13) *Na hi bhikṣukāḥ santiti sthālyo nādhiśriyante na ca mṛgāh santīti yavā nopyante* PM. p.21.

(14). *Na hi sutukṣṇā'pyasidhārā svayam cchettumāhityavyāpārā* NM. p.183.

(15) *Prayojananamudiśya na mandopi pravartate* NM. 205.

(16) *Uṣṭralaguḍanyāya* ND. p.6.

(17) *Vadhyaghātakanyāya* NM. p.18

(18) *Vṛścikabhiyā palāyamāno viṣamāmukhe nipatitaḥ* NM. p.223.

(19) *Yādṛso yakṣastādṛso valiḥ.* NM. p.355.

APPENDIX B

Epigrams in the Works of Ānandabodha

Kaḥ khalu anukūlam ācarati pratikūlamācaret. NM. p.194

Grahaṇanibandhanaḥ hi cetanavyavahāraḥ na a-grahaṇāt yuktaḥ bhavitum NM. p.67.

Na khalu pracaṇḍabhāskara abhisantapta-śarīrasya upakartum upadhīyamānaḥ dahanaḥ tadanukūlatāmācarati. NM. p.220.

Na hi taskarāparādhāt sādhūnām bandhaḥ nyāyaḥ sādhukṛtāt vā sukṛtāt taskarāṇām NM. p.283

Na hi prayojanānuvarti pramāṇam. pramāṇānuvarti eva tat NM. p.236

Nivṛttiḥ hi nivṛttimatbhāvapūrvikā, NM. p.353.

Na khalu adhigate api tṛptisādhane bhojanādau-atīte vartamāne va pravṛttiḥ, nāpi bhaviṣyati, Sāmudravit akhyāte pravṛtyunupalambhāt. NM. p.186

Yasya hi parāpekṣam svarupam na tat parāpratītau pratīyate NM.p.228.

Sampratipannena eva hi pramāṇena vipratipannaḥ bodhanīyaḥ. NM. p.210.

Sarvatra dṛṣṭānusāriṇī kalpanā prasarīsarīti. NM. p.181

Sarvam hi yo jānāti sa sarvajñaḥ svagocara sūratvāt sarvānubhavānām NM. p.127.

APPENDIX-C

QUATATIONS IN ĀNANDABoDHA'S WORKS

1.	akke cet madhu vindeta kimartham parvatam vrajet	NM p.343	untraced
2.	agnihotram juhuyāt swargakāmaḥ	NM p. 190	"
3.	aṅgulyagram svamātmānam na ātmanā spṛṣṭumarhati	NM p.183	"
4.	aṇ-matubini samāsa-viśeṣāṇām sannihita-viśeṣā bhidhāyitam aṅgikurvāṇā vaiśvadevī āmīkṣā daṇḍī kamaṇḍalumān ityādi api akhaṇḍārthavṛttitāyām udāhāryāḥ	NM p. 264	(from some work of Vācas-pati)
5.	ata eva ca vidvatsu mucyamāneṣu santatam/ brahmāṇḍa-loka jīvānām anantatvāt aśunyatā//	NM p. 333	Untraced
6.	atidurāt-sāmipyāt-indriyaghātat manonavasthānāt/ saukṣmyāt vyavadhānāt abhibhavāt samānābhihārātca//	NM p. 78	SK VIII
7.	atrāym puruṣaḥ svayaṁjyotiḥ	PM p.13	Bṛhadāraṇyaka Up.4.3.9
8.	ananyalabhyaḥ tu śabdaḥ	NM p. 184	untraced

9.	anaśnan anyaḥ abhicākaśīti	NM p.16	Muṇḍaka Up. 3.1.1
10.	anena jīvena ātmanā	NM p.309	Chāndogya Up. 6.3.2
11.	antanyūnātiriktatve yujyata parimāṇavat/vastuni aparimeya tu nūnam teṣām asambhavaḥ//	NM P. 333	untraced
12.	andham tamaḥ praviśanti ye avidyāmupāsate/ tatobhūya iva te tamo ya u vidyāyām ratāḥ//	NM p. 338	Bṛhadāraṇyaka Up.4.4.10
13.	anyatheyamanālambā labhamānodayam kvacid/ hanyādekaprahāreṇa bāhyārtha-parikalpanam//	NM p. 121	untraced
14.	anyathaikanivṛtyā anyavinivṛttiḥ katham bhavet/ nāśvavān iti martyena na bhāvyam gomatā api kim//	NM p. 13	untraced
15.	api ca janma eva buddeḥ vyāpāraḥ arthāvagraha-rūpāyāh/	NM p.35	BR p.45
16.	apekṣitopāyata eva vidhiḥ iṣṭo manīṣibhiḥ/	NM p. 256	BR III.104
17.	Ayam ātmā brahma	PM p. 13	Bṛhadāraṇyaka Up. 2.5.19
18.	vā yat viruddha-dharmādyāsaḥ kāraṇabhedaḥ ca	NM p. 48	Untraced
19.	alābhe mattakāśinyā dṛṣṭā tiryakṣu kāmyatā	PM p.2	untraced

20. avidyā kṣetram uttareṣām prasupta-tanu- vicchinnodārāṇām	PM p. 2	Yogasūtra II.4
21. avidyāstamayo mokṣaḥ sā saṅsāra udāhṛta	NM P. 271	Br.III 106
22. aśvatthamenam suvirūḍhamūlam asaṅgaśastreṇa dṛḍhena chitvā/tataḥ padam tat parimārgitavyam yasmin gatā na nivartanti bhūyaḥ/	PM. p.22	Bhagavadgitā 15,3
23. asaṅgo hi ayam puruṣaḥ	NM p.324 Bṛhadāraṇyaka Up.4.3.15	
24. asaṁvittau vitteḥ na khalu tadupādhi- vyavahṛtiḥ pratītau anyasyām prasabham anavasthā prasarati	PM p.15	untraced
25. asaṁvedyamānaḥ api duḥkhābhāvaḥ sauṣuptaduḥkhābhāva iva puruṣārthaḥ	NM p.277	untraced
26. asarvagata-dravya-parimāṇam mūrthiḥ	NM p. 184	"
27. ahṛdayavācām ahṛdayā eva prativācobhavanti	ND p.2	"
28. ācāryavān puruṣo veda	NM p.314	Chāndogya Up.6.14.2
29. ātmanaḥ ākāśaḥ	NM p.21 Taittirīya	Up. 2.1.1
30. ātmanaḥ tu kāmāya sarvam priyam bhavati	PM p. 2	Bṛhadāraṇyaka Up. 2.4.5
31. ātmā vā are draṣṭavyaḥ	PM p.19	" " 2.4.6
32. ātmā eva ajñānahāniḥ vā	NM p. 357	untraced

33.	āarurukṣoḥ muneḥ yogam karma kāraṇamucyate/ yogārūḍhasya tasyeva śamaḥ kāraṇamucyate//	PM p.22	Bhagavadgīta 6.3
34.	iṣṭopāyatādhiyā hi mama idam kāryam iti buddhyā svatantraḥ pravartate	NM p. 195	NVp.38
35.	iha khalu saṅgati-saṁvedanāpekṣā...vyāmoha brahmavādinām	NM pp. 155-162	PP pp. 240-242
36.	eka eva devaḥ	NM p. 25	untraced
37.	eka eva hi bhūtātmā bhūte bhūte vyavasthitaḥ/ ekadhābahudhā ca eva/ dṛśyate jalacandra-vat//	NM p. 26	Brahmabindu Up.11
38.	eka eva ayam paramātmā	NM p.7	untraced
39.	ekam eva advitīyam	NM p.266 PM p.4	Chāndogya Up. 6.2.1
40.	ekam kasyacit anyasya dvayam eva prakāśakam/ atyantam anapekṣasya na ekam api astu kā kṣatiḥ//	PM p. 14	Untraced
41.	etasva eva ānandasya anyāni bhūtāni matram up-jivanti	PM p.1	Bṛhadāraṇyaka Up.4.3.22
42.	evamvidhe api viṣaye har-sahetvantarm āśṁkamānā jananī jāra-śaṁkaya svakīyāna api brāhmaṇatvam prati saṁdihānā na adhikārabhājo brāhmaṇocitāsu kriyāsu iti kṛtam mīṁāṁsābhyāsa-pariśrameṇa teṣām	ntraced	(from some work of NM p.163 Vācaspatimiśra)

43. evam somya sa ādeśaḥ	ND p.7	Chāndogya Up.6.1.6
44. kartavyatā ekārtha-samavāyinī samīhitasādhanatā vidhiḥ	NM p. 197	untraced (from some work of Vācas-patimiśra)
45. kaṣāyapaktiḥ karmāṇi jñānam tu paramā gatiḥ/ kaṣāya karmabhiḥ pakve tato jñānam pravartate//	PM p.22	untraced
46. kasya avidyā yaducchittiḥ muktiḥ iṣṭā parātmanaḥ/vidyāsvabhāvataḥ ayuktā sā ataḥ jivaḥ na bhidyate//	NM p. 309	"
47. kāyena manasā buddhyā kevalaiḥ indriyaiḥ api/ yoginaḥ karma kurvanti saṅgam tyaktvā ātmaśuddhaye//	NM p. 343	Bhagvadgītā 5.11
48. kāryatvena niyojyam ca svātmani prerayan asu/ niyoga iti mīmāṁsā niṣṇātaiḥ abhidhiyate//	NM p. 192	PP p. 441
49. kāryam eva ca vaktṛṇām jyāyaḥ-sama- kaniyasām/ pravartyāpekṣayā bhedāt praiṣādi- vyapadeśa-bhāg//	NM p. 187	PP p. 430
50. kāryam bādariḥ asya gatyupapatteḥ	NM p. 351	B.4.3.7
51. kiṅtu vastvantarānusandhāna-śūnyatayā sāmānyaviśeṣarūpatā na pratīyate	NM p.177	untraced

52. kiṅtu svayam kleśarūpam karma yat kāryatām vrajet/ phalasādhanatā tatra kāraṇam tena kāryatā//	NM p. 195	PP p.439
53. kṛtisādhyam pradhānam yat tat kāryam abhidhīyate/ tat ca mānāntareṇa api vedyam odanapākavat//	NM pp.188,203	PP p. 431
54. kṛtyuddeśyatā eva iṣṭopāyasya vyaktidhīḥ uktā/	NM p. 195-196	NV p. 39
55. kriyādibhinnam yat kāryam vedyam mānāntaraiḥ na tat/ ato mānātarāpūrvam opūrvam abhidhīyate//	NM p. 191	P p. 441
56. gauḥ na padā spṛṣṭavyā/	ND p. 8	untraced
57. janana-maraṇa-karaṇānam pratiniyamāt-a yugapatpravṛtteḥ ca/ puruṣabahutvam siddham traiguṇya-viparyayāt ca//	NM p. 18	SM XVIII
58. jñānāt eva ca kaivalyam prāpyate yena mucyate/ karmaṇā badhyate jantuḥ vidyayā ca vimucyate//	NM p. 338 PM pp.21,23	untraced
59. tat-paricchinnatti tataḥ anyaś vyavacchinnatti, tṛtiya-prakārābhāvam sūcayati	NM p. 40	"
60. tat-praptihetuḥ jñānam ca karma ca uktam mahāmuneḥ	NM p.340 PM p. 23	(from the work of Parāśara) un-traced
61. tat tvam asi	NM P.18	Chāndyogya Up. 6.8.7
62. tapo vidyā ca viprasya niśśreyasakaram param/	NM p.341	Manusmṛti 12.104

63. tameva vidvān amṛta iha bhavati nānyaḥ panthā ayanāya vidyate	PM.p. 21	Śvetāśvatara Up. 3.6
64. tameva bhāntam anubhāti sarvam	NM p. 319	Kaṭha. Up. 5.15
65. tasmāt sarveṣu kāleṣu mām anusmara yudhya ca	NM p. 340	BHagvedgīta 8.27
66. darśapūrṇamāsābhyām svargakāmo yajeta	NM p. 212	untraced
67. duḥkhāhānāya ca yuktam sukham duḥkhātmakam varam/ na hi kaścit padārthajñaḥ mohasiddyai pravartate//	NM p. 280	"
68. duḥkhābhāvaḥ api nāvedyaḥ puruṣārt iṣyate/ na hi mūrcchadyavasthārtham pravṛtiḥ dṛśyate sudhīḥ//	NM p. 277	"
69. dvā suparṇa...	ND p.7	Muṇḍaka Up. 3.1.1
70. dvitīāt vai bhayam bhavati	PM p.20 ND p.7	Bṛhadāraṇyaka Up. 1.4.2
71. dharma-rajjvā vrajet ūrdhvam pāpa-rajjvā vrajet adhaḥ/ dvayam jñānāśinā chitvā videhaḥ śāntimṛcchati//	NM p. 352	untraced
72. dharmāt sukham ca Jñānam ca jnānāt mokṣaḥ ad-higamyate	NM p. 343 PM p.22	untraced

73. dharmeṇa gamanam urdhavm gamanam adhastāt bhavati adharmeṇa/ jñānena ca apavargaḥ viparyayāt iṣyate bandhaḥ//	NM p. 282	SM XIIv
74. na karmaṇā na prajayā na dhanena tyāgena eka amṛtatvam ānaśuḥ/	PM p.22	Mahānārāyaṇa Up.8.14
75. na ca svādhigata-tatpriye taddhīḥ iti klṛptavāt avadhṛtiḥ, tatra eva ca anekasya sambhavāt, suto jātaḥ prasūta ta sukham priyā	NM p. 164	NV p.44
76. na bhāvaḥ na api abhāvaḥ kiṅtu anirvācyā eva avidyā//	NM p.318	untraced
77. na sa kalpayitum śakyaḥ tatsiddheḥ laukikāt api/	NM p.231	BR III. 85
78. nahi nari śṛṅgam bhāti gavi iva	NM p. 109	IS p.39
79. na hiṅsyāt sarvā bhūtāni	NM p. 152	untraced
80. nānātmānaḥ vyavasthātaḥ	NM p. 4	Vaiśeṣika sūtra 3.2.20
81. nānyatra kāraṇāt kāryam na cet tatra kva tat bhavet	PM p.4	IS 1.3
82. nānyatra sarvasmtyāgāt mokṣam vindanti mānavāḥ/	PM p. 22	untraced
83. nitya-naimittikaiḥ eva kurvāṇo duritakṣayam/ jñānam ca vimalīkurvan abhyāsena tu pācayet//	PM p. 23	"
84. niyojyaḥ sa ca kāryam svakīyatvena budhyate	NM p.191	PP p. 433

85.	nirvikalpakena sāmānyaviśeṣau dve vastunī pratipadyamānena api tayoḥ bhedaḥ na pratyetum śakyate	NM p. 177	untraced
86.	niṣpāditakriya karmāṇi aviśeṣābhidhāyinaḥ sādhansya sādhananyāyātipātaḥ	NM p. 259	"
87.	neha nānasti kiṅcana	NM p. 266 PM p.4 ND p.7	Bṛhadāraṇyaka Up. 4.4.19
88.	padam svadharmam vyutkramet anyasiddhārthatā anyathā	NM p. 234	Br p.103
89.	pūrvāt parabalīyatvam tatra nāma pratīyatām/ annoya-nirapreksạ̄ṇām yatra janma dhiyām bhavet//	NM p. 151	untraced
90.	paurvāparye pūrvadaurbalyam prakṛtivat	NM p.150	Jaimini-Sūtra 6.5.54
91.	pradipasya iva nirvāṇam vimokṣaḥ tasyaḥ tāyinaḥ	NM p. 270	untraced
92.	Pramāṇam anubhūtiḥ sā smṛteranyā smṛtiḥ punaḥ/ pūrva-vijñāna-saṁskāra mātrajam jñānam ucyate//	NM p. 223	PP p. 42
93.	pravartakatva tu śabdārthaḥ sarvatra avyabhicārāt//	NM p. 229	untraced
94.	prasakta-pratiṣedha sati anyatra a-prasaṅgāt śiṣyamāna sampratyayaḥ pariśeṣaḥ//	Nyāyabhāṣya on Nyāyasūtra II.5	aNM p. 230
95.	prāṇā vai satyam...	ND p.7	Bṛhadāraṇyaka Up.2.1.20

96. phalasādhanatā nāma yā sā naiva ca kāryatā/kāryatā kṛtisādhyatā punaḥ/ kāraṇatvam phalotpāde te bhidyate parasparam//	NM p. 189	PP p. 425
97. brahmaṇyādhāya karmāṇi saṅgam tyaktvā karoti yaḥ/ lipyate na sa pāpena padmapatramivāmbhasā//	NM p. 343	Bhagavadgītā 5.10
98. bhāvāntaram abhāvonyo na kaścit anirūpaṇāt	NM p.86	untraced
99. bhāvāntaram abhāvo hi kayācittu vyapekṣayā	NM p.86	"
100.bhūtiḥ yeṣām kriyā sā eva kārakam sā eva ucyate	NM p.35	untraced
101.maṇi-pradīpa-prabhayoḥ maṇibuddhyā abhidhāvatoḥ/ mithyājñānāviśeṣe api viśeṣaḥ arthakriyām prati//	NM p.148	PV p. 2.58
102.madhu paśyasi durbuddheḥ prapātam kim na paśyasi	NM p. 77	untraced
103.mā bhut ayam mānasa-pratyakṣagocaraḥ...prakāśate	NM pp. 132	PP p. 334
104.māyām tu prakṛtim	ND p.7	Śvetāśvatra Up.4.10
105.mithyābhāvena bhūtam kim mithyānāśāt na naṅkṣyati	NM p.359	IS VIII.2
106.mūlakṣayakarīm prāhuḥ anavasthām hi dūṣaṇam	NM p. 49	untraced
107.yajñena devān āpnoti vairājam tapasā punaḥ/ sannyāsāt brahmaṇaḥ sthānam vairāgyāt prakṛtau layaḥ//	NM p. 337	untraced

108. yathā annam madhu-saṁyuktam madhu ca an-nena saṁyutam/ evam tapaḥ ca vidyā ca saṁyuktam bheṣajam mahat//	NM p. 340 PM p.23	(It is recorded as from Dakṣa, but is not found in the printed text of Dakṣa-smṛti
109. yadā karmasu kāmyeṣu striyam svapneṣu paśyati/ samṛddhis tatra jānīyat tas-min svapna-nidarśane//	PM p. 16	Chānpya Up. 5.2.9
110. yaḥ pratītivirodhaḥ tu sa sva-doṣaḥ udāhṛtaḥ/ sāmānādhikaraṇyena bodhāt rūpyam idam sitam//	ND p. 12	BR.III 149
111. yastāvat pratipattā....paraśarīre anumīyate/	NM pp. 27-28	PP p. 345
112. rūpaiḥ saptabhiḥ eva badhnāti ātmānam ātmanā prakṛtiḥ/ sā eva ca puruṣasyārtham vimocayati ekarūpeṇa//	NM p. 283	SM LXIII
113. vatsa-vivṛddhi-nimittam kṣīrasya yathā pravṛttiḥ ajñasya/ puruṣa-vimokṣa-nimittam pravartate tad-vadavyaktam//	NṀ p. 287	SM LVII
114. vijñānam ānandam brahma	NM p. 136 PM pp. 1,13	Bṛhadāraṇyaka Up. 3.9.34
115. vidyām ca avidyām ca yaḥ tat veda ubhayam saha/ avidyayā mṛtyum tīrtvā vidyayā amṛtam aśnute//	NM p. 338	Īśāvāsya II

116.vidhānam pratiṣedham ca muktvā śabdaḥ asti nāparaḥ/ vyavahāra sa ca asatsu na iti prāptā atra mūkatā//	ND p.2	untraced
117.vidhi-nimantraṇāmantraṇādhīṣṭa..	NM p. 227	P III.3.161
118.viṣṇuḥ upāṁśu yastavyaḥ	PM p.19	untraced
119.vairagyāt prakṛti-layaḥ	PM p. 19	untraced
120 vairāgyāt prakṛti-layaḥ saṁsāro bhavati rājasāt rāgāt/ aiśvaryāt avighātaḥ viparyayāt tadviparyāsaḥ//	NM p.282	SM XIV
121.vyasanāni durantāni samavyayaphalāni ca/ aśakyāni ca vastūni nārabheta vicakṣaṇaḥ//	NM p. 276	untraced
122.vyutpattiḥ api kārya arthe vyavahārānusāriṇī/ kiṅtu nirdhāraṇāmātram veda-vākyavimarśajam//	NM p. 192	PP p. 446
123.śabda-jṅānānupāti vastuśūnyaḥ vikalpaḥ/	NM p. 109	Yogasūtra 1.9
124.sarva-pratyaya-vedya vā brahmarūpa vyavasthite/ prapañcasya pravilayaḥ śabdena pratipādyate//	NM p. 298	BR IV 3,4
125.satyasya satyam teṣām eṣa satyam	NM p. 7	Bṛahadāraṇyaka Up.2.1.20
126.satyena labhyaḥ tapasā hi esa ātmā samyag jñanena brahmacaryeṇa nityam	NM p. 340	Muṇḍaka Up. 3.1.5

127.sadasat-ubhaya-anubhayādi-prakāraiḥ anirvācyatvam eva hi avidyānām avidyātvam	PM p.10	untraced (It is from the Brahmatatva samīkṣā of Vācaspatimiśra, which is not available now).
128.sannāsāt brahmaṇaḥ sthāna	PM p. 22	untraced
129.sarvātmanārthaḥ jñāna kenacit na hi gṛhyate	NM p. 127	BR III 138
130.saḥ vā eṣa puruṣaḥ annarasamayaḥ anyaḥ antaraḥ ātmā prāṇamayaḥ anyaḥ antara ātmā manomayaḥ	ND p.7	Taittirīya UP 2.1.1
131.sāmānya-viśeṣau dve vaśtunī pratipadyamānem pratyakṣam upapadyate	NM p.177	untraced
132.sūcakaḥ ca hi śruteḥ ācakṣate ca tadvidaḥ	PM p. 16	B 3.2.4
133.so'sya paramaḥ ānandaḥ etasya eva ānandasya, anyāni bhūtāni mātrām upajīvanti	PM p.1	Bṛhadāraṇyaka 4.3.32
134.syāt etatevam yadi ad-vaitam kasyacit pramāṇasya gocaraḥ....rātrisatravat	NM pp. 290-296	PP p. 336-341
135.svabhāvena hi karmāṇi duḥkhotpādana- hetubhūtāni teṣu kāryatvāvagamaḥ phala-sādhanatāvagama-nibandhanaḥ/	NM p. 195	PP p. 429

APPENDIX D

List of Verses Composed by Ānandabodha in his Works

Nyāyadīpikā

1) *Yadbhāsānikhilam vibhāti viṣayo*
yo na svayaṁ jyotiṣām
Yasyāhurbhuvanodbhavasthitilayān
lilāmayānsurayaḥ/
Yaṁcāgocaramāmanantimanasām
vācām ca visvātmane
tasmai śuddhasukhādvitīyavapuṣe
sasvannamo viṣnave// p.1

2) *Srotṛmohātimirāpahāriṇī*
sadhnoti nikurumbadīdhitiḥ/
śābdanirṇayasadarthabhāsikā
dīpikeyamamalāvidhīyate// p.1

3) *Yasyām prasādamabalambya jagadguruṇā*
mapyaskhalad bahuguṇā prasaranti vācaḥ/
sā vedasāśastraparinirmitavandvadehā
bhūyādṣamagravaradaiva sarasvatīva II

Pramāṇamala

1. *Ānadamātmānamasatyabhedam praṇamya vijñānatanum mukundam/ prasādhane tasya sadopayuktām pramāṇamālām racayāmi ramyām//* p.1

2. *Tataparatvāt parattvācca nirdoṣatvātca vaidikam/ pūrvasya bādhakam, nāyam sarpa ityāptavākyavat//* p.4
3. *Vimatam tāttvikasvāntarbhedahīnam mittattvataḥ/ yadittham tattathā yadvat kham tathedam tatastathā//* p.4
4. *Sati caivam prapañco'pi syādavidyāvinirmitaḥ avidyāto vibhinnatve jaḍatvādrajusarpavat/ jāḍyadṛśyatvahetubhyām mithyātvam vā prasādhyatām/ prāgukta eva dṛṣṭānto mithyātvam ceha bādhyatām//* p.11
5. *Pratyakṣādipramāṇām prāmāṇyam vyāvahārikam/ āśrityāyam prapañcaḥ syādalikopi pramāṇavān// advaitāgamavākyam tu tattvāvedanalakṣaṇam/ pramāṇabhābam bhajatām bādhavaidhuryahetutaḥ//* p.12
6. *Parataśca pramāṇatvaparijñāne'navasthiteḥ/ parihāram prayatne'pe na pasyāmaḥ sabhākṣamam//* p.12
7. *Vimatā dhīḥ samādhārakālasvajñānahānitaḥ/ na hīnā vyavahāreṇa dhitvādavimatā yathā//* p.13
8. *Evaṁcābhedasaṁsidhau saṁvitsvābhāvyasambhavāt/ ātmanaḥ svaprakāsatvamanīrvāryaiti sthitam//* p.15
9. *Jaḍatā dṛśyatācāstu satyasyaiveti cenmatam/ samvityasambandhe dharmyasiddhiprasaktitaḥ//* p.16
10. *Tasmādadtvaitavijñānasukharūpe pramāṇatām/ brahmaṇi pratipadyante vedānta iti sāmpratam //* p.19
11. *Evamānandarūpo'yam vijñānatvāt svayam prabhuḥ/ viṣṇurātmātmanaḥ śrutvā vimokṣāya nīrupyate//* p. 20
12. *Avidyāstamayo mokṣa nityānandapratititaḥ/ niḥseṣaduḥkhocchedācca puruṣārthaḥ paro mataḥ//* p.21
13. *Avidyāstamayo mokṣa bhavedvidaikahetukaḥ/ yuktyā śrutismṛtibhyām ca svīkarttavyo manīṣibhiḥ// sadādibhyaśca bhinno'sya prakāraḥ pariśeṣataḥ/ yathāsamupapadyeta tathaiva parikalpyatām//* p.24
14. *Pramāṇamālā guṇasamgateyamapeta doṣā vihitā dareṇa/ prasādhayantīparam puṁāsa prakalpatām pārthitasiddha ye vaḥ//* p.24

15. *Ātmasvabhāvamadhikṛtya mukundameṣā/ mānābhidhānanavaranta manojñamālā// Ānandabodhayatinā nidhinā guṇānām/ ānandahe turakalaṅkadhiyāṁ vyadhāyi// p.25*

Nyāyadīpāvali

1. *Jagadaṅkurakandāya viśadānandamūrttaye/ galitākhilabhedāya namaḥ śāntāya viṣṇave// p.1*
2. *Dustarkatimiraśreṇīvidāraṇaviśāradām/ ṛcirām nyāyadīpānāmāvalim racayāmyaham// p.1*
3. *Vidhānam pratiṣedham ca muktvā śābdo'sti nāparaḥ/ vyavahāraḥ sa cāsatsu neti prāptātra mukatā// p.2*
4. *Śrīmadānadabodhasya vibudhānandadāyīnī/ Śravantya'mṛtadhāreva sevyatām kṛtibhiḥ kṛtiḥ// p.8*
5. *Sevantām matimāntaḥ sarasvatīcandrikām ānandabodhakṛtinaḥ prasarantim pūrṇadikcakram// p.15*

Nyāyamakranda

1. *yadbhāsā nikhilam vibhati viṣayo yo na svayaṁ jyotiṣām/ sasyāhurbhuvanodbhavastitilayā lilamanānsūrayaḥ//*

   Yaṁ cā' gocaramāmananti manasām vācāṁ ca visvātmane/ tasmai śuddhasukhādvitīyavapuṣe sasvan-namo viṣṇave// p.2
2. *Nibandhapuṣpajālāni samālocya prayatnataḥ/ sannyāmakarandānām saṁgraha kriyate mayā// p.3*
3. *Pratyakṣepi pratikṣetram bhedaḥ puṁsām pramāṇataḥ/ pratyetavyagate bhede na prametyadhunācyate// p.31*
4. *Ittham nirastanikhilapratikūlaśaṁkād vedāntavākyanika-rānnikhilopi bhedaḥ/ śakyo niṣeddhamiti siddhamanā-dyavidyā tadvāsanāviracitabhūmamātrasiddaḥ//p.56*
5. *Sati caivam prapañcopi syādavidyā vijṛmbhitaḥ/ jāḍyadṛśyatva hetubhyām rajatasvapnadṛśyavad// p.128*

6 *Māyāmayatvasiddhau ca prapañca sva pramāṇataḥ/ pratyakṣādi prāmāṇānām prāmāṇyam vyāvahārikam// p.145*

7. *Advaitāgamavākyantu tattvāvedanalakṣaṇam/ pramāṇabhāvam bhajate vādhavaiduryahetutaḥ// p.145*

8. *Iti vigalitadoṣo mānabhāvaḥ śrutīnām/ niratiśayasukhātmanyadvitīye prakāśe,/ nanu paramatakārye vedaleśopi matyam/ bhajata iti vadāmastatra saṁgatyajogād// p.179*

9. *Nanvānandādiśabdānā maikārthyānupapattitaḥ/ advaitānanandaniṣṭatvam vedāntānāmapyuktimad// p.247*

10. *Lakṣārthabhedābhāvepi vyavacchedyavibhedataḥ/ vijnānamānandapadayoḥ praryāyavyarthatā kutaḥ// p.260*

11. *Avidyāstamayo mokṣa iti tāvatsamarthitam/ tena mokṣābhyupāyatvam vidyāyā na tu karmaṇām// p.336*

12. *Nanvavidhyākṣateḥ sattve saddvitīyatvamātmanaḥ/ mithyābhāve tvanirmokṣo mūlāvidyāvyavasthiteḥ// p.352*

13. *Nānānibandhakusumaprabhavāvadāta/ nyāyāpadeśamakarandakadamba eṣaḥ/ ānandabodhayatinā nidhinā guṇānā mānandaheturakalaṅkadhiyām vyadhāyi // p.360*

14. *Sevantām matimantaḥ sarasvatīm candrikām viśadām/ Ānandabodhakṛtinaḥ samayantīmāntaram timiram// p.360*

15. *Ānandabodhasukaveḥ sūktim ke nābhinandanti/ no cedarūcinidānam matsarasamjñam mahāpittam// p.360*

APPENDIX E

SYLLOGISMS EMPLOYED BY ĀNANDABODHA IN HIS TEXTS

PRAMĀṆAMĀLĀ

Ānando duḥkhābhāvo na bhavati tada nirūpyatvāt yadittham tattathā yathā ghaṭaḥ yadvā, ānando bhāvarūpaḥ pratiyogyanirūpyatvāt ghaṭavat p.1

Ānando bhāvarūpaḥ sātisayatvāt duḥkhavat p.1

Jīvasca paramānandasvabhāvaḥ parama premāspadatvāt uktasādhyo na bhavati, nāsāvuktasādhanaḥ yathā ghaṭaḥ na cāyam uktasādhano na bhavati tasmānna noktasādhya iti p.2

Jīvāḥ paramātmanastatvato na bhidyante ātmatvāt paramātma vat p.3

Vivādāspadībhūtāni bhogāyatanāni ubhayavādyavivādāspadasyaiva bhogāyatanāni bhogāyatanatvād prativādibhogāyatanavad p.3

Vivādādhyāsitā jīvāḥ prativādinastatvto na vyatirivyante jīvatvād ātmatvād vā prativādivat p.3

Vivādādhyāsito bhedo mithyā, bhedatvāt darpaṇādigatamukhādi bhedavaditi p.7

Vivādapadam bhedasamvedanam mithya bhedasamvedanatvāt svapnabhedasaṁvedanavaditi p.7

Vivādādhyāsitā pravṛttiḥ purovartti gocara rajatajnānā pūrvika rajatecchādhīnapurovarttipravṛttitvāt samyagrajatapravṛttivat p.

Vivādādhyāsitam rajatadhī padam rajatavyavahāra adatvāt yadittham tattathā yathā samyak rajatam p.9

Vivādāpadamanirvāryam bādhyatvāt yaduktasādhyam na bhavati, na taduktasādhanam yathātmā na tathedamuktasādhanam na bhavatīti tasmānnedam noktasādhyamiti p.11

Avacchedakaścāyamātmā na svāśrayavyāpyo bhavitumutsahate vastudvādasidhārāvat p.13

Samveditā hi na svātirekisaṁvidadhīna prakāśaḥ samvitkarmatāmantareṇā parokṣatvāt saṁvedanavat p.13

Samvit svāntargatabhedasunyā bheopādhimantareṇāvibhāvyamāna bhedatvādākāsavat p.15

Vivādādhyāsitaḥ śabdavyut pattigocarḥ prameyatvādubhayābhima taprameyavat p.17

Vedaḥ siddha evārthe pramāṇam, pramāṇatvāt cakṣurvat p.18

Vijñānādivākyam akhaṇḍārthaniṣṭham lakṣaṇavākyatvāt pṛthubughnodarā kāro ghaṭa etyādivākyavat p.19

NYĀYADĪPĀVALI

Vivādapadam mithyā dṛśyatvāt yadittham tattathā yathobhayavādyavivādapadam rajatam tathaitat, tatasthathā p.1

Vandhyāsuto vaktā na bhavati acetanatvād pāṣāṇavat p.2

Vivādādhyāsitā pravṛttiḥ purovartti gocararajatajñānapūrvikā rajatecchādhīnapurovarttipravṛttitvat yaduktasādhanam taduktasādhyam yathā samyagrajatapravṛtti sthatheyam tatastathā p.8

Vivādādhyāsitam rajatavijñānam yathārtham jñānatvādubhayavādisiddhasamīcīnarajatajñānavat p.13

NYĀYAMAKARANDA

Ātmā dravyatvavyatiriktāparajātyādhārabhedena nānā, aśrāvaṇaviśeṣaguṇādhikaraṇatvād yaduktasādhanam taduktasādhyam yathā atmaktavidhayā nānā śarīrātma sambandasabandhitvād sarīravad p.6

Vivādapadāni śarīrāṇi svasaṁkhyā saṁkhyeyātmabhirātmavanti śarīratvāt sampratipanna śarīravad p.6

Vivādāspadam mityam jaḍatvād yadittham tattathā yathā kumbhādi p.21

Vivādāpadāni śarīrāṇi ubhayavādya vivādāspadenaivātmanādhiṣṭhitāni jīvatsarīratvād yaduktasādhanam taduktasādhyam yathobhayavādya vivādāspadam śarīram tathā cemāni tasmāduktasādhyāni p.29

Ātmā dravyatvavyatiriktāpārajātyādhāna bhedana nānā na bhavati nityatvād vibhutvād niravayavadravyatvād vā gaganavad p.30

Vivādapadam bhedasaṁvedanam na pramāṇanibandhanam anirūpita pramāṇakatvād bhedasṁvedanatvād vā svapnabhedāvabhāsanavad p.55.

Idam smaraṇamanākalitarajatasyānutpadyamānatvād yaditthām tattathā yothobhayavādyavivādāspadam rajatasmaranam p.62

Yathārthāḥ sarve vivādāspadībhūtāḥ pratyay pratyayatvātsaṁpratipannasamīcīnapratyayavad p.65

Vivādādhyāsitam rajatavijñānam purovarttivastuviṣayam rajatārthi onastatraniyamenapray taka tvādubhayavādāspadarajatavijñāna vat p.72

Vivādapadam-anādyanirācyopādānam vipakṣe vādhakopapattau satyām kāryatvād yadyuktasādhyam na bhavati na tadyathoktasadhanam yathobhayavādya vivādāspadam vastu p.124

Samveditā na samvidadhīnaprakāśaḥ samvitkarmaṇāmaṇtareṇā parokṣatvāt samvedanavaditi p.135

Vijñānamarthaprakāśasamaye prakāśate tadupādhāvanantaram sandehā-yogyatvād arthavad p.138

Vivādapadāni na kāryānvitasvārtha niyatasāmarthyāni padatvāt kāryapadavat yadvā kāryam na samastapadasāmarthya pratiyogī anvayātirikta tvādubhayavādyavivādāspanda padārthāntaravaditi p.168.

Vedaḥ siddha evārthe pramāṇam pramāṇatvāt pratyakṣavat p.256.

Tattvamasivākyamakhaṇḍārthaniṣṭamakāryakāraṇadravya varttitva sati sāmānādhikaraṇatvāt so'yam devedatta iti vākyavat p.269.

SANSKRIT GLOSSARY

Akhaṇḍa : Individual

Akhaṇḍārtha: Impartite sense

Akhaṇḍārtha Vṛtti: Impartite psychosis of the mind.

Akhaṇḍopādhi: An attribute which is not a *jāti* but similar to it.

Akhyāti: The Prābhākāra theory of error according to which all cognitions are valid. It contends that the error in illusory experience consists in the non-apprehension of the difference between the presented object and the represented idea.

Agrahaṇa: Non-apprehension.

Ajāti: Theory of no creation.

Atiprasaṅga: Over-extention; too-wideness of a defining mark.

Ativyāpti: Over-applicability being too wide.

Atyantābhāva: Absolute non-existence.

Atyantāsat: Non-being out-and-out.

Advitīya: Without a second

Adhikaraṇa: Substratum.

Adhiṣṭhāna: Substratum, Support.

Adhyāsa: Superimposition.

Aṇu: Atom; Minute part.

Aṇuparimāṇa: Atomic size.

Anāncam: Infinite.

Anavasthā: Regressus infinitum.

Anirvacanīya: Inexplicable; Indescribable.

Anirvacanīyatā: Indefinability.

Anupalabdhi: Non-cognition, Non-recongintion.

Anubhava: Practical experience of the infinite.

Anubhūti: Consciousness, Knowledge.

Anumāna: Inference.

Anuvyavasāya: Secondary or introspective congnition.

Anvaya: I. Method of agreement.

Anvayavyatirekin: Having both similar and contrary instances.

Anyathā: Something other than what it is.

Anyathākhyāti: The Nyāya-Vaiśeṣika and Bhāṭṭa theory of error according to which the error in illusory experience consists in apprehending something as otherwise.

Antaḥkaraṇa: Internal organ.

Aparokṣajñāna: Direct and immediate knowledge (intuition) of *Brahman*.

Apūrva: Unseen result.

Abādhita: Non-sublated

Abhāva: Non-existence

Arthāpatti: Presumption, regarded as an independent means of knowledge.

Asat: Non-existence

Asatkhyāti: The Śūnyavādī Buddhist's (Mādhyamika) theory of error according to which the illusory error consists in apprehending the wholly non-existent as existent.

Asiddha: Unfounded.

Avacchinna: Limited.

Avacchedaka: Limitor.

Avacchedavāda: Vācaspati's view that *jīva* is but a seeming delimitation of the eternal pure *ātman* by *avidyā*.

Avidyā: Māyā, the cosmic principle which gives rise to the world.

Avidyā-nivṛtti: The removal of nescience.

Ahaṁ-kāra: I-notion.

Ākāṅkṣā: Expectancy

Āgama: Verbal or scriptural.

Ātmakhyāti: The Vijñānavādī Buddhist's (Yogācāra) theory of error according to which the illusory error consists in apprehending a subjective idea as an external object.

Ānanda: Bliss.

Ābhāsavāda: Sureśvara's view according to which *jīva* is but a semblance of *Brahman*.

Āvaraṇa› Concealment.

Āśraya: Locus.

Āsatti: Contiguity.

Upacāra: Metaphore

Upapatti: Logical tenability

Upādānakāraṇa: Material cause.

Upādhi: Adjunct.

Karma: Grammatical object expressed by accusative etc.; defined as what the agent seeks most to obtain through his actions.

Kuṭastha: Immutable pure consciousness which is the ground of all change.

Guṇa: Quality

Gaurava: Heaviness.

Jīvanmukti: Release even when one is alive

Jīvāśrita avidyāvāda: The view that *jīva* is the locus of *avidyā*

Jñānakarmasammuccayavāda: The theory that the combination of knowledge and result rituals *(Jñānakarma)* is a means to *mokṣa.*

Tātparya: Intention.

Tādātmya: Sameness of nature

Tulāvidyā: Derivative nescience.

Dṛśyatva: Objectivity.

Dharma: Property, character.

Dharmin: The charaterized, (property) possessor.

Nididhyāsana: Continued contemplation on the Truth.

Nirvikalpaka-jñāna: Cognition whithout mode.

Pakṣa: Locus of an inference.

Prakaraṇa: Context.

Pratibimbavāda: The Vivaraṇa view that the *jiva* is but a reflection of *Brahman* in *avidyā.*

Pratiyogin: (i) Successor (the second term of a relation); (ii) counter positive of a negation.

Pratyakṣa: Perception.

Pramāṇa: Means of obtaining valid knowledge.

Prasaṁkhyāna: Repeated contemplation on the nature of the Ultimate Reality.

Prātipadika: Meaningful mominal base or stem.

Prātipadikārtha: Base-meaning such as generic property etc.

Prātibhāsikasattā: Illusory Reality.

Pāramārthika: Absolutely Real, the ultimate.

Brahnajñāna: The realisation of *Brahman.*

Brahmāśrita-avidyāvāda: The view that *Brahman* is the locus of *avidyā.*

Bhāvarūpa: Existence of something positive.

Bhavanā: Productive activity, expressed by verbal ending and the chief qualificand of relations in verbal cognitions.

Mahāvākya: The great saying of the scriptures, the hearing and continued contemplation of which leads of *Brahman*-realisation.

Māyā: Avidyā, Cosmic principle which gives rise to world-illusion.

Mithyā: Neither existence *(sat)* nor non-existence *(asat)* but different from both *(sadasatvilakṣaṇa).*

Mūlāvidyā: Primal nescience.

Yogyatā: Semantical competency, one of the necessary conditions for verbal cognition.

Lāghava: The law of simplicity or parsimony.

Vijñānavādin: One who contends that the Real consists of a series of ideas *(vijñānas)* and that it is momentary.

Vipakṣa: A negative instance; a locus where the probandum is known to be present.

Viparitakhyāti: The Bhāṭṭa theory of error according to which the illusory error is one of commission. The error arises as a result of confusion of one thing for another.

Vibhakti: Case ending or post nominal affix referring to the *kāraka* and non-*karaka* relations.

Vikṣepa: Distortion.

Vyāpti: Pervasion.

Vyāpāra: Action or operation or movement.

Vivartavāda: The theory that the worldly existence is an illusory a appearance of *Brahaman.*

Vividiṣā: The desire to know *Brahman*.

Viṣaya: Object of nescience.

Vṛtti: Mental modification.

Vṛttijñāna: Knowledge of the psychosis.

Sapakṣa: A locus where the probandum is known to be present.

Savikalpaka-jñāna: Cognition with mode.

Suṣupti: Deep sleep.

Svayam-prakāśa: Self-illumined.

Svataḥ-prāmāṇyavāda: The theory advocates that validity of knowledge is self-constituted.

Sādhya: Probandum; action to be accomplished.

Sāmānādhikaraṇa: Co-present; present in the same locus.

Hetu: Probans.

GENERAL INDEX